MICHAEL McKINLEY

VIKING

VIKING
an imprint of Penguin Canada

Published by the Penguin Group
Penguin Group (Canada), 90 Eglinton Avenue East, Suite 700, Toronto, Ontario, Canada M4P 2Y3

Penguin Group (USA) Inc., 375 Hudson Street, New York, New York 10014, U.S.A.
Penguin Books Ltd, 80 Strand, London WC2R 0RL, England
Penguin Ireland, 25 St Stephen's Green, Dublin 2, Ireland (a division of Penguin Books Ltd)
Penguin Group (Australia), 707 Collins Street, Melbourne, Victoria 3008, Australia
(a division of Pearson Australia Group Pty Ltd)
Penguin Books India Pvt Ltd, 11 Community Centre, Panchsheel Park, New Delhi – 110 017, India
Penguin Group (NZ), 67 Apollo Drive, Rosedale, Auckland 0632, New Zealand
(a division of Pearson New Zealand Ltd)
Penguin Books (South Africa) (Pty) Ltd, 24 Sturdee Avenue, Rosebank, Johannesburg 2196, South Africa

Penguin Books Ltd, Registered Offices: 80 Strand, London WC2R 0RL, England

First published 2012

1 2 3 4 5 6 7 8 9 10   (C)

Copyright © Canadian Broadcasting Corporation, 2012
Foreword copyright © Ron MacLean, 2012

Cover photographs courtesy of CBC

Photo credits on page 319 constitute an extension of this copyright page.

Manufactured in the U.S.A.

LIBRARY AND ARCHIVES CANADA CATALOGUING IN PUBLICATION

McKinley, Michael (Michael B.)
   Hockey night in Canada / Michael McKinley.

Includes index.
ISBN 978-0-670-06698-8

1. Hockey night in Canada (Television program) 2. Television broadcasting of sports—Social aspects—Canada. I. Title.

GV742.3.M35 2012   070.4'497969620971   C2012-903283-2

Visit the Penguin Canada website at **www.penguin.ca**

Special and corporate bulk purchase rates available; please see
www.penguin.ca/corporatesales or call 1-800-810-3104, ext. 2477.

ALWAYS LEARNING   PEARSON

For my daughter, Rose,

and all the girls and boys who are

the next generation of hockey players.

Their love of the game was learned beside us,

long before skate was put to ice,

through that magic of sound and light called

Hockey Night.

Contents

PREGAME

by Ron MacLean

Foreword

Leo Tolstoy described art as a means of communion among people. He explained that just as words convey one's thoughts and experiences and serve to unite people, art does something similar, but with feelings. *Hockey Night in Canada*, the show, the good old hockey game, is a feeling. Made real, symbolic, made better because of the words added throughout the years. Words that were sometimes thoughts. Stories and opinions. But also words that were sound effects. Foster Hewitt taught Bob Cole the four levels of intensity, Danny Gallivan invented words, and Dick Irvin gave them a sense of history. To "dangle" used to mean skating fast, nowadays it represents stickhandling. Feelings and thoughts that have become a communion among Canadians. In a word, art.

Over time, we developed a national friendship that is entertainment, sometimes an education and always a connection of the best kind. You cannot be lonely with us. We are all drawn to the show, like moths to a flame. Such a long-lasting relationship would seem a daunting ideal. But it lasts because the feelings are anchored snug. There is a saying "Life's short, Art is long." If I say that reminds me of a Norman Rockwell or a Group of Seven setting, the image you conjure is instant.

But those associations took time to plant. And that's how it is with us. Sixty years.

It is a show that allows us to break bread with our ancestors. It links the generation who saw ghostly images of the players back in 1952–53 with present day viewers, watching their high-definition big-screen televisions with Dolby sound. The technology has changed. We can follow our favourite team via Twitter, on smart phones or streaming over the internet, and *Hockey Night* has embraced those innovations. But for however many ways the dish is served, it's still cooked up around the hot stove. *Hockey Night in Canada* slides us easily into a warm and cozy past.

I've been with the telecast twenty-seven years. I should have grown up long ago. And yet on many Saturday nights, I still picture myself doing what I did as a child, rushing out to purchase my snacks. Sunflower seeds, red licorice and a pop. Making sure I was seated in time to see the "opening" of the show. And so just before we get on with our story, I thought I would reprise one other aspect of the fan worship of my youth. Hockey cards. That was the closest thing we kids had to an interactive experience. I could check out each player's birthplace, size and statistics. Of course I'd only look at the cards during commercial breaks. My favourite cards were the first and second team all-star cards, honouring the best performers of a given season. To this day, I often show my cards on the show when telling stories.

So I am going to pick twelve voices of *Hockey Night* I believe worthy of an all-star card—twelve men whose words not only gave us an outward depiction of things, but also their inward significance. It's going be Team *Hockey Night in Canada* versus Team *La Soirée du Hockey*. And you would love your chances in Game 7 with either crew.

TEAM *HOCKEY NIGHT IN CANADA*

LW—René Lecavalier—"Il lance … et compte!" "Et devant le but. Et le but de Henderson. Avec trente-quatre secondes encore!" Thirty years of elegance.

C—Foster Hewitt—"Hello, Canada." "Henderson takes a wild stab at it. He shoots, he scores! Henderson has scored for Canada." He stands alone.

RW—Jim Robson—"There is going to be that seventh game. We'll hope they can patch Linden up and get him in that one. He will play. You know he'll play. He'll play on crutches. And he'll play at Madison Square Garden on Tuesday night. The game is over!" Plus his famous shout-out to shut-ins. Beloved.

LD—Don Cherry—Don became the Canada in our show and was always on a mission to make it fun. "Tolstoy! What are we doing here?"

RD—Gilles Tremblay—The finest teacher at Radio-Canada. Hall of Famer.

G—Dick Irvin—The last line of anything at *Hockey Night* belongs with Dick. Between his father and himself, a century of keeping score. Inarguably our guardian of what the show means.

TEAM *LA SOIRÉE DU HOCKEY*

LW—Bob Cole—"They're going home. We went to Russia and took it all. Now they're going home." "Stand up and cheer, Canada." "There's a new kid on the block, the Edmonton Oilers by name." "Oh baby!" Case closed.

C—Richard Garneau—Brilliant narrative and cool. When Jacques Lemaire bristled at Garneau's criticism of his play in Minnesota, Richard said to Jacques, "How did you hear about it?" Lemaire said, "My family listens!" The next night in St. Louis, Garneau did the entire sixty-minute broadcast without mentioning Lemaire once! He's a legend.

RW—Danny Gallivan —"1:27 remaining in regulation time, Boston 4, Montreal 3. Lafleur's coming out rather gingerly on the right side, gets it to Lemaire, back to Lafleur. He scores!" Then not a word as the crowd convulses. Inimitable!

LD—Howie Meeker—"Golly gee whiz, Jiminy Crickets, standing on a pier he couldn't put a puck in the ocean!" The way he talked and his use of the telestrator made him the first superstar analyst.

RD—Brian McFarlane—"The best sports production in the world is *Hockey Night in Canada*, and their best is Brian McFarlane. That is why we got him."—Scotty Connal, NBC Sports. Historian, author and creator of Peter Puck.

G—Dave Hodge—Dave's the one who spoke to me. I idolized his work. I could never mirror his edge, but I borrowed his approach to detail. It is technically true I owe my career to Dave moving on. The fact is, I owe him even more for the inspiration.

So those are my all-stars, but as you'll read there are many more, and often they're not names or faces we'd recognize. They are the production and technical wizards behind the camera.

Foster Hewitt believed he was just lucky. I'm guessing all of us feel that way. It's not something you explain. The height of art is to conceal art. Those of us framed by the artists who keep creating *Hockey Night in Canada* would simply wish to say thank you. Here's to Saturday nights. To communion. Enjoy.

FIRST PERIOD

Hockey Night in Canada was already a powerful character in the Canadian imagination when it stepped onto the stage of television in 1952. For nearly three decades, millions of Canadians, Americans, and Newfoundlanders had made a date with the radio every Saturday night—at dinner time in Vancouver, and at (extended) bedtime for children in St. John's—to hear Foster Hewitt spin tales of the icemen. So sacred was their place in the national drama, some thought television would ruin the weekly story with its cold, myth-censoring eye. But as this new medium of TV would soon show, hockey was a game that loved the electronic limelight. What was already a national passion would now become an obsession, as *Hockey Night in Canada* invented a new way to look at an old game.

In the Beginning ...

If Foster Hewitt hadn't existed, it would have been necessary to invent him. But instead, he invented himself, and intersected with history in a way that allowed him to make history himself. By inventing *Hockey Night in Canada*.

Hewitt, an Upper Canada College prep schooler, University of Toronto boxing champion (a flyweight at 5'7" and 112 lbs), and general radio nut, was just 21 years old when the first hockey radio broadcast came from Toronto's Arena Gardens on February 8, 1923. The first NHL game on radio came out of the same arena on February 14. The Toronto St. Patricks delivered a bitter valentine to the Ottawa Senators, 6–4.

Hewitt's excited, nasal tenor finally penetrated the ether two days later, when he broadcast the Toronto Argonauts game against the Kitchener Greenshirts. And the fact he was there at all was a combination of luck, work, and an opportune family connection.

Hewitt's father, the formidable W.A., sports editor of the *Toronto Daily Star*, had told his son that the *Star* was going to start a radio station. Hewitt, obsessed by the broadcasting power of the new medium, left his job with a radio manufacturer, quit his arts-faculty studies at U of T, and, not hurt by his father's position, began as a *Star* beat reporter. Waiting for his radio chance.

On March 28, 1922, the *Star* broadcast its first live radio "entertainment" program, a Toronto concert beamed out as far as London, Belleville, Buffalo, and Rochester. CFCA Radio was born three months later, and, in an early example of convergence, the newspaper promoted its radio station and vice-versa. This cross-promotion was done, though, with such amateur sensitivities that it seems not from another century, but from another planet, with the reigning idea being that paid advertising was intrusive on the privacy of listeners.

Foster Hewitt was the voice of *Hockey Night in Canada* before it even had that name. He enshrined the show in the Canadian imagination in a career that spanned forty years.

5

Foster Hewitt announcing a game from his Gondola in Maple Leaf Gardens, 1933.

However, privacy was not an issue when CFCA, after a few months of running news and music, needed to expand its programming to lure more ears to the enterprise. Hewitt, now working on radio assignments, loved the suggestion that CFCA broadcast a hockey game. But that idea was quickly frozen by the paper's skeptics: hockey was too fast and complicated to explain to people who couldn't see it. Radio was thought to be a passing fad. And probably the clincher, no one in the sports department wanted to volunteer for the doomed mission.

A few weeks passed before the cold idea thawed fast (broadcasting decision-making hasn't changed a lot in the past century). As Foster was shuffling homeward after an eleven-hour shift at the *Star*, his boss, Bruce Lake, handed him the radio assignment by extolling convergence: the broadcast had been advertised in the paper. So Hewitt broke a date with his sweetheart, Kay How, then hustled to the arena on Mutual Street and, fortified with a five-cent hot dog, met up with history.

As he would do for years to follow, Hewitt recapped the first two periods for his radio audience, then did a live broadcast of the third period. The concept of "live," however, was fraught with difficulty and doubt. His radio bosses, like others in the nascent industry, were wary of crowd noises spoiling the product.

HOCKEY BEFORE RADIO

Hockey broadcasting did not begin with the radio. Stanley Cup competitions between Montreal and Winnipeg at the end of the nineteenth century saw large crowds gather to hear telegraphed updates of the game. Foster Hewitt's father, W.A. Hewitt, promoted the Paragon Score Board in 1901, on which a professional announcer would dramatically read out telegraphed play-by-play of World Series baseball games to theatre crowds, who, enraptured, watched a board onstage light up to show players on base, where the ball was hit, types of pitches, and so on

The *Toronto Star* newspaper ventured into the new medium of radio in the 1920s.

(interestingly, W.A. Hewitt's commercial sports broadcasting venture occurred at about the same time that, as the powerful secretary of the Ontario Hockey Association, he was banning hockey players from taking money for playing the game).

So Hewitt was sealed into a glass box at rinkside, three feet square and four feet high. Squatting on a stool with sawed-off legs, Hewitt had to wipe the glass windows of his cubicle so he could see through the fog made by his body heat colliding with the rink's chill. It made the players look as if they were "floating on clouds."

Foster Hewitt literally "called" his first game by describing the action not into a microphone, but into a telephone. About ten minutes before going live, Hewitt took the receiver off the hook of a phone in his "broadcast booth," spoke to the telephone operator and his engineer, synchronized watches, and then left the receiver to hang, keeping the line open. He would need only the mouthpiece of the phone to do his broadcast, which would then be relayed through the CFCA transmitter.

It was a good thing that Hewitt wasn't using the receiver. Phone lines were shared in those days, so other callers and the operator were squawking at him to get off the line, or to ask what number he wished to call, all while he was trying to call the game. But he couldn't hear them. All he could hear as he sat in that tiny glass box, his knees up to his chin, was a scary voice in his head telling him that no one was listening.

But people were listening—then, and onward, for half a century, as he

A cartoon from the 1920s wittily dramatizes the visual power of radio.

chronicled the travails and the triumphs of the icemen. No one knows for certain if Hewitt coined his famous "He shoots, he scores!" on that first night in 1923, though he thought he might have. But that's the way myths begin, and so, for this epic story of the union between a hot game and a cold country, brokered and impassioned by the images hymned over the dark winter airwaves, when Foster Hewitt opened his mouth to begin his first radio broadcast it was already game on. The show didn't have a name, yet, but it had found its voice.

XWA (later CFCF) received Canada's radio broadcast licence in 1919, and by 1922, there were nearly 10,000 radio sets in Canadian homes. In the spring of 1922, the Hewitts went to the first-ever radio show in Detroit, where they marvelled at Henry Ford's ten-tube radio—largest in the world—and where Foster managed to convince a manufacturer to sell him thirty-five Tecla crystal radio sets, which he imported to Canada, and sold at a profit. Radio was so popular in both Canada and the United States that an amendment was made to the Radiotelegraph Act, allowing only British subjects to apply for radio licences in Canada in order to prevent U.S. domination of the airwaves. Of course, radio waves don't carry passports, something that Hewitt acknowledged with his signature opening to his broadcasts: "Hello Canada and hockey fans in the United States and Newfoundland!"

This state-of-the-art 1931 radio is also a fine piece of living room furniture around which families gather to hear Foster Hewitt call games from the brand new Maple Leaf Gardens.

Radio Days

A flying coat, gambling, Foster Hewitt, and golf. It's an unusual quartet, but it gave figurative birth to the first incarnation of *Hockey Night in Canada*—the radio show that skated through the winter ether to capture the imagination of the country.

It almost didn't happen because of the scrappy temperament of one of the most epic characters in Canadian history, Conn Smythe. A bantam-weight Toronto Orangeman who could start a brawl with his own shadow, Smythe so annoyed the German soldier taking him prisoner after Smythe's plane crash-landed in World War I that the German shot him twice, point blank. Smythe's thick flying coat saved him. And it saved *Hockey Night in Canada*.

On his return to Toronto after the war, Smythe combined knowledge gleaned as a varsity hockey player and coach at the University of Toronto with his lifelong love of risk. He gambled on hockey, won big, and with the profits created the Toronto Maple Leafs in 1927.

Enter Foster Hewitt.

Hewitt had grown up seven years behind Smythe in Toronto, and they had crossed paths in the sporting and social world. So when Smythe became total boss of the Leafs in 1928, he made a deal with Hewitt, nicknamed "The Voice," now a radio star in Toronto. Hewitt, who called hockey, football, and horse racing for CFCA, would become the exclusive broadcaster of Leafs games.

In June 1929, Smythe was playing golf on a modest nine-hole course in Orchard Beach, near Ontario's Lake Simcoe, with Jack MacLaren, an advertising executive. Smythe had visions of a grand home for his popular hockey team, something swanky where people could dress up as if going to the opera. And MacLaren had visions of the money that could be made by selling advertising in Smythe's daydream rink.

2

CANADA'S GREATEST SPORT PALACE

Maple Leaf Gardens, Toronto

The building, completed in 1931, is 350 feet by 282 feet, and its dome is 154 feet high. There are no pillars to obstruct the view. Seating capacity is 12,466; record hockey attendance 14,886. Ice surface (see sketch) is 200 feet by 85 feet. At either end are wire nets to protect spectators from wild shots on goal. Centre ice is marked by a circle. Dots shown on sketch indicate line-up positions of players. Lines across the ice are the blue lines. Broadcasting gondola is on the west side, sixty ... feet back from the ice.

HOW YOUR IMPERIAL OIL HOCKEY BROADCAST REACHES YOUR RADIO

By speaking into his microphone, the announcer creates faint electrical vibrations. A copper wire carries these to the Gardens' radio control room. Similarly, the cheers of the crowd are brought by wire from microphones hanging up in the rafters.

In the control room, the faint electrical vibrations from these two wires are first "amplified"—that is, increased in strength. Then they are "mixed", or blended, in just the right proportions, and sent out over another wire to the key station, which relays them to the network.

6,000 miles of double line carry Imperial Oil Hockey Broadcasts across Canada. Another double line stands by for emergency. A single line provides telegraphic communication between all stations. Total—30,000 miles of copper wire, strung on 300,000 telegraph poles.

Every hundred miles or so, the broadcast is "boosted" slightly in volume for the next stage of its wire journey. When it reaches a radio station, it is given a tremendous "boost"—sending it flashing through the air to your home.

More than 150 radio engineers are employed across Canada each Saturday evening in helping to bring you these Imperial Oil Hockey Broadcasts.

OIL HOCKEY BROADCAST NIGHT

| 6 P.M. PACIFIC STANDARD TIME | 7 P.M. MOUNTAIN STANDARD TIME | 8 P.M. CENTRAL STANDARD TIME | 9 P.M. EASTERN STANDARD TIME | 10 P.M. ATLANTIC STANDARD TIME | 11 P.M. NEWFOUNDLAND STANDARD TIME |

HOCKEY BROADCAST STATIONS AND TIME ZONES

6 p.m.	CBR Vancouver CJIC Kamloops CKOV Kelowna CJAT Trail		
		CHAB Moose Jaw CKCK Regina	
7 p.m.	CJOC Lethbridge CFAC Calgary CJCA Edmonton CKBI Prince Albert CFQC Saskatoon	8 p.m.	CKX Brandon CKY Winnipeg
		9 p.m.	CKPR Fort William CKGB Timmins CJKL Kirkland Lake CFCH North Bay CKSO Sudbury

(1) Substitute CRCT during early weeks of season.

(1)	CBW CKCL CKY	Windsor Toronto Toronto
(2)	CBL CFRB	Toronto Toronto
(2)	CKCL CFRC CBO	Toronto Kingston Ottawa
(3)	CFNB CBM CBF	Montreal Montreal
(3)	CRCK	Quebec

(2) Only station carrying mid-week games in Toronto during regular schedule.

(3)	CRCS CJBR	Chicoutimi Rimouski
10 p.m. (3)	CHNC CFNB CHSJ CFCY CHNS CJCB	New Carlisle Fredericton Saint John Moncton Charlottetown Halifax Sydney

(3) Quebec network carrying French language broadcasts.

EVERYWHERE IN CANADA ... SATURDAY NIGHT

N.H.L. SCHEDULE 1937-38

HOME GAMES READ ACROSS ★ ★ ★ ALL RADIO BROADCAST GAMES SHOWN IN RED AWAY GAMES READ DOWN

	MONTREAL	CANADIENS	TORONTO	AMERICANS	RANGERS	BOSTON	DETROIT	CHICAGO
MONTREAL	Imperial	Tu. Nov. 11	Tu. Nov. 23 Sa. Feb. 26 Th. Mar. 1	Tu. Nov. 6 Tu. Jan. 6 Th. Mar.	Tu. Nov. 2	Tu. Dec. 7 Sa. Feb. 19	Tu. Dec. 14 Tu. Feb. 22	Tu. Feb.
CANADIENS	Sa. Dec. 7 Su. Feb. 6 Th. Feb. 19	Oil	Su. Dec. Tu. Dec. 30 Su. Feb. 20	Su. Nov. 18 Su. Jan. 2 Su. Feb. 13	Su. Dec. 4 Su. Jan. 22 Su. Feb.	Su. Dec. 23 Su. Jan. 29	Su. Dec. 19 Su. Jan. 9	
TORONTO	Sa. Dec. 11 Su. Feb. 19 Sa. Mar.		Products	Tu. Dec. 21 Sa. Feb. 18 Tu. Mar. 15	Sa. Dec. 18 Sa. Feb. 15	Th. Dec. 2 Th. Jan. 27	Th. Nov. 11 Th. Jan. 15 Th. Feb.	Sa. Nov. 13 Sa. Jan. 8 Sa. Feb. 12
AMERICANS	Su. Dec. 12 Su. Jan. 9 Su. Feb. 27	Tu. Nov. 16 Tu. Feb. 1 Su. Feb. 20	Su. Nov. 14 Su. Jan. 16 Sa. Feb. 26	Make	Su. Nov. 28 Su. Jan. 23 Su. Feb.	Sa. Nov. 20 Su. Jan. 16	Su. Dec. 5 Su. Mar.	Su. Nov. 21 Sa. Jan. 22 Su. Feb. 20
RANGERS	Su. Nov. 21 Tu. Dec. 28 Su. Feb. 13	Tu. Nov. 23 Tu. Feb. 8	Su. Nov. 28 Su. Feb. 6 Su. Feb. 20	Sa. Nov. 14	More	Su. Nov. 18 Su. Jan. 9 Sa. Mar. 19	Su. Nov. 14 Su. Jan. 23	Th. Nov. 18 Su. Feb. 3 Su. Mar. 10
BOSTON	Tu. Dec. 21 Su. Jan. 16 Tu. Mar. 15	Su. Nov. 21 Su. Jan. 16 Tu. Feb. 22	Tu. Dec. 14 Th. Jan. 20	Su. Dec. 19	Fri. Dec. 3 Su. Feb. 13	Friends	Th. Dec. 16 Su. Jan. 30 Su. Mar. 6	Su. Nov. 28 Su. Feb. 6 Su. Feb. 13
DETROIT	Su. Dec. 5 Su. Jan. 16 Tu. Feb. 15	Su. Nov. 14 Su. Jan. 9 Su. Feb. 27	Su. Nov. 21 Su. Jan. 2 Su. Feb. 13	Su. Nov. 21 Su. Jan. 9 Su. Mar. 20	Su. Dec. 19 Su. Jan. 30 Su. Feb. 20	Su. Dec. 12 Th. Feb. 10	Every	Su. Dec. 19 Th. Dec. 30 Su. Mar. 13
CHICAGO	Su. Dec. 12 Su. Jan. 30 Th. Mar. 10	Su. Dec. 5 Su. Jan. 2 Su. Feb. 20	Su. Nov. 14 Su. Jan. 30 Su. Feb.	Su. Dec. 2 Su. Jan. 23 Su. Feb.	Su. Nov. 21 Su. Jan. 16 Su. Feb. 27	Su. Dec. 19 Su. Jan. 23 Tu. Mar. 1	Su. Nov. 28 Th. Dec. 9 Su. Feb. 13	Day

IMPERIAL OIL HOCKEY BROADCAST

NATIONAL HOCKEY LEAGUE GAMES ON THE RADIO

BROUGHT TO YOU ON BEHALF OF YOUR NEIGHBORHOOD IMPERIAL OIL DEALER...
HE WILL BE GLAD TO HAVE YOUR COMMENTS

Sat., Nov. 6 — Americans at Toronto	Sat., Jan. 22 — Boston at Toronto
Sat., Nov. 13 — Chicago at Toronto	Sat., Jan. 29 — Detroit at Toronto
Sat., Nov. 20 — Boston at Toronto	Sat., Feb. 5 — Boston at Toronto
Sat., Nov. 27 — Montreal at Toronto	Sat., Feb. 12 — Chicago at Toronto
Sat., Dec. 4 — Canadiens at Toronto	Sat., Feb. 19 — Americans at Toronto
Sat., Dec. 11 — Rangers at Toronto	Sat., Feb. 26 — Rangers at Toronto
Sat., Dec. 18 — Americans at Toronto	Sat., Mar. 5 — Montreal at Toronto
Sat., Dec. 25 — Detroit at Toronto	Sat., Mar. 12 — Canadiens at Toronto
Sat., Jan. 1 — Canadiens at Toronto	Sat., Mar. 19 — Americans at Toronto
Sat., Jan. 8 — Rangers at Toronto	
Sat., Jan. 15 — Chicago at Toronto	

IMPERIAL DEALER

BROADCAST OVER CKCL ONLY
Th. Nov. 4—Detroit at Toronto   Th. Feb. 3—Canadiens at Toronto
Th. Jan. 13—Montreal at Toronto   Th. Feb. 7—Montreal at Toronto

EVERY SATURDAY NIGHT 9 P.M. EASTERN STANDARD TIME

The stock market crash that cratered into the Great Depression was four months away, so Smythe and MacLaren, dreaming of their mutual glories, shook hands. And so *Hockey Night in Canada*, though still just a gleam in the eye, would soon become a reality.

Despite the hardships of the Depression—or perhaps because of them, as Smythe cannily topped up workers' wages with Maple Leaf Gardens shares—workers broke the ground for Smythe's dream on June 1, 1931. Five months later, on November 12, 1931, the bands from the Royal Grenadiers and the 48th Highlanders played "Happy Days Are Here Again" to an audience of more than 13,000 hockey fans, many of them wearing evening dress. The thought of donning a Leafs jersey, face paint, and a backwards ball cap would have been as ludicrous to them as the idea of broadcasting hockey had been to some of the Gardens board of directors.

As difficult as it is to believe today, where media coverage serves to fuel public attendance at sports events, Smythe had faced arguments that broadcasting the Leafs' games on radio would keep people away from the arena.

He had swatted down the naysayers with Foster Hewitt. The Voice had filled the Mutual Street Arena with his play-by-play of Leafs games, even if the radio audience joined in at 9:00 P.M. Eastern, about when the second period began.

When Smythe was trying to raise money for the Gardens, he had his assistant Frank Selke put together special game programs for the 1930–31 season. Smythe asked Hewitt to pitch the programs on air, emphasizing their drawings of the proposed arena. Hewitt's power was such that Smythe sold 91,000 programs that season, three times more than expected.

Hewitt was aware of his own power. Despite an off-air demeanour so modest that his fans didn't recognize him as he walked the concourse of Maple Leaf Gardens, Hewitt was a tough negotiator. After all, he had been a U of T varsity boxing champion. So, when he agreed to be the voice of the Leafs in their new home, he won the right to produce the games through Foster Hewitt Productions. He also had approval rights over anyone else who wanted to broadcast or film in the building. And he won the right to negotiate advertising time with sponsors, take his cut, and hand the rest over to Smythe. What that cut was, Hewitt never said.

Imperial Oil advertising cards tell fans everything they need to know about the 1937–38 NHL schedule, the season's radio broadcasts, and even how the game makes it through the airwaves to their radios.

Hewitt first tried to woo the British American Oil Company as the hockey show's sponsor, but BA's new president was a baseball fan. General Motors, though, was looking to spend money, and MacLaren Advertising connected them to Foster Hewitt. The deal decreed that MacLaren would buy exclusive rights to Maple Leafs games, broadcast exclusively by Foster Hewitt, and sell them to General Motors. The cost: $500, at a time when Maple Leafs gate revenues were close to $200,000.

The Leafs lost that first game in their Gardens to the Chicago Black Hawks, and the radio broadcast was almost lost, too. Three stations were to carry it, with the feed coming from the powerful 5,000-watt CKGW, a Westinghouse station controlled from the United States. When Westinghouse discovered their scheduled program had been cancelled for a hockey game, they pulled the plug. So, with about thirty minutes to broadcast time, the circuitry was hastily re-routed by Bell Telephone technicians from the Gardens through CFCA. And Hewitt went live, just in time, from his silver tube, nicknamed the Gondola.

It took courage just to get to the Gondola. Hewitt had to walk several metres above the ice along an initially handrail-free catwalk, then descend a steep ladder. After handrails were installed, it was still a frightening trip. Once Hewitt turned to see his intermission guest, Hollywood tough guy George Raft, desperately clinging to the handrail, refusing to let go. Conn Smythe, for all his bravado, never even tried to visit the Gondola.

But from it, 56 feet above the ice, Hewitt became Homeric, hymning the exploits of the icemen over the airwaves of the Canadian National Railway's network. The *General Motors Hockey Broadcast* was his own opera, his voice soaring on the roar—or falling with the silence—of the crowd. By the end of 1933–34, Hewitt's hockey broadcast could be heard over a twenty-station radio network from Canada's east to west coasts, as could hockey broadcasts from Montreal. By 1936, there were nearly 900,000 radios in Canada—and four people listening to each, for a potential audience of almost 3.5 million people in a country of 11 million.

And at the start of the next season, Imperial Oil took over as sponsor when General Motors' American president didn't see how hockey could sell automobiles. On January 1, 1937, the Canadian Broadcasting Corporation was born, and it became the national carrier for what would soon become known to all across the land—and, as Maestro Hewitt would remind listeners, in the United States and Newfoundland—as *Hockey Night in Canada*.

Fans flipping the Charlie Conacher poster on page 11
would find this handy pocket-sized NHL schedule.

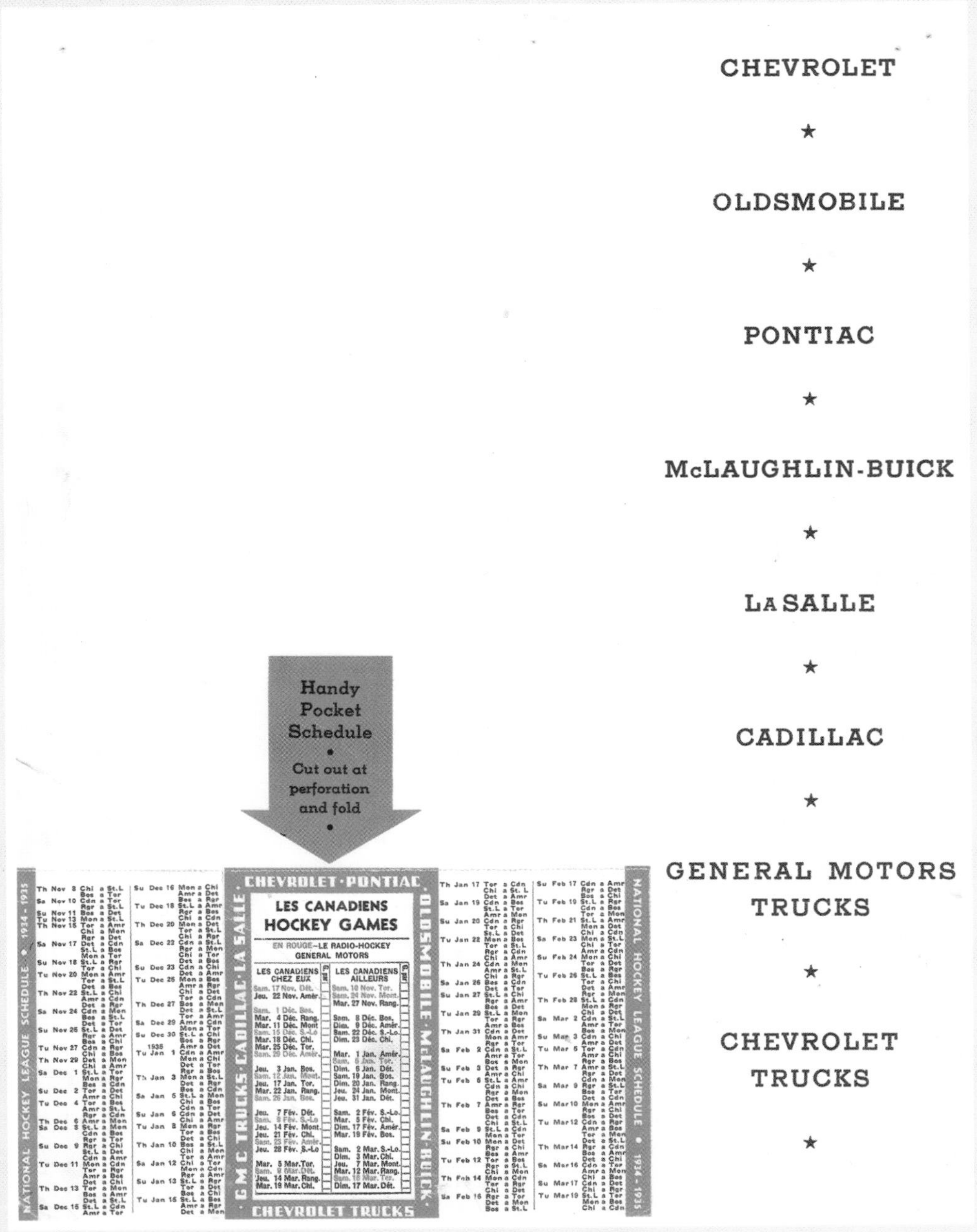

CHEVROLET

★

OLDSMOBILE

★

PONTIAC

★

McLAUGHLIN-BUICK

★

LaSALLE

★

CADILLAC

★

GENERAL MOTORS
TRUCKS

★

CHEVROLET
TRUCKS

★

Handy
Pocket
Schedule
•
Cut out at
perforation
and fold
•

War

On Saturday, February 17, 1940, an extraordinary experiment took place at Maple Leaf Gardens. On the surface of things, it seemed another winter Saturday in Canada: the Toronto Maple Leafs took on the Montreal Canadiens, and up in the Gondola, Foster Hewitt called the play-by-play, which ended in Toronto's 3–1 victory. This time, though, Hewitt's broadcast was being recorded for a mission of national importance. The recording was a test run for a program that would transmit the *Imperial Oil Hockey Broadcast*, as it was now called, to Canadian troops in the U.K. preparing to fight Hitler.

Precisely at 9:00 P.M., a "sapphire cutting needle was dropped on the shining virgin surface of a 16-inch blank transcription disk." Each disk could record seventeen minutes of Hewitt's broadcast, so CBC technicians kept changing disks until Hewitt signed off "at 10:32½ P.M."

Then Hewitt and more than a dozen engineers, technicians, and producers tried to squeeze the 92½-minute broadcast into a thirty-minute hockey night record. In fact, the mission was even more streamlined: there would be twenty-six minutes of game highlights, and four minutes of scene-setting.

There was a problem: no one had done this before. In a game where four goals were scored, and were obvious selections for the condensed broadcast, what else could the production team choose to include? More importantly, how should they do it?

Conn Smythe, World War I veteran, creator of the Maple Leafs and arch-patriot, sees the hockey player as a warrior in training. Here he shakes hands with Leafs' captain Syl Apps on September 8, 1940, at Niagara camp. Looking on are Phil Stein, Red Horner, and Clarence "Hap" Day. Smythe will echo the war to end all wars by marshalling the Sportsman's Battalion, made up of Canadian athletes during World War II.

The answer lay in the essence of radio: sound. One of the team would listen for the ebb and flow of crowd noise, and cross-reference it to a graphic chart of logged play. Where the crowd made noise on the graphic chart, Hewitt's accompanying play-by-play would be selected. The condensed disk would then be transmitted to England via a shortwave broadcast across the Atlantic Ocean. The BBC would receive the hockey highlights, and re-broadcast them in the evening to lonely Canadians longing for the pleasures of home.

That the effort was being made at all was a testament to the power of both hockey and Hewitt. Nazi Germany had launched their stunning blitzkrieg on Poland on September 1, 1939. In February 1940, the Allies were engaged in the Phoney War (thus called because of sea and air action, but little on the ground) with the Nazis. The war would become starkly real in the spring, with the disastrous Battle of Dunkirk, the fall of France, and the Battle of Britain.

Hockey's importance to Canada, especially in the darkness of the war years, is beautifully caught by author Morley Callaghan, walking one snowy night in late December 1942 to Maple Leaf Gardens. Callaghan encounters a group of boys playing shinny, and though a stew of ethnicities, he sees them all as Canadian kids. And he sees how, as the country prepares for total war, hockey sustains it: "Hockey is our winter ballet and in many ways our only national drama," he wrote. "When the Germans were at the gates of Moscow the Russians were still listening to the plays of their classic dramatists, weren't they?"

Still, the man who ran the Maple Leafs thought the "national drama" provided just the kind of incentive that the fighting machine needed. So Conn Smythe, the arch-patriot who put the maple leaf badge that he and his fellow Canadians had worn in the "war to end all wars" on the sweater of his hockey team, created the Sportsman's Battalion. Smythe dragooned hockey—and football and baseball—players, as well as a lacrosse team, golfers, and a few sports reporters, into uniform to take them off to war.

Smythe's patriotism was at the heart of a national debate about who should be signing up to fight. The last thing that the National Hockey League wanted was a repeat of the casualty lists from World War I, when the pages of newspapers across the British Empire were littered with pictures of the corpses of athletes killed in battle. So hockey players from the NHL and other senior leagues were drafted into action as players. The idea was to keep morale high at home and overseas by having them play hockey for civilians and troops alike.

Though ninety NHLers had joined the army by 1944 (and 500,000 Canadians by 1945), the Canadian high command saw hockey, and Hewitt's broadcasts, as far more important for the psychological health of the country than seeing hockey players in harm's way.

Not only did Hewitt and the production team provide the comfort of a cherished weekly hockey night in Canada, but in 1941 the hockey radio broadcast showed how powerful it had become in just two decades. When Japan attacked Hawaii on December 7 of that year, panicked Canadian military officials demanded binoculars for Canada's defence of its own West Coast in the face of what they believed was an inevitable Japanese onslaught. When Canada's binocular industry couldn't provide enough pairs, the military turned to Foster Hewitt.

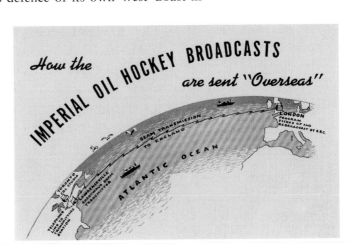

Hewitt and Imperial Oil made three appeals for binoculars during the hockey broadcast: on December 20 and 27, 1941, and on January 3, 1942. Despite the fact these pleas came during Christmas and New Year's, by January 17 the military asked Hewitt to "lay off for a week." They had already received 400 pairs of binoculars, and the binocular inspectors couldn't keep up. Despite Hewitt making no more requests for binoculars, and indeed, asking people to stop sending them, the military had received 1,116 pairs by the end of January. It was more than enough.

And Hewitt's broadcasts to Canadian troops gave those far away and facing violent death a consoling connection to home, one that reached the unlikeliest places. An RCAF Flight Lieutenant wrote to his wife in November 1944 that he'd heard Hewitt's condensed call of the Leafs–Canadiens game, while flying high above the earth on a reconnaissance mission. "Score being 2–0 for the Leafs. Pretty good reception, eh?"

Even the Nazis noticed. Radio Arnhem, a Netherlands station under German control, would join the BBC's transmission of Hewitt's broadcasts. Their announcer, known by Allied troops as Calamity Jane, would announce the switch to the BBC in order to present a feature "of special interest to Canadians."

An illustration from Imperial Oil's magazine reveals how hockey broadcasts go to war.

After each broadcast, the Nazi propaganda machine would appeal to the Canadian listeners to follow Hewitt's voice back to where they belonged. "Why not call off the war and go home?" Hewitt had a defiant response, opening his 1944 pre-Christmas overseas hockey broadcast with his usual greetings to Canadian troops, "and an extra big hello to Calamity Jane of Radio Arnhem."

Soldiers listening to Hewitt's hockey broadcasts in the U.K. a month before the Allied invasion of Europe. Hockey broadcasts were not only good for morale on the homefront, but also for soldiers serving overseas. The Nazis even picked them up, thinking they would make the Canadian troops throw down their weapons and go home. The tactic served only to remind the Canadians of why they were fighting.

Hockey broadcasts made their way to Nazi-occupied Europe via a complex process: highlights of Hewitt's game broadcasts were merged, with Hewitt's bridging commentary, to form a condensed package that was sent out from the CBC control room via telephone lines to the shortwave beam-transmitting station at Lawrenceville, and then onward to troops serving in Europe.

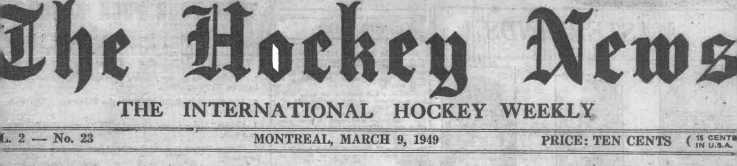

The Hockey News

THE INTERNATIONAL HOCKEY WEEKLY

L. 2 — No. 23   MONTREAL, MARCH 9, 1949   PRICE: TEN CENTS (15 CENTS IN U.S.A.

WILL VIDEO HURT HOCKEY?

N.H.L. President Warns TV May Keep Fans Home

By SYD THOMAS

MONTREAL, Que.— Television lost another round in its battle with sporting interests this week when President Clarence Campbell of the National Hockey League came out flatly with the charge that the new entertainment medium was a definite threat to the winter sport.

The N.H.L. chief asserted that television would adversely affect attendance by keeping present and prospective fans at home, and would further harm the game by presenting the less attractive features while missing out on the speed and skill which make the sport such a thrilling spectacle for rink-goers.

"Fights, injuries, boarding and other rough tactics are the easiest to catch on television," President Campbell told THE HOCKEY NEWS in an interview. "On the other hand, the fast end-to-end rushes, the skilful, attractive features of the game are most difficult to portray because of TV's limited field of view. This is not a proper representation of the overall action, and certainly can't be doing the game any good."

"This is especially important, since all the surveys taken so far have shown hockey to be one of the most popular forms of TV entertainment. But, if the television fans are going to get the impression hockey is made up only of fights and injuries, the game will suffer.

Regarding attendance, the league leader said that the future course of action would depend entirely on how television

(Continued on page 12)

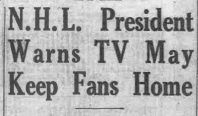

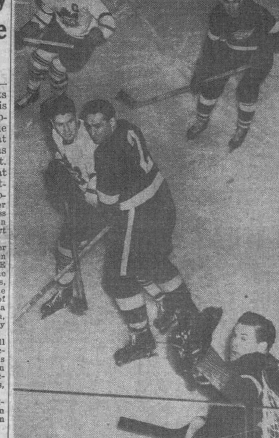

BETTER THAN VIDEO

THRILLING N.H.L. ACTION is caught by the cameraman in Maple Leaf Gardens as Toronto Maple Leafs tangle with various opponents. The Turofsky lens here shows some of the fast-paced plays which the rink-side observers see every game, but which the viewer of a television screen often misses.

Goalmouth scrambles, m

1952

In September 1952, the CBC added light to sound, and broke into the brave new world of television broadcasting. On September 6, CBFT went on the air at 4:00 P.M. in Montreal with the film *Aladdin and His Lamp*, followed by a cartoon, Jean Cocteau's drama *Oedipus Rex*, a news piece, and a variety show—in both official languages.

Two days later, CBLT began broadcasting at 7:15 P.M. in Toronto (the station's identification sign briefly inverted, and backwards) with a preview of the night's broadcast. It was followed by a weather report, the Uncle Chichimus puppet show, and the station's opening ceremonies. On the same night, the Boyd Gang obliged TV's demands for immediacy by escaping from the Don Jail. This launched both a massive manhunt and a news piece, narrated by Lorne Greene, on the bank robbers who had killed a Toronto police officer in March (and who would be captured eight days later, with two of the four gangsters hanged for the murder in December).

Nearly 150,000 Canadians tuned in on small, grainy black and white TV sets to the Toronto broadcast in a country that was on the cusp of significant social change. Canada's 14.5 million citizens were still largely white and ethnically aligned with the Union Jack or the fleur-de-lys, but the cultural mosaic was about to acquire exotic tiles from across the planet.

In 1949, NHL President Clarence Campbell echoed the views of many in professional hockey's boardrooms when he said that TV would hurt hockey by reducing attendance in arenas. The new medium's power would soon be realized by the NHL in the very place people feared it would be harmed: the balance sheet.

Canada, perceived as a land of bounty and peaceful promise while the smoke of a devastating war still clouded optimism in Europe, offered pristine hope, despite the winters. And so they came, first from the mother country, the United Kingdom, as well as from Europe, South Africa, and the Antipodes. Within the decade, as the Immigration Act of 1952 was reformed to emphasize education and family rather than race, Canada's cultural complexion grew richer with immigrants from Asia, South Asia, and the West Indies.

Despite having men and women still at war in Korea in 1952, Canada was forging a new sense of identity after the hardships of World War II. It was an identity based less on definition as a colony than as a country with its own ambitions, and the muscle to make them real. In the same year that Elizabeth was crowned Queen of Canada (the start of her reign preceded *Hockey Night in Canada*'s television debut by about nine months), Vincent Massey became Canada's first home-grown Governor-General.

The Old Age Security Act was introduced, while Lester B. Pearson, not yet a Nobel laureate or a Prime Minister, became President of the United Nations General Assembly. And the Edmonton Mercurys won Olympic gold in hockey in Oslo in February, the sixth of seven times in which Canada had triumphed on Olympic ice (the Soviets were to change all that by entering Olympic ice hockey four years hence).

Yet one of the other most significant events in Canada of 1952 was the untimely death of Harold Innis, the man whom Marshall McLuhan considered his messiah. Innis's life as an evangelical Baptist farm boy, a seriously wounded World War I artillery signaller, and a scholar of economics and history all combined in wondrous alchemy to make him a pioneer in the field of media theory.

Innis, a professor of political economy at the University of Toronto, divided media into those of time—hand-written and oral—and space—radio and TV and mass circulation newspapers. He believed the time-based media were more durable and socially constructive, imparting ideas that lasted over generations. Media of space were ephemeral, and prone to the vagaries of the marketplace through advertising. As such, they had less cultural resonance.

Innis's disciple, Marshall McLuhan, refined these ideas through his notion of "hot and cool" media. Hot media, such as film, did all the work for a viewer, while "cool" media, such as television, required more effort to derive meaning on the part of the viewer.

OPENING NIGHT

CBC stepped through the electronic curtain of television in September 1952. Performers waited backstage before CBLT's Toronto debut on the night of September 8. Director Drew Crossan could well have told the rapt group that they were about to journey into outer space once they stepped in front of the cameras behind the curtain. In the front row, a 20-year-old Glenn Gould, in white tie and tails, looked both skeptical of, and awestruck by, the journey ahead in this new platform for his talents. It is one that would disseminate his genius to the planet in a way no other medium could.

Toronto's portentous CBLT broadcast studio on English Canadian television's opening night, 1952.

The Toronto skyline from the 1950s on the Channel 9 logo—the *Hockey Night in Canada* television broadcast was coming right up.

Brand new 20-inch screen and cabinet—a real steal at $349 (black and white, of course).

Advertisements surround the rosters of Toronto and Boston in this program insert for the first televised game in English on November 1, 1952. Soon advertisers will be selling their wares on TV itself during games.

A modern *Hockey Night in Canada* broadcast studio—a multi-tasker's dream.

While McLuhan advanced his hot and cool media notions in the 1960s, the idea that TV viewers would apply their efforts anywhere that they could was already a powerful notion in 1952. And it was a prime mover of the CBC's rush to have a voice in the cool medium.

Television broadcasting had been a reality since the 1920s. General Electric broadcast *The Queen's Messenger*, the world's first live television drama, on its experimental station from Schenectady, New York, via shortwave as far as Los Angeles, in 1928. Television's power had begun to express itself through regular New York City broadcasting by the American companies CBS in 1931, and NBC in 1939. Two years later, NBC and CBS received commercial licences to create broadcasting networks, and by 1951, Americans from coast to coast could watch television.

The problem for Canadian cultural mavens such as Innis and McLuhan was that Canadians were watching those U.S. networks, too. People living in Ontario's Golden Horseshoe region had access to stations in Buffalo. Those in the Lower Mainland of British Columbia had Bellingham and Seattle, and Windsor-area residents could watch TV shows broadcast from Detroit. By the time the CBC entered television history, *The Globe and Mail* reported that 85,000 TV sets would be sold to Canadians that year. By 1954, there were a million sets in the country, or one for every fifteen people.

So the CBC's arrival was timely in many ways. Innis's ideas of culture being endangered by this spatial media were prescient in a way that still resonates in Canada, always needing to define itself by being different from the cultural elephant below the border. Those viewers of this cool medium in its infancy would be doing the interpretive work to provide meaning to TV's content.

Another problem that Canadian historians had grappled with in such a vast country was locating and placing the idea of "here" in the Canadian identity. So the medium that let Canadians see their stories, their heroes and villains, and share the passions of their country, came to be in September 1952. *Hockey Night in Canada* was more than a TV show in competition with football and baseball beamed up from the south. It became the cool lens through which Canadian viewers could watch the cool game, and through which they would see themselves for the next six decades—and counting. Suddenly, "here" was everywhere.

Hockey Night in Canada on Television

W hen Conn Smythe saw a closed-circuit telecast of a hockey game in 1952, he was not impressed. Despite Foster Hewitt's expert play-by-play of a Memorial Cup game in Maple Leaf Gardens, Smythe snarled at the TV screen, "If that's what hockey looks like on television, then the people of Toronto won't be seeing it."

Smythe's comment reveals much about his absolute power over the Leafs— indeed, over the city of Toronto—but also of the state of things in 1952, when CBC stepped into the world of TV. The first producers of *Hockey Night in Canada* pretty much had to invent the wheel when it came to televising hockey, despite the fact that the medium had been around for decades. So, how do you show hockey on television in a way that makes all the excitement and drama of a live game play the same way in the living rooms of the nation?

In 1952, Gerald Renaud was a 24-year-old sports editor for *Le Droit* newspaper in Ottawa, and also had a radio show on CKCH in Hull, Quebec. Renaud's brother-in-law, a producer of TV drama at the august National Film Board of Canada, told him that the CBC were looking for someone to produce TV sports in Montreal. Renaud applied, and to his great surprise, got the job. Which is how he found himself on October 11, 1952, producing Canada's first televised hockey game between Montreal and Detroit, featuring the sport's most fabled Number 9s, Maurice "Rocket" Richard and Gordie Howe.

Dark and intense, with a strong jaw and hot eyes, Renaud looked as if he could have been related to Rocket Richard, and indeed, he played hockey, too, though at a far less exalted level. Novelist William Faulkner famously said in *Sports Illustrated* that The Rocket's eyes as he closed in on a goal had "the

A CBC camera captures the action in a game between Toronto and Montreal— the historic rivalry becomes visual for the nation.

28

5

George Retzlaff, *Hockey Night in Canada*'s pioneering visionary, exits a broadcast truck in the 1950s.

passionate glittering fatal alien quality of snakes." Renaud's eyes, on the other hand, had to see the game that The Rocket and Howe played so brilliantly, and then translate that vision through a camera lens, so that viewers could see their brilliance, too.

Indeed, Renaud's broadcasting philosophy was simple: he wanted to place the cameras so that he—and so the viewer—had an ideal seat from which to watch the game. Since there was no one to ask about how to televise hockey, he read books on TV production, and drew diagrams of where he thought the cameras should go. In June 1952, he tested his ideas on a closed-circuit ping pong game, which moves fast, like hockey.

From there Renaud moved to baseball, and then, finally, in the city where the Canadiens are virtually a religion, to hockey. His mission was to get the Habs on TV with style and flair, reflecting the play of the team itself. Renaud decided that he needed three cameras to succeed, all of them close to centre ice. Camera Two was wide-angle, giving coverage of the entire rink. Camera One was for medium shots. Camera Three, directly at centre ice, was for close-ups, and for action in each defensive zone.

Four years later, Renaud added another camera, at ice-level, near the Zamboni entrance. This "goal camera" caught the action around the nets, but had to be used discreetly. If the director used the goal camera too much, it could disrupt the flow of the play. But if the director got it right, then the goal camera caught exciting action close-up. Best of all, it could follow a puck from a stick into the goal net, an angle that had often been lost in the days before four cameras.

Three weeks after the Montreal debut of hockey on TV, it was Toronto's turn. The man who produced TV hockey's first English telecast had an advantage: not only did he have the precedence of Renaud's broadcast, but he had some experience with cameras.

George Retzlaff had come from Germany to Canada as a four-year-old in 1927. His father planned to take up farming, which he had never done before, in order to scoop up the money shimmering in the Canadian wheat fields. When that didn't work out, the family moved to Winnipeg, and Retzlaff wound up working in radio.

The driven, Teutonic Retzlaff eventually moved into production, and in 1951 his ambition and ability propelled him to Toronto. There he worked as a cameraman, a lighting technician, a floor manager, and a producer. "I was mostly intrigued by the camera work," Retzlaff recalled [to George Gross in

Montreal's Elmer Lach faces off against Detroit's Dutch Reibel. For the first time, Canadians are seeing a televised face-off. Also on the ice are some of hockey's heroes of the day—Montreal's "Punch Line" featuring Maurice Richard and Detroit's "Production Line" with Mr. Hockey himself, Gordie Howe.

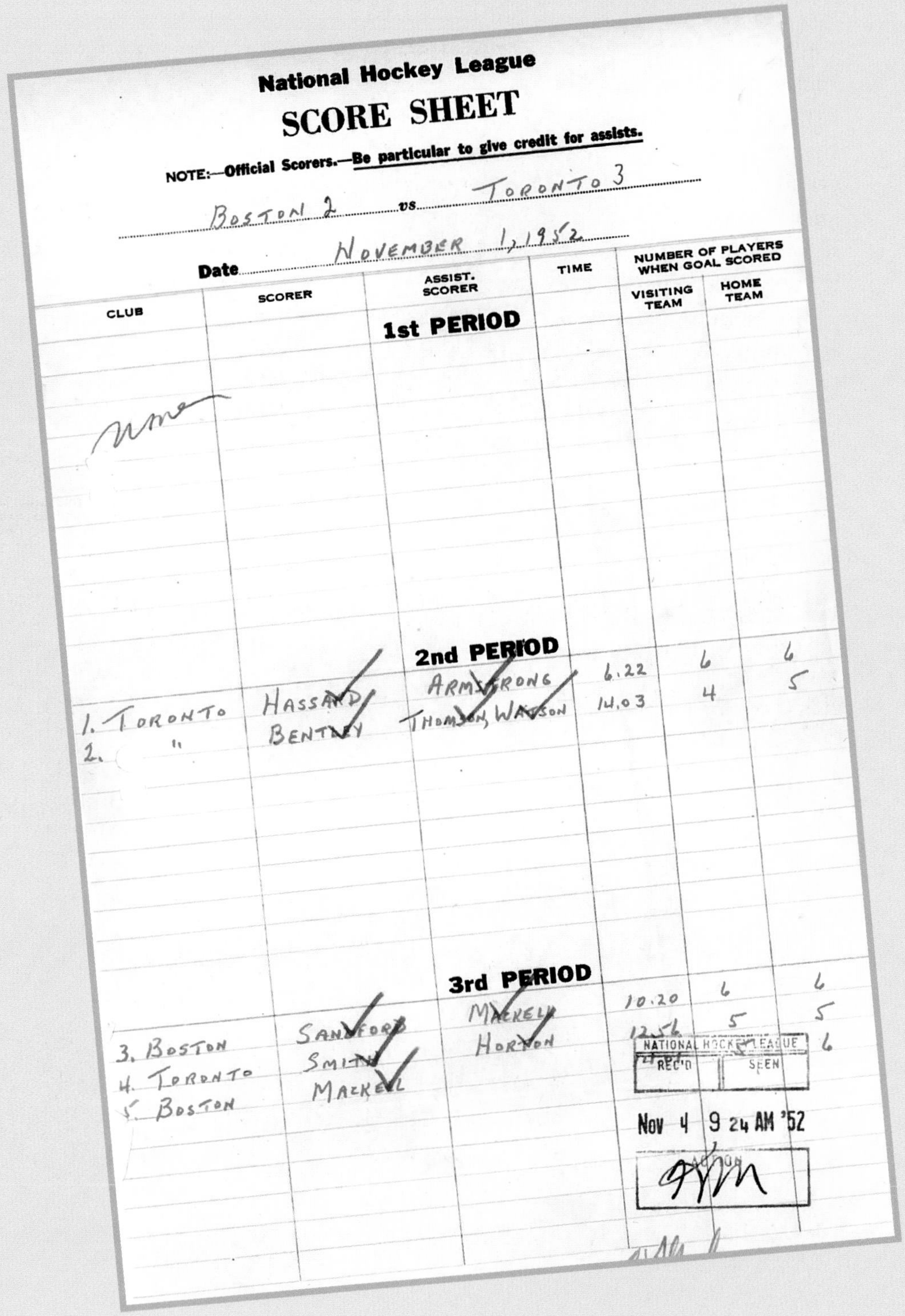

The official score sheet from the first *Hockey Night in Canada* game televised in English.

National Hockey League

SCORE SHEET

NOTE:—Official Scorers.—Be particular to give credit for assists.

BOSTON 2   vs   TORONTO 3

Date NOVEMBER 1, 1952

CLUB	SCORER	ASSIST. SCORER	TIME	NUMBER OF PLAYERS WHEN GOAL SCORED	
				VISITING TEAM	HOME TEAM
		1st PERIOD			
		2nd PERIOD			
1. TORONTO	HASSARD	ARMSTRONG	6.22	6	6
2. "	BENTLEY	THOMSON, WATSON	14.03	4	5
		3rd PERIOD			
3. BOSTON	SANDFORD	MACKELL	10.20	6	6
4. TORONTO	SMITH	HORTON	12.56	5	5
5. BOSTON	MACKELL				6

NATIONAL HOCKEY LEAGUE
REC'D   SEEN

Nov 4 9 24 AM '52

1969], "because I liked to try new ideas, unusual shots, and different camera angles."

Retzlaff had rejected the idea of installing a camera in Foster Hewitt's Gondola. The steep angle, he said, would make players look as if they were skating uphill. He also said no to Conn Smythe's suggestion—insofar as Smythe made "suggestions"—to place cameras opposite each other in the middle of the rink. The effect would be dizzying, with the picture cutting back and forth, but in effect showing the same action.

So, despite his love of the new, Retzlaff used Renaud's three-camera model, and produced the first NHL hockey telecast in Maple Leaf Gardens—and the city—that would become *Hockey Night in Canada*'s physical, not to mention spiritual, centre for more than forty years.

A 1950s *Hockey Night in Canada* cameraman—dressed as Conn Smythe meant Maple Leaf Gardens patrons to dress—operates state-of-the-art technology.

In a great and enduring irony that still raises the neck hairs on producers of TV sports, *Hockey Night in Canada*'s first English television broadcast aired on November 1, 1952, at 9:30 P.M., in the middle of the second period between Toronto and the Boston Bruins—just after Toronto's Bob Hassard had scored. The grand debut had missed the goal by seconds.

Later in life, Hassard recalled the event with amusement. "It was a trivia question forever, that apparently I scored the first goal that was ever televised," he later reminisced. "But the truth of it is that the goal had just gone in about two or three seconds before [the TV] came on and we were just patting each other on the back.... I didn't score the first goal on TV and really Max Bentley scored it later on in the game."

So, excited viewers thus just missed seeing their first Leafs goal on this exciting medium of TV, though they heard about it via Foster Hewitt's simultaneous TV and radio play-by-play. Indeed, Hewitt himself had been the subject of doubt as a TV broadcaster, as skeptics thought television would expose the "fictions" he'd inserted to make radio play-by-play more dramatic. In the end, Hewitt called the television games the way he called radio, and generations of play-by-play callers have done much the same. Telling us about what we're seeing.

Toronto won its first TV match 3–2, and Montreal had won its game 2–1, three weeks earlier. Montreal would go on to win the Stanley Cup that season, but as Renaud recalled, Rocket Richard provided a special challenge to producers of TV hockey. "You watch closely as Richard takes the puck. You know anything can happen," he told *Blueline Magazine* in 1955. "He's hard to keep up with, but you have to anticipate a play." And so, in summarizing The Rocket he summed up the lot of *Hockey Night in Canada* television producers ever since, who are still using the template invented by Renaud and Retzlaff, sixty years ago.

Above and right: These CBC broadcast trucks from the 1950s were forerunners of the mobile studios the network uses today.

1965, outside Maple Leaf Gardens.

First Period

Early Intermissions: The Hot Stove League

As soon as hockey took to the airwaves, its producers realized they had a new challenge. Even the perfect hockey game, with no whistles, would now run a clean seventy-five minutes. There would be sixty minutes for the game, and then another fifteen minutes to fill during the second intermission. Hard as it is to imagine today, *Hockey Night in Canada* games began on TV in the second period until 1968. There was only one live intermission on air.

For radio, the challenge was easier, as listeners took whatever came out of the radio—a hot, information-heavy medium, said Marshall McLuhan—and let their imaginations do the rest. Hewitt's radio play-by-play created legends and heroes for a generation who would never see their ice gods play, except in the mind's eye. Intermission fillers like the orchestras led by Joe DeCourcy and Luigi Romanelli were musical interludes to Hewitt's opera on ice.

But in 1939, C.M. Passmore, co-director of MacLaren Advertising's radio department and the man who christened Foster Hewitt's Gondola, realized that more could be done with the interval. Passmore created the Hot Stove League, featuring hockey experts having a chinwag around a hot stove on a winter night.

Hockey rinks, both indoor and out, had long featured a rest area where skaters could warm themselves next to a pot bellied stove. While pro baseball also featured a Hot Stove League during its winter hiatus, hockey's pundits were in season, and they were good radio—they knew their stuff and delivered it with a light, jocular touch.

Indeed, things were so loose in the radio studio that Hot Stover Harold "Baldy" Cotton, a former NHLer and then a hockey scout, once used his coffee cup as an ashtray. He was so engrossed in his dissection of the second period

Howie Meeker (centre) speaks to *Hockey Night in Canada* host Jack Dennett during a recreated Hot Stove League segment, featuring an actual hot stove.

that he failed to notice his windy oratory had roused the ashes into flame, now licking at his sleeve.

When hockey came to television, the intermission came with it. Smooth, professional Murray Westgate could kill three minutes with his Esso commercials. The supremely talented artist George Feyer could entertain with his live drawings that illustrated Westgate's narration of an Esso fable—the hare and the tortoise was one, in which Esso fuels the slow-moving reptile to victory with its high performance gasoline.

But what to do with the rest of the time? Hugh Horler, then vice-president of MacLaren, reckoned that importing the Hot Stove League would solve the problem. He had a studio built replicating a general store, with a real hot stove in the middle of it, which the host—eventually Leafs great Syl Apps—would stoke by scooping in wood. Guests would enter through a door to the right of the TV audience, and a bell would ring, announcing the newcomer.

What had worked on radio, though, was stilted on television. The producers tried other gimmicks, such as dressing the Hot Stovers Cotton and Apps in

Wes McKnight interviews The Cisco Kid.

MORE THAN A GAME

Things changed during the 1957–58 season, when the Hot Stove League vanished and player interviews took over. Teams had become more willing to let their players speak on TV, now recognizing the worth of selling the star value of their club on *Hockey Night in Canada*. Team executives appeared, too, as did others in the hockey world, such as the renowned Père Athol Murray, de facto hockey Pope of Notre Dame College. In keeping with what was popular in that time, "The Cisco Kid," complete with his western gear, was interviewed during the 1959 NHL semi-finals. The following season, Tom Foley, with his videotaped highlights, became a regular but most welcome part of the intermissions. Another popular feature was the Hockey Quiz, with comedian Johnny Wayne as a chain-smoking participant. Like popular quiz shows *Front Page Challenge* and *What's My Line?*, the Hockey Quiz panel had to guess at the answer by asking questions themselves, while the audience, in on the answer, was entertained by their often comic efforts.

Johnny Wayne, of *Wayne & Shuster* fame, ponders a question on the intermission feature Hockey Quiz, helped out by a bit of nicotine.

ill-coordinated hayseed duds, but the Hot Stove crew seemed tight and self-conscious. To be sure, segments in which they handed each other photos of the great players—which the audience couldn't see—didn't help. They also had no access to replays to deconstruct, as the replay hadn't been invented. So they wound up talking about plays the audience had also seen, without being able to illustrate their points. Or worse, they *didn't* talk about plays that the

Bandleaders Joe DeCourcy and Luigi Romanelli and their orchestras provided musical interludes during game intermissions before TV realizes its own power to provide visual features and interviews that help tell the story of the game.

Foster Hewitt broadcasts from his Gondola, made to look like the living room of the fans watching at home. There is nothing behind the blinds but concrete.

audience *had* seen. The Hot Stovers had to hustle over to the studio from Maple Leaf Gardens to make the intermission sequence, and so missed some of the second period.

Westgate's regular interruptions to do a commercial or announce the start of the third period were a welcome relief to everyone, except for Conn Smythe. The boss of the Leafs and builder of Maple Leaf Gardens had no time for dramatic convention when it came to appearing on the Hot Stove. Though gifted as a self-dramatizer, Smythe barrelled around the fake door and onto the set. When Westgate entered to announce the third period, pinging the doorbell, Smythe snarled, "Here comes the gas man. Time to go." And then he did.

One of the grand ironies of the Hot Stove League for Westgate was that he first met *Hockey Night in Canada* next to a real hot stove. "I'm from Regina, and we used to meet at the corner store down at the end of the road every Saturday night and listen to the radio," he recalled. "There was a hot stove in the centre [of the store], and in the cold of the winter, we'd come and all hang around in the evening, and listen to *Hockey Night in Canada*. I never thought I'd ever come near Maple Leaf Gardens!"

But there he was, wrangling Leafs greats such as Apps and Teeder Kennedy, when he wasn't selling gas, or narrating for the artist Feyer, or listening to Lorne Greene read a surprisingly witty *Hockey Night in Canada*-ized version of "'Twas The Night Before Christmas," with a wayward reindeer winding up in a flying gondola with Foster Hewitt. So *Hockey Night in Canada*'s intermissions carried on with the Hot Stovers, the wandering Esso minstrel, Westgate, and whoever turned up to help them invent the hockey intermission.

The Instant Replay

George Retzlaff had a problem. It was 1955, and three years into *Hockey Night in Canada*'s success on television, but he could see that viewers weren't seeing enough. Sure, they could watch a game live, in black and white, through a glass in a box. But no matter how dramatically Foster Hewitt called the play, or how entertaining the intermissions were, viewers still couldn't see great goals, or great plays, again. There was no such thing as "instant"—or even pretty quick—replay.

In 1955, the CBC used kinescope technology to film games in 16 mm from a telecast. They would then ship that footage to wherever it needed to be seen a day or two later, somewhere like Calgary or Edmonton, perhaps, as CBC Television wouldn't reach the Rockies until 1957. The process was cumbersome, and of no real help to Retzlaff, whose restless mind saw what he needed, but not the means to make it happen.

He had risen to direct CBC Sports by learning all aspects of TV production, and his "geek" side ensured that he kept up with the galloping technological developments and demands of TV. When he learned that a "hot processor" had been invented that could develop kine film fast, Retzlaff had his eureka moment.

"Once the goal was scored, it took half a minute for that length of film to be developed," says Ray Waines, a long-time CBC Sports cameraman who worked with Retzlaff. "Then that portion was cut and transferred wet to a 16 mm telecine projector system. Then he had to wait for a break in the game, to play back that goal at regular speed. Of course, George would have had to get the announcers ready to explain to the viewers what they were seeing and that it wasn't another goal!"

Two of *Hockey Night in Canada*'s inventors—George Retzlaff and Foster Hewitt—celebrate their achievement.

The inventor of the "creepy peepy" as captured through his own lens. On the right is Frank Selke Jr.

Retzlaff was as canny about corporate politics as he was about television, and didn't tell anyone other than his crew what he was up to. So, Hugh Horler and Ted Hough, his overseers at MacLaren Advertising, were as surprised at the result as Retzlaff's television crew, who gasped in delight when they saw TV's first replay.

Except Horler and Hough weren't delighted. Indeed, Retzlaff was excoriated for his revolutionary idea. He suspected the brain trust at MacLaren was angry because they didn't want Toronto broadcasts to look different from Montreal's and create any perception that one child was more loved than the other. Hough later protested that, no, he was annoyed because Retzlaff's secret ploy didn't allow him to promote the idea, and so win more viewers and sell more advertising.

The truth is likely a mix of both, but astonishingly, Retzlaff's replay technology was shelved. Instead, film features on intermissions were common throughout the 1950s. Host Ed Fitkin (later an executive assistant with Jack Kent Cooke's Los Angeles Kings) presented the first videotape footage from the game that viewers were watching during the intermission of the Toronto Maple Leafs home opener on October 10, 1959.

Surprisingly, the Leafs had been pioneers in using film since the 1940s. Don "Shanty" McKenzie, a former Toronto Argonauts football player who had served as a Sergeant Major in Conn Smythe's World War II Sportsman's Battalion, had become building superintendent of Maple Leaf Gardens after the war. In 1945, he was sent to the green seats, near the top of the Gardens, to film their home games on a 16 mm camera. Leafs players then watched the game film, and Toronto coach Clarence "Hap" Day would make sure they saw their mistakes—prefiguring the "teaching" use of video that became common in the NHL and other sports in the 1970s and 1980s.

Even so, it wasn't until the 1965 NHL semi-finals that the replay came back to stay. By then, U.S. networks were also experimenting with replay, but Ty Lemberg, a Retzlaff staffer from CBC Sports, developed a technique that allowed for even faster viewing of a play that needed to be seen again.

"Two VTR [video tape recorder] machines were placed beside each other, one to record and the other to play back," says Ray Waines. "They were joined

Hockey Night in Canada lost one of its first, and most promising, hosts when Tom Foley was killed in a car accident. Here Tom Foley is showing the public what videotape looks like.

by a piece of plywood with a series of rollers that delayed the 2-inch-wide videotape from getting to the playback VTR for about 10 seconds."

Right after a goal was scored, the switcher—whose job is to switch between cameras—cut to the playback VTR and the *Hockey Night in Canada* viewers then saw the previous ten seconds again, as an instant replay.

It was quick, and clearer than the kinescope replays. The ten seconds of footage was an arbitrary amount decided on by the technicians. They could have shown a minute, if they wanted, but there was no way to jump ahead of the footage, so they picked ten seconds as enough time to give context to a goal or save.

In those same 1965 playoffs, Retzlaff revealed another dazzling new gizmo. During an intermission, he demonstrated a hand-held camera—or "creepy peepy" as it was then referred to—which opened up all kinds of possibilities, such as rinkside or locker room interviews.

And if that wasn't enough, the CBC experimented with its first colour telecast in the 1965 playoffs, in a game between the reds and the blues, Toronto and Montreal. Colour television came to stay at the start of the 1966–67 season, though viewers still couldn't watch a game from the opening puck drop. Toronto goalie Terry Sawchuk watched the game from the bench, wearing sunglasses against the bright new television lights.

That same season, the slow-motion replay was born, and though choppy, it, too, added a new way of looking again at a live game. But it was the introduction of the replay that truly elevated sports broadcasting on television. The replay allowed for nuance and reflection, giving rise to the next generation of hockey analysts and allowing producers to be more confident in their creation of story lines, and to show viewers what they wanted them to see.

Anyone who doubts the power of the replay need only observe the Jumbotrons or giant video screens in almost every major sports arena or stadium. Now the experience of attending a game live is enhanced by being able to watch the replay of a goal missed—while out getting beer or texting a friend about what a great game it is. Even players look up to the Jumbotron replay after a play, to see what they just did. It's an ironic reversal of the old concern that fans wouldn't come to games if they could watch them on TV. Now, fans and players alike come to games knowing that the in-house replay will let them watch the game as if they were watching it on TV. Thanks to *Hockey Night in Canada*.

The view from the "creepy peepy" on the infamous steps in Chicago leading from the dressing room to the ice.

Six decades separate these CBC rinkside cameras. Though similar in size, the bottom camera, from today, offers its operator much more broadcasting firepower.

The Making of The Big M

*H*ockey *Night in Canada* made talent spotting a virtue—especially as it grew in confidence and scope. The show needed material to fill its intermission slot, and what better way to enhance the power of the telecast than by showcasing players in short feature films?

As *Hockey Night in Canada* approached its fifth birthday on TV, George Retzlaff and his fellow producers had seen players quickly made into even greater celebrities by the power of television. Early in the 1957–58 season, they took it a step further, and engaged in a risky bit of celebrity-making themselves by featuring the raw-boned son of a Croatian miner on *Hockey Night in Canada*, their fingers crossed in hope that the kid would last longer with the Leafs than his three-game stint the previous season.

Frank Mahovlich was such a tempting junior prospect in 1953 that scouts from the NHL were crowding the road to Timmins, Ontario, to try to sign the 15-year-old. The Detroit Red Wings offered his father a five-acre fruit farm on the Niagara Peninsula. The elder Mahovlich was insulted—*he* wasn't going to play hockey for the Red Wings. His boy Frank was the talent. And he needed a good education. So Frank Mahovlich took the Toronto Maple Leafs scholarship to St. Michael's College, where he was so impressive off and on the ice that he made it onto the Leafs straight out of school.

Mahovlich appeared in intermission feature profiles in October of the 1957–58 season, his first full one in the NHL. Indeed, the *Hockey Night in Canada* cameras were there to catch the 19-year-old packing for his first road trip with the Leafs. Mahovlich, dark, lean, and classically handsome in his white shirt and tie, shows off the puck on his bedroom dressing table, commemorating his first goal in the NHL.

Handsome and talented Frank Mahovlich was made for television and soon he would become a featured player on *Hockey Night in Canada.*

Hockey Night in Canada profiles Toronto Maple Leafs rookie Frank Mahovlich in an intermission feature during the 1957–58 season. In the bottom photo you can see a young Peter Mahovlich.

During his career, Frank Mahovlich would be accused of moodiness any time he wasn't pumping pucks into the net or skating as fast as spectators demanded from his prodigious talent. Indeed, he would be treated for acute depression within the decade, but even in this rookie feature, the seed that something is wrong is sown when the announcer cheerily proclaims over the pensive player's profile: "Some people say when they see him play that he never smiles much." On cue, Mahovlich turns his head toward the camera and flashes a smile. The announcer continues, "But he's got one here, and a big one for his mom."

Mrs. Mahovlich enters, portly and bustling in her dress and apron, and helps her 6'1" son into his blazer. The camera then follows young Mahovlich outside, introducing viewers to his 11-year-old brother, Peter, a future NHLer himself who plays for the Leaside Lions Pee Wees. On a ladder nearby, Mahovlich's father installs a storm window on the tidy brick house that his hockey-playing son has scored for the family in the Toronto suburb of Leaside. It's the perfect picture of Canadian suburban life in the 1950s, whence *Hockey Night in Canada*'s viewers come.

Mahovlich gets into his car, and drives himself off to Montreal, to face the Canadiens, for whom he'll also one day play. Though he doesn't say anything in the feature, the footage speaks loudly about what the Leafs think of him: a solid young man from a nuclear family, on whose broad shoulders rest the hopes of years to come.

Mahovlich will score twenty goals in his rookie season, and win the Calder Trophy as the NHL's top first-year player. And he'll win four Stanley Cups with Toronto, and two more with Montreal. He'll also be featured again, many times, on *Hockey Night in Canada*, but here and now in 1957, he's a star in the making, thanks to his play on the ice, and *Hockey Night in Canada*'s flexing of its star-making muscles.

The Electronic Skyway

If you had wanted to watch *Hockey Night in Canada* live in Vancouver in 1954, your 10" black and white television might have been able to pick up the show from a station in Washington State. The signal from Toronto would snake its way south, and along the U.S. microwave network, and if you were close enough to the U.S. border, then your antenna could connect with the signal.

If you and your television were farther north, then you had to wait until the kinescopes—the filmed versions of the telecast—made it out to the West Coast for re-broadcast. *Hockey Night in Canada* might have been a dependable, necessary, national event on radio. But television—as far as people living on the western side of the Rockies were concerned—was still like the settling of the far west itself, an adventure.

And then, on Canada's birthday in 1958, everything changed. Not just for *Hockey Night in Canada*, but for every other live program that the CBC broadcast from the country's far east to the far west. On July 1, one hundred and thirty-nine microwave towers, spanning 6,275 kilometres from Sydney, Nova Scotia, to Victoria, British Columbia, linked up to form an "electronic skyway." Now the CBC could send *Hockey Night in Canada* from coast to coast in one-fiftieth of a second. It was like magic.

Canada and the age of telecommunications were meant for each other. With 9,984,670 square kilometres, Canada is the second largest country,

A railroad physically linked Canada from coast to coast in the nineteenth century and in the middle of the twentieth century, an electronic skyway did the same, showing Canadians the national drama via *Hockey Night in Canada*.

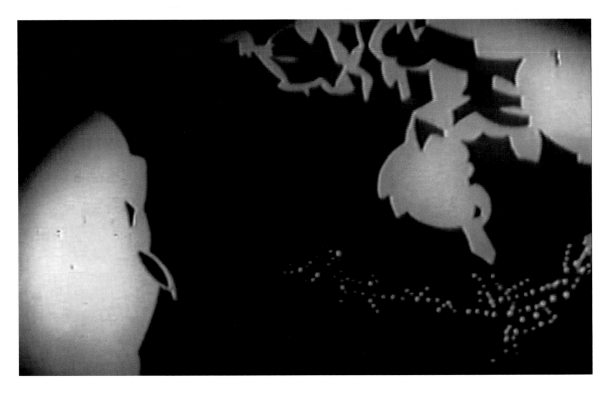

The lights reveal Canada's broadcasting areas—and where Canadians can get television—before the country is linked by TV in 1958.

geographically, in the world. The United States is third, just 200,000 square kilometres smaller than Canada. In 1958, the U.S. was home to nearly 175 million people; Canada, to 17 million. The electronic skyway was more than a technological marvel for Canadians—it was a profound cultural link among a sparse population stretched across a vast landscape.

Microwave technology was one of the by-products of World War II research, developing from discoveries connected to radar. The idea behind the microwave system was complex: TV camera images would be re-arranged into electronic pieces, sped along the electronic skyway at 186,000 miles per second, and then re-assembled for broadcast.

Since microwaves travel in a straight line, and not along the earth's curve, the towers, spaced forty-eight kilometres apart, had to be "visible" to each other, so rocks were blasted, trees were cut down, and towers ranged in height from nine to one hundred metres. The Trans-Canada Telephone System began the $50 million construction project in 1954, and by 1956 had connected Manitoba to the system, with Alberta following in 1957, British Columbia in 1958, and Newfoundland in 1959. By the middle of that process, the project had transformed Canada into the world's premier nation of television viewers, based on population.

HOCKEY TV ON THE WEST COAST

On Saturday, October 4, 1958, viewers in Vancouver could join *Hockey Night in Canada* for the first time via the electronic skyway. Given the time zone difference, the NHL All-Stars versus the Stanley Cup champion Canadiens began at 6:00 P.M. Vancouver time. The season started the following Saturday, with Montreal taking on Detroit. *Hockey Night in Canada* would be a dinnertime companion to millions of British Columbians even after the Canucks joined the NHL in 1970. Their games now began at 5:00 P.M. so eastern viewers could see them in prime time. In 1995, with the arrival of doubleheaders, West Coast viewers could watch the eastern game at 4:30 P.M. Pacific time, and the western game at 7:30. The development changed Saturday night rituals for millions of western viewers—and for those Canucks, Oilers, and Flames fans in Newfoundland, who now began their western telecast at midnight.

Canadians celebrate their first Canada Day linked from sea-to-sea by television.

10

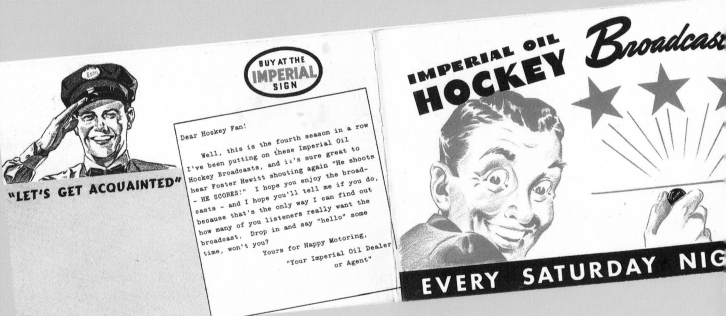

"LET'S GET ACQUAINTED"

BUY AT THE IMPERIAL SIGN

Dear Hockey Fan!

Well, this is the fourth season in a row I've been putting on these Imperial Oil Hockey Broadcasts, and it's sure great to hear Foster Hewitt shouting again "He shoots - HE SCORES!" I hope you enjoy the broadcasts - and I hope you'll tell me if you do, because that's the only way I can find out how many of you listeners really want the broadcast. Drop in and say "hello" some time, won't you?

Yours for Happy Motoring,

"Your Imperial Oil Dealer
or Agent"

IMPERIAL OIL Broadcast
HOCKEY

EVERY SATURDAY NIG

Murray Westgate and Happy Motoring

Murray Westgate was as much of a star on *Hockey Night in Canada* as some of the game's greatest names. He didn't score goals like Frank Mahovlich and Jean Béliveau, or stop them like Johnny Bower and Charlie Hodge. However, for sixteen years—or three times the average length of an NHL career—Westgate came into Canadian homes each Saturday, his warm baritone and easy smile wishing "Happy Motoring!" to millions on behalf of Imperial/Esso. Or rather, of MacLaren Advertising, who had also made the transition from radio to television as purveyors of the show that would soon be called *Hockey Night in Canada*.

Westgate had come to Toronto in 1947, via a circuitous route from his hometown of Regina. When World War II broke out in 1939, Westgate signed up for the thing that would get him as far from the prairies as he could imagine: the Royal Canadian Navy. He served for six long years as the adjutant to a staff officer, but it was no desk job. Instead, Westgate zigged and zagged the perilous North Atlantic, seeing ships afore and aft blown to smithereens by Nazi U-boats.

He emerged unscathed and headed west, first successfully dodging the amatory torpedoes of his next boss, a Vancouver theatre director. There he trod the boards with the likes of Ted Follows, and graced CBC Radio airwaves with his mellifluous charm. But Toronto offered more acting opportunities. As Westgate saw it, "If you want to grow strawberries, you've got to go where they grow them."

In Toronto, he snagged some small radio parts; then, thanks to a friend's neighbour being an Imperial Oil PR man, he landed a gig playing an Imperial Oil dealer for the company's in-house films, to be screened at sales conferences.

Murray Westgate was gas jockey to the nation—and much more than that—in his role as Esso pitchman and *Hockey Night in Canada* star for sixteen years. Here he introduces the Essomatic credit card.

"I was supposed to be the good dealer, and the bad dealer was across the street, all scruffy and messed up," Westgate recalls, laughing at the premise in his cozy room at Sunnybrook Veterans Residence in Toronto, where the sharp 94-year-old now lives.

Westgate, tall, forthright, and confident, created the perfect Esso dealer, and made several promotional films for the company. When TV arrived, he suddenly found himself screen-testing for the role he had already been playing on film. He passed the test, and soon he was selling the virtues of Imperial Oil via hockey every Saturday night—for $75 a night, at a time when a gallon of gas cost 25 cents.

It was just like being back in the theatre. "When we did it live I got the script in the afternoon at the CBC studio and I had to memorize it," Westgate says, pausing for effect. "It was three minutes long" (which, for an actor, is about the same length as Hamlet's "To be or not to be" soliloquy). Eventually, live commercials included teleprompters, which Westgate says were prone to malfunction. His solution: to tape his script to the back of a can of Marvel-Lube

Motor Oil, then hold up the can and read the script while pretending to study the can.

After the arrival of teleprompting, Westgate's commercials were recorded at the CBC studios on Jarvis Street. His live hits at Maple Leaf Gardens had him introduce the Hot Stove League, the intermission gabfest of pundits and former players that moved from radio to television in 1952, lasting until 1959.

When his sixteen-year TV run began, Westgate would speak from a faux Esso station in the studio, using charts, photos, and the help of the Hot Stove Leaguers to do his job. One classic commercial shows Westgate introducing the Esso credit card to the team. Though credit had been around for centuries, the 1950s saw the rise of the magic plastic card with which people get into debt with ease.

In the commercial, Westgate, with the flair of a magician, pulls the cover off a credit card imprint machine, while a bemused Harold "Baldy" Cotton, a former NHLer who won a Stanley Cup with Toronto in 1932, and his fellow Hot Stovers murmur in a mix of skepticism and wonder. The cover turns out

Murray Westgate offers viewers motoring tips during an intermission.

Murray Westgate takes a customer call at his studio gas station—to talk hockey.

to be a flag announcing the Essomatic card. Westgate runs Cotton's Esso card through the machine, explaining how its use will have him on his way much faster—"a real boon to Happy Motoring."

Westgate's fame grew with time, and so did his fee, rising to a "couple of thousand" a show, though never with a contract. He would just get a phone call every September, telling him that *Hockey Night in Canada* was about to begin, and back he'd go for another season of being the nation's favourite gas jockey.

His success, though, bred resentment among acting snobs. They saw no hypocrisy in sneering at those who acted for money in commercials while respecting those who did so onstage, or in film. "I was very active as an actor, but I had a little trouble because actors didn't do commercials in those days," Westgate recalls. "I remember one Saturday morning up at our cottage I was reading *The Globe and Mail*, and Stratford was playing then, and a big-shot actor in Stratford was being interviewed, and my name came up and he said, 'Murray Westgate! He should be ashamed of himself, doing commercials.'" Westgate harrumphs at the memory. "I did it to make a living!"

Westgate forgets the name of the actor who sneered at him. But in the funny way time sorts out insults, today people vividly remember the acting genius of Murray Westgate, who seemed so real as an Esso dealer that for decades people asked him for car advice when they bumped into him.

When the end of his Esso promotional career came at the beginning of the 1967–68 season, with an expanded NHL and a change in *Hockey Night in Canada* sponsorship, it came with a rather shabby silence. "There was no phone call, that's all," says Westgate. "I had a long run. Things change, you know?"

And so he moved on, appearing onstage and onscreen, and winning an Actra Award in 1979. He also made a comeback commercial in the early 1970s, replacing his peaked hat with an Esso ball cap, but sliding right back into the iconic status he'd created as *Hockey Night*'s honest, friendly, and competent

Esso dealer. Indeed, through Westgate's character, the values he projected became those of the show. He wasn't playing on the ice, but the people who knew the game best knew Westgate's value as a performer.

"At the end of the period the teams came filing out to their dressing rooms," Westgate says. "I was usually standing at the boards watching them come in, because I had already introduced the commercial, and it was on tape. So Gordie Howe comes by, with one of his pals, sweat pouring off their faces, and he looks at me and then looks at his friend and says, 'There's the guy with the best job in the league!'"

Murray Westgate promotes an Esso offer.

A Family Affair

The broadcast booth in Air Canada Centre, a far cry from the humble Gondola, is named in homage to the man whose voice lit up Canada from Maple Leaf Gardens.

In December 1936, *Hockey Night in Canada*'s radio broadcast suddenly had a new play-by-play man. Rather, it had a play-by-play boy, when 8-year-old Billy Hewitt took over from his famous father for a few minutes to call the action for Young Canada Night. On the last Saturday game before Christmas, patrons of Maple Leaf Gardens were encouraged to bring their own children, or friendly loaners, to a Leafs game. And so Billy Hewitt got to live the fantasy of hockey-mad children across the continent, sitting next to the great Foster Hewitt in the Gondola, and spinning magic over the winter airwaves.

Much of the younger Hewitt's life was the stuff of sporting fantasy. His grandfather, W.A., sports editor and Ontario Hockey Association executive, could talk about any sport under the sun with the boy—and he was on speaking terms with many of the day's athletic Apollos. His father was the best known— and most beloved—voice in Canada, entertaining the nation each Saturday night with the exploits of the icemen.

Even Hewitt's school days were gilded with hockey privilege. Each Saturday morning, Billy's Upper Canada College prep school team practised at Maple Leaf Gardens. In a gesture far removed from the hermetically sealed athletes of today, the Leafs would be having a light skate at the same time. Charlie "The Big Bomber" Conacher, a star power forward, would playfully scare the prepster goalie by unleashing his cannonball slapshot at the kid—missing wide, on purpose.

Twenty-two years later, Bill Hewitt, as he was then known, joined *Hockey Night in Canada* as part of the team for the Leafs' opening game against Chicago on October 11, 1958. Foster Hewitt introduced his son to the audience

Years later, Foster Hewitt interviews his grandson, Bruce, at Young Canada Night in Maple Leaf Gardens.

as a fellow professional: Bill would take over the television play-by-play, while Foster stayed on as the first Toronto "colour" man.

Foster Hewitt stayed next to his son for three years, and then switched to radio only. His was a heavy torch to pass, despite the younger Hewitt's skill at calling games. He sounded just like his father had sounded when he invented the prototype broadcast more than thirty years earlier: a nasal tenor, rising with the crowd's highs, and falling with its lows. The younger Hewitt was also blessed with an eagle eye, and was so accurate from his vista up in the Gondola that any doubters in the broadcast truck were humbled when they viewed a replay. They saw that Hewitt's naked eye had seen what the powerful, unblinking camera had seen, making his the right call, nine times out of ten.

Watching Bill Hewitt in early intermission interviews, though, reveals a man who is in his father's thrall. Though well into his thirties, he defers to "Dad" and seems like an awkward, nervous teenager, looking to his father to show him the way. So, for the 1963–64 season, *Hockey Night in Canada* reprised the colour commentator's job and auditioned various sports writers alongside Bill Hewitt in the broadcast booth.

Two seasons later, Brian McFarlane would sign on as the regular Toronto colour man, and stay there for the next quarter century. His professionalism and vast knowledge of the game allowed Hewitt to do what he had been wired to do: tell the viewers what was happening in front of their eyes, in a way that would make the obvious seem fresh.

But the younger Hewitt yearned in some primal way to escape the life for which he had been destined as an 8-year-old, calling Christmas games beside his father. So he took flying lessons, and his father didn't approve. "It seems silly, learning to fly," he said.

Hockey Night in Canada thought otherwise. They sent Brian McFarlane up in the air with Bill Hewitt during a flying lesson to film an intermission feature. It finally showed a human side to their automatic play-by-play man—a mixture of old silent film footage of barnstorming daredevil pilots, intercut with Hewitt flying and landing the plane, and McFarlane kissing the tarmac in relief.

When Hewitt won his wings shortly afterward, *Hockey Night in Canada* broadcast the feature, showing that Bill Hewitt could literally fly.

Foster Hewitt was not amused. Invoking noble lineage, he told his son that as his successor to the throne of *Hockey Night in Canada*, tempting fate in a private plane was folly. And so he banned his 45-year-old son from the one hobby that seemed to bring him joy.

Bill Hewitt went into a slow dive. A master of the play-by-play universe when there were only six teams, NHL expansion had caused him to struggle with player names. And then one night in the 1981–82 season, he plummeted. Hewitt was calling an exhibition game when suddenly he confused players— they all looked the same. He had suffered rapid weight loss in the weeks preceding the event, and would lose 50 pounds before the dive was stopped.

While Ted Reynolds interviews Toronto Maple Leafs star goalie Johnny Bower in full gear in the studio between periods, Ed Chadwick, Toronto's backup goalie (right), uses his appearance on *Hockey Night in Canada* to signal to his daughter as he had promised to wave to her during intermission.

But it wasn't reversed. Nor was the medical reason for his alarming descent ever revealed, leading to cruel speculation that Hewitt was under the influence of drugs or alcohol or both. In all likelihood, he'd suffered a breakdown. He took a leave of absence from hockey. In his year away from the game, he decided he didn't want to come back. As he had done when he first brought young Billy to the microphone, Foster gave his blessing for his son's leaving of it. And with that, the Hewitt dynasty's end was in sight.

TV and Players' Unions

On November 2, 1957, Gus Mortson returned to Toronto and fired a very public shot in the revolution that would lead the NHL to a new promised land. It wasn't the first shot in the war, but *Hockey Night in Canada* caught it. And captured the end of one era and the beginning of another, where players would no longer be in economic bondage to team owners.

Mortson had won four Stanley Cups with Toronto and an all-star spot every season since he entered the NHL in 1946. He was known as "Old Hardrock"— partly because of his origins in northeastern Ontario's mining country, but mainly because he was as tough as the rebar that supported the mine shafts. He and another hardrock, Gordie Howe, are the only two players ever to fight each other at the gentlemanly All-Star Game. In his thirteen NHL seasons, Mortson racked up an astonishing 1,380 penalty minutes—he never backed down from a battle.

It was no surprise that he was on board when a fellow northern Ontario mining kid, Ted Lindsay, started organizing players to take on the NHL owners. Lindsay, a Detroit Red Wings all-star, had been appointed to the board of the NHL's Pension Society in 1952, full of hope. Finally, the owners were going to treat the players as partners. The owners quickly killed that idea, refusing to let the players see the books to their own pension fund, begun in 1947. The players were contributing 20 percent of their annual salaries to the fund, and the NHL added $600 a player from All-Star Game revenue. The All-Star Game was one which the players played for free.

It was a revolutionary time for professional athletes. A "players' association" had begun in major league baseball in the United States, so Lindsay flew to New York to talk to the lawyers who had helped the ball players organize.

Toronto's Hall of Fame goalie Walter "Turk" Broda celebrates with boss Conn Smythe.

Gus Mortson mock salutes Major Conn Smythe (sitting a few rows back), owner of the Toronto Maple Leafs and ardent opponent of the nascent players' union.

There he learned what was going to drive the revenues of all professional sports: television.

The NHL owners maintained that they didn't make any money from TV, nor did they make anything from paying customers. This was patently false: Conn Smythe saw so much money in television that after just one TV season he raised the fee from $100 per televised Leafs game to $450,000 over three years. And the other owners knew it.

The players knew almost nothing. The owners controlled information, and players were strongly discouraged from speaking to players on other teams. It was considered a kind of treason. But Ted Lindsay saw beyond the smokescreen of pieties. So, when Lindsay and player representatives from those other teams held a press conference in New York on February 12, 1957, to announce the birth of a players' association, they had signed up every player in the NHL except for Toronto star Ted Kennedy—who was retiring.

The owners wanted to meet this new association after the 1957 playoffs, so Mortson—who, after six years in Toronto, was unhappily traded to Chicago in 1952—and his fellow player reps went down to Florida. In the meeting, Mortson found himself sitting at the far the end of a long table, ready to explain what the players' association wanted. And the man sitting beside him was Conn Smythe, the man he used to play for as a Cup-winning all-star.

"I guess he thought he was still a Major in the army and he was going to lead," Mortson recalled. "Every time I said something, he'd get red in the face and start yelling at me, 'We can't do that! We're not going to do that!'"

That summer, the owners had their revenge. Ted Lindsay was traded to Chicago, as was the Toronto player rep, Jim Thomson. His replacement on the Leafs, Tod Sloan, would also be dispatched to the Black Hawks. The Hawks were kept in the NHL basement—accidentally on purpose—by owner Jim

Norris, who also owned Detroit, and was the majority shareholder in Madison Square Garden, effectively controlling the New York Rangers. The fact that players had to pay their own travel and moving expenses when traded was a further insult.

The Black Hawks made their first Toronto visit of the season on November 2, 1957, and *Hockey Night in Canada*'s cameras caught Mortson giving a two-handed slash to a Leaf breaking in on goal. Mortson skated directly to the penalty box, while teammates stood with their skates toeing the line of a semi-circle painted from the boards out between the penalty boxes. Foster Hewitt explained to the viewers that if a player crossed that line—say, to get at another player in the penalty box—he would be fined $25. As the annual NHL salary was $8,000 in 1957, this would be the equivalent of fining a 2012 NHL player $6,146 for literally crossing a line.

Mortson had barely taken his seat in the penalty box, which was not protected from the crowd by plexiglas, when the crowd in front of the camera rose to get a better look at a commotion involving a fan.

The "fan" turned out to be no fan: it was Conn Smythe, who had left his private box (nicknamed by the disgruntled "the Berchtesgaden," after the German Alps where Hitler had a residence) to sit rinkside. And he was haranguing Mortson, still seething over his role in forming a players' association.

"Take it to your lawyers in New York!" Smythe yelled repeatedly, equating the two-minute penalty, which Mortson wasn't protesting, with a union formed to break the owners' cartel.

"So I stood up and said, 'Major!' and I gave him the salute," Mortson recalled. Everyone watching, in the Gardens and especially on TV, had seen a player stand up for himself. They couldn't see Smythe in the picture, but they didn't need to. And though he was smiling, Mortson finished his salute by cocking his fingers into an imaginary gun. He didn't "shoot" at Smythe, but it didn't matter. The shot had been fired.

Bonus Coverage

*H*ockey Night in Canada was seven years old in 1959, pushing the boundaries of what sports television could do. When its cameras caught a nasty event which rippled on long past the end of the telecast, the show would get an unsentimental lesson in just how far the league that it was celebrating would push back.

At the end of a Stanley Cup semi-final game in which Boston defeated Toronto on April 4, 1959, *Hockey Night in Canada* switched live to "bonus coverage," another innovation in the heady early days of television broadcasting. Now viewers were whisked in the blink of an eye from Maple Leaf Gardens to Chicago Stadium to join the playoff game in progress between Montreal and Chicago. And it was high drama: Chicago had to win to avoid elimination.

Play-by-play man Danny Gallivan welcomed the Toronto audience as the second period was ending, with the two teams locked in a close game. The third period, though, provided more bonus coverage than anyone could have imagined. When referee Roy "Red" Storey failed to call a penalty for a trip on Bobby Hull late in the game, the extroverted Chicago fans let Storey have it, with insults about his eyesight and his mother. With just over a minute left, Montreal's Claude Provost scored the game-winning goal for Montreal and the 20,000 Chicago fans erupted in fury, incited by Hawks coach Rudy Pilous.

Bottles, papers, a chair, and general mayhem rained down on Storey, as the *Hockey Night in Canada* cameras watched him skate to centre ice, away from the shower of debris. Then, from the right side of the screen, a fan ran full tilt onto the ice to attack Storey from behind. It was the second such attack, and Montreal defenceman Doug Harvey speared the prone fan in the head while Storey skated away.

The two Reds—Kelly and Storey—debate the finer points of officiating with team officials.

Imperial Oil opened the game in the 1950s by splashing its logo over the action—anticipating the electronic advertising boards of the next millennium.

The riot continued for another twenty minutes. Storey appealed to NHL President Clarence Campbell, sitting rinkside with Chicago owner Jim Norris, for direction. Storey already had a difficult history with Campbell and arena violence, for he was the referee on March 17, 1955, when the "Richard Riot" broke out in the Montreal Forum and spilled onto the street. As tear gas spread through the Forum, Campbell cancelled that game, on advice from the fire department. On this night in April he was no help at all to the referee under attack. He wouldn't even look at Storey, much less speak to him.

The following day, the league president had found his voice, and criticized Storey to the newspapers, saying the referee's inept actions led to the violent outcome. Storey, a multi-sport athlete who had won two Grey Cups as a Toronto Argonaut, his talent so stellar that he received offers to play in the NFL for New York and Chicago, was also one of the most senior and respected NHL referees. But no more. He vowed he would never referee another game in Clarence Campbell's NHL.

Hockey Night in Canada saw a great story, and invited "Red" Storey to come on the show to tell his side of it, during a Stanley Cup finals intermission of a game between Toronto and Montreal. Attending the *Hockey Night in Canada* production meeting, though, was Ken Reardon, an all-star defenceman with the Montreal Canadiens during the 1940s. Reardon was now an executive with the Canadiens, and he was at the meeting to represent the interests of both Montreal and the NHL owners.

Reardon's presence was an astonishing reality of constraints imposed by the NHL on the still new medium, ostensibly to preserve the integrity of the game, but in reality to avoid making the league look bad by exposing the truth. So NHL owners could ban *Hockey Night in Canada*'s personnel from their arenas for any reason they liked. And Reardon saw trouble looming—for himself at least—if he didn't let his employers know what the show had planned.

Reardon probably phoned his boss, Frank Selke Sr., in Montreal, who then alerted Conn Smythe in Toronto, who then roused Clarence Campbell. No matter what the trajectory, word came down from on high: Red Storey could talk to all the reporters he liked, but the results of what they wrote had limited power. His comments would be seen only in the cities in which the sportswriters published. *Hockey Night in Canada*'s voice, however, went all across the country, and into the northern United States. So Storey was not to be given any television exposure for his version of the truth. *Hockey Night in Canada* was faced with a hard choice: interview Storey on camera, or have access dry up to Canada's two NHL teams, and maybe others. Storey did not go on the show.

Storey had his revenge when he joined the *Hockey Night in Canada* crew as an analyst in 1970, a position he colourfully fulfilled—while moonlighting as the *Hockey Night in Canada* Santa Claus—for the next decade.

Legendary referee "Red" Storey found himself at the centre of many battles, but one of the worst came in Chicago in 1959. When Montreal scored to put Chicago on the edge of elimination from playoff contention, a fan leapt from the stands to attack Storey.

The Rocket Wins
His Last Stanley Cup

It is Thursday, April 14, 1960. *Hockey Night in Canada* is a few months short of its eighth birthday, and by now, it has realized its own power in telling the national story. The *Hockey Night in Canada* telecast begins, as they all did then, in the middle of the game at 9:00 P.M., but this time with a great sense of drama. An announcer, his voice low and portentous, tells the viewers that things are different tonight, that history has eclipsed routine. Or rather, that *The Man from Blackhawk*, an American drama series about an insurance investigator in the wild west, and *Close-Up*, a CBC public affairs program with a high-octane roster of Canadian journalistic talent—Pierre Berton, Patrick Watson, Jack Webster—will be pre-empted. And then another announcer happily explains why: "It's playoff time in Canada!"

An oval on a black screen flashes with the Esso sign, then *Hockey Night in Canada*'s logo slides out toward the viewer. Esso's "Happy Motoring" song begins, playing over cars driving in Toronto at night, illuminated by flashing Esso service station signs. These cars, filled with happy Esso customers and hockey fans, drive in front of Maple Leaf Gardens, lit up with the spectacle within. A graphic and an announcer tell us that Toronto and Montreal are playing Game 4 of the Stanley Cup finals.

And then suddenly we're inside the rink. The Canadiens are in white, the Leafs in black (or blue, if you're there live), and they're in the middle of what could be the Cup-clinching match. It seems extraordinary now, when the idea of a broadcaster missing any portion of a Stanley Cup game on purpose could only be tied to licensing fee wars with a cable company. The hunger for TV sport was there, then, too, for as soon as the nation's TV screens heated up with

Maurice Richard after winning the Stanley Cup on April 14, 1960, at Maple Leaf Gardens.

75

Celebrated Radio Canada broadcaster René Lecavalier, who called games for *La Soirée du Hockey*, interviews the man who was like a battle standard for the Québécois, Maurice "Rocket" Richard.

the hockey game, the TV ratings across the country spiked upward—nearly 77 percent of TV sets tuned in to Canadiens' games in Montreal alone.

This sophisticated mix of a dramatic beginning and a benevolent sponsor illuminating the way to the temple in a busy big city at night (Toronto then had an estimated population of 1.7 million people, but was still second city to Montreal's 2 million) elevate the *Hockey Night in Canada* broadcast to a plane occupied by high culture. This isn't a game. This is unscripted drama in an arena to which the viewer has special access thanks to the eye of the camera.

The Montreal Canadiens do the rest, winning the Cup, with ease. They celebrate as if this hadn't—since the spring of 1956—become an annual ritual. They embrace a Hall of Fame roster: goalie Jacques Plante, Jean Béliveau, Bernie "Boom Boom" Geoffrion, and the guy who tied him as playoff points leader, Henri Richard, "The Pocket Rocket," little brother of the great Maurice.

But it's Maurice who skates to the table at centre ice, where the Stanley Cup sits, and wraps arms that have held the Cup seven times before around it, as if this is his first time. When league president Clarence Campbell walks onto the ice to present the Cup, he's even more lustily booed by the well-dressed crowd than some more recent NHL bosses. Richard responds to Campbell's arrival by skating away, to join his mates. Campbell has been an antagonist to Richard for years, even suspending him from the 1955 Stanley Cup playoff for punching a linesman. The suspension, and its circumstances, were seen as English colonial injustice, sparking riots in Montreal and possibly even, as some scholars have argued, Quebec's Quiet Revolution.

Then Richard skates back to join Campbell, and the camera catches men on the ice behind him holding a large homemade banner with the Montreal logo, and "Compliments de Tom St. Jean." Apparently, this is not from the

The Man from Blackhawk, a popular U.S. drama about an insurance investigator, was bumped aside by the Stanley Cup final on *Hockey Night in Canada*.

Rocket Richard doesn't mind shaking hands with his frequent tormentor, NHL president Clarence Campbell, to accept his eighth—and last—Stanley Cup.

nationalist Société de St-Jean Baptiste, but from Sudbury's francophone community. One of its bearers pushes away a competing banner, borne by a man dressed as a wizard, with a cape and pointy hat, reading "Victory for Our Canadians." These standard bearers engage in a pushing and tugging match to get in front of the camera. The two solitudes, claiming the Cup on national TV.

Richard is the model of gentlemanly comportment, shaking Campbell's hand, and holding up the microphone to the cheers of the crowd. And then he seems to take witty revenge on all those in Toronto who have accused him throughout his career of all kinds of flaws: of brittleness, for his many injuries; of cowardice, for not fighting in World War II (he tried three times and was rejected); of not being a Leaf, though Conn Smythe tried his best to make him one after the war. Richard is a high priest in Montreal. He has no interest in defrocking himself.

So he takes the microphone and says, "Ladies and Gentlemen, it's always nice to win the Cup outside of Montreal. But the best place to win it is right here in Toronto." There's a smattering of uncertainty, as if the crowd isn't sure whether they've just been insulted. Richard clears up any misunderstanding quickly. "Because the people are really nice, they give us a nice hand any time we score, and they really give us a good hand all the way through the series."

Then he switches to French, and the crowd he's just thanked for being good sports boos him. As photographers scrum around, he and Plante hug and kiss the Cup on its white-clothed table, with the wizard character trying to get in the photo before being shooed away. Richard moves to pick up the Cup, but a Leafs official intercepts him and wheels the table and the Cup away.

Richard skates off the ice, toward the dressing room. It will be the last time anyone will see him wear the Montreal sweater. He's 38, and slowing down. Come September, he'll hang up his skates. Richard has played his last game, and *Hockey Night in Canada* watches him exit the stage, a champion still.

Willie O'Ree and *Hockey Night in Canada*

On January 18, 1958, Willie O'Ree broke the "colour barrier" to become the first black man to play in the NHL—the last of the four major sports leagues to have such a barrier. *Hockey Night in Canada* filmed O'Ree, in the gold and black of Boston, skating around the Forum during that Saturday game against Montreal, as well as the Prime Minister of Laos, Prince Souvanna Phouma, on a state visit to Canada, watching approvingly. "The Montreal Forum was different and special that night," O'Ree recalled. "The lights were brighter and the ice whiter. The fans seemed more elegant and nobody called me any names."

Even though this was a momentous occasion, *Hockey Night in Canada* didn't actually speak to O'Ree until 1961. And it was O'Ree who brought up the elephant in the studio, midway through a five-minute interview with host Ward Cornell. O'Ree was recounting his arrival in the NHL—two games for the Bruins in 1958, and then the minor leagues until what would be forty-three games in 1960–61—and mentioned that his Quebec coach, Phil Watson, told him he could be "the Jackie Robinson of hockey."

Cornell, whose sombre "moonlighting undertaker" style belied a sharp sense of interviewing, let O'Ree continue, but every adult viewer would have immediately felt the power of this reference. Robinson had crashed through the colour barrier of Major League Baseball when he joined the Brooklyn Dodgers in 1947. And hockey could have cracked the nasty segregation of major league sports even earlier with Herb Carnegie.

Carnegie, born in Toronto to Jamaican parents, was such a talented centreman that future Canadiens legend Jean Béliveau wouldn't dare miss a game when Carnegie and his Sherbrooke team came to town in the 1940s. Béliveau, inspired, would emulate his hero later on the backyard ice rink.

Willie O'Ree was, unknown to the league, 95% blind in his right eye. He still managed four goals and ten assists in forty-five games.

15

Carnegie caught the eye of Conn Smythe while playing for a Toronto junior team in 1938, and impressed the Leafs' boss so much that Smythe wanted him for Toronto. The problem: his colour. The story Carnegie always told had Smythe offering $10,000 to the man who could turn Carnegie white. Sordid and shameful though the racism Carnegie—and other black players—experienced in hockey was, it was largely economics that kept him out of the NHL. The New York Rangers offered him a contract in 1948, but he could make more money playing in the minors, and there he stayed.

O'Ree, on the other hand, had dreamed of playing in the NHL since his boyhood in Fredericton, New Brunswick. He listened to Foster Hewitt as a kid during World War II, and imagined himself tearing up Maple Leaf Gardens one day. And now, early in 1961, O'Ree was on *Hockey Night in Canada*, telling a pensive Ward Cornell what it was like.

"In terms of this business of being the Jackie Robinson of hockey," Cornell begins, head down, arms folded across his beefy chest, "have you had any troubles?" It's then that Cornell raises and swivels his head to look O'Ree in the eye. And what had at first seemed dismissive—"this business of being"—

suddenly opens up into a startling moment, where *Hockey Night in Canada* raises the window to let decades of the game's racism begin its escape.

"No, none that you could say were troubles," O'Ree replies, his own head down. "I've heard a few jeers," he adds, looking up to smile at Cornell, "but I guess all hockey players get that."

And then, ever so casually, Cornell asks, "When you're on the road, whom do you room with?"

"Well, I've been rooming with Charlie Burns," O'Ree replies.

"Good," says Cornell, then moves on to what he claims is his most pressing query, the fate of the basement-dwelling Bruins. But it's this offhand question about roommates that would have revealed much to an audience at the time, who were well aware of the naked discrimination that many U.S. hotels showed to "people of colour." O'Ree's guileless answer revealed that his away-game lodging wasn't a problem for anyone—himself included. And so, with great subtlety and economy, Cornell takes the viewer right through the Jim Crow laws of the United States, which were still keeping blacks, so the racist legislators had it, "separate but equal."

And so O'Ree's historic interview on *Hockey Night in Canada* becomes remarkable for its ordinariness. Of course, he's of interest to everyone because he doesn't look like the other players, but the brilliance of the interview is that by the end of it, he seems not only like the rest of them, but like one of the best.

That 1960–61 season would be O'Ree's last with the Bruins, and with the NHL. Despite playing forty-three games for Boston, and being told to go home and have a great summer until training camp started, O'Ree was dealt to the talent-rich Montreal Canadiens. In the six-team NHL, he knew his chances of cracking Montreal's line-up were slim. And what the Canadiens (or anyone else) didn't know was that O'Ree had lost 95 percent of the vision in his right eye in 1956 when a puck hit it during a junior game.

Ward Cornell was looking into the eyes of a one-eyed player, who kept his blindness a secret so he could keep doing the thing he loved. It's a great irony of O'Ree's career that the real story was not how people saw him, but what he could have done in the NHL had *he* been able to see out of both eyes. But for the *Hockey Night in Canada* viewers on that Saturday night in 1961, seeing and hearing O'Ree treated like any other player was as significant as if he had been one of the greatest players to ever lace up skates.

16

Danny Gallivan

If Foster Hewitt was hockey's Homer, hymning the heroic exploits of the icemen across five decades of winter, then Danny Gallivan was the game's James Joyce. In rapturous love with the English language, Gallivan invented new words and romanced old ones to elevate any hockey game he called into a riotous, full-throated drama. It didn't matter if Montreal—the team he covered most for his extraordinary thirty-two-year career with *Hockey Night in Canada*—was winning 10–0 or losing by the same difference. Every game was a gleeful adventure, where pucks came "cannonading" off sticks; players deked their way out of danger with "spinneramas"; Bobby Hull had a "bombastic" shot, which goalies robbed in the broad daylight of TV with "larcenous" saves.

Gallivan was born one of thirteen children to a poor Sydney, Nova Scotia, coal shipper and his wife on an epic Wednesday: April 11, 1917, the middle day of the three-day battle for Vimy Ridge. Four divisions of Canadian troops fought together under Canadian command for the first time, and with imagination, planning, and bloody-mindedness won a stunning World War I victory. Indeed, the battle is said to be Canada's coming of age as a country, and while the infant Gallivan was oblivious to the war in Europe, his role in shaping the country's sense of itself was to be as original and stubborn as that of the victors of Vimy.

Ralph Mellanby, *Hockey Night in Canada*'s legendary executive producer, said Gallivan was so hard-headed that he refused to give up his old microphone when headset microphones were introduced to the crew. Gallivan had a more practical reason: he didn't like to be bothered by producers in the truck, whispering in his ear, and saw the headset as a distraction.

Mellanby indulged him, allowing Gallivan to hold the old microphone— which wasn't plugged in—while calling the play through the new one. On

Danny Gallivan chats with another legend, Henri "The Pocket Rocket" Richard.

Danny Gallivan and his Radio-Canada counterpart René Lecavalier present Henri Richard with a miniature of himself holding the Stanley Cup. He would win eleven Cups—more than any other player in NHL history.

his first broadcast with the headset mike, Gallivan interviewed statistician Ron Andrews, then celebrating his twentieth anniversary with *Hockey Night in Canada*. The problem, of course, was that Gallivan interviewed Andrews with his cherished old microphone—so no one listening heard a thing from the statistician.

Gallivan, though, was heard throughout the land as he bounced around the broadcast booth, following the play with his body and calling the action with his formidable brain and his lilting voice. After graduating from high school, he had sweated for two years in front of the blast furnace at the town's Dofasco steel plant, to earn his college tuition. After graduating from St. Francis Xavier University in Antigonish, Nova Scotia, Gallivan taught high school algebra and English, and intended to make teaching his career. But when war came, he went overseas with the Canadian Armed Forces.

When he returned home, he was offered a baseball tryout by the New York Giants. A talented pitcher, Gallivan realized he would never rise above the minor leagues. So he returned to Halifax. He had done some play-by-play at his university radio station, and wound up calling the hockey exploits of a junior team, St. Mary's. He was discovered by the wider hockey world while calling a Memorial Cup game between Halifax and Montreal, and in 1952, he stepped into the world of *Hockey Night in Canada*.

It was a step fraught with peril. Danny Gallivan had never seen an NHL game when he was asked to broadcast one. He went to the Montreal Forum the night before his first broadcast to check out the Canadiens. The following morning, a Saturday, he staked out the lobby of the Detroit Red Wings' hotel.

"I seated myself in the lobby, and watched them as they came out of the elevator," he recalled. Gallivan tried to memorize their faces so he'd recognize them in the broadcast booth later. "When they skated out on the ice it was a disaster. From that 60-, 70-feet perch, the fellows whom I saw in the lobby of that hotel didn't look the same. I recognized about three. Kelly with his red hair, Leswick didn't have any hair, and Gordie Howe. So I didn't panic. I said there's a job waiting for me in Halifax...."

Everything went well until the third period, when Detroit scored a goal. Gallivan announced the scorer: Floyd "Busher" Curry. "They gave me a spotter, marvellous gentleman, Elmer Ferguson, and he'd never seen a game from that area. And he said to me, 'I think that was Butch Bouchard' and it just dawned on me that Bouchard does have wavy hair like Curry. And I suffered it out because the first announcement was in French, and I didn't know what they were saying. Finally they said in English, 'Goal by Curry!' and I was beside myself and Fergie said, 'They all look the same from here.'"

Gallivan's genius was to make sure each game was the same, but different. He moved from radio to television in 1953, and did play-by-play until his retirement in 1984. *Hockey Night in Canada* teamed him up with cerebral, encyclopaedic colour man Dick Irvin Jr. in 1966. With his impeccable pedigree as the son of the NHL player and coach who won three of his four Stanley Cups behind the Montreal bench, Irvin paired with Gallivan to form one of the most dynamic sports broadcasting teams of the modern era.

Yet the bookish Gallivan never forgot history, nor the quasi-religious place he and his fellow broadcasters occupied in hockey-crazed Canada. "Anybody who has ever worked in the field of hockey broadcasting owes Foster Hewitt an invaluable debt of gratitude for what he has done," Gallivan recalled after his retirement. "He blazed the trail, and we have all been disciples ... he showed us the way."

Ward, Bobby, and Wayne

On February 27, 1963, *Hockey Night in Canada* showed how deeply its reach went into the Canadian hockey community by showcasing two of the game's most prodigious young talents: 17-year-old Wayne Carleton of the Toronto Marlboroughs, and 14-year-old Bobby Orr of the Oshawa Generals.

During an intermission of a Toronto–Chicago game, interviewer Ward Cornell introduced the segment as part of a national week celebrating minor hockey. Then, drolly, he presented the duo beside him as "a couple of gentlemen who've played a little bit of minor hockey." Cornell, despite his often dour demeanour, flashed a smile to let the audience know that he was in on the joke. And that this was not the last they were going to see of the minor hockey players before them.

Though it would have been easy to lavish puffery on the talented pair, Cornell, a former English and history teacher, came to interviews prepared. He also asked short, specific questions that gave his subjects the chance to answer. And the two teenagers were surprisingly expansive, especially when Cornell began by asking about the business of hockey.

Both Carleton and Orr had been wooed by the likes of Scotty Bowman in Montreal, as well as by other teams. Carleton, earnest in a shirt and tie and Marlboroughs crested blazer, had chosen to play with Toronto. For the Beeton, Ontario, lad, it was "close to home."

Orr, though, is much more interesting, in part because of what he says, and in part because of what we know now (which Cornell knew then). Wearing a three-piece suit and a serious expression, Orr replied that "Boston is building their team, and I'd like to be a part of their building."

There was a lot more truth behind that truth.

The Bruins had had their eyes on Orr since Boston Bruins GM Lynn Patrick, along with Wren Blair, a coach for their minor league affiliate in Kingston, were scouting 14-year-old players at a bantam tournament. By chance, they saw a 5'2", 110 pound, 12-year-old peewee who was clearly the best player on the ice. Blair hurried from the stands to find out the boy's name—and whether he'd given any NHL team his rights.

Robert Gordon Orr had not, so the Bruins quickly befriended Orr's family and "protected" Bobby from other teams. In 1962, Bobby Orr signed a "C" form—a standard contract which gave Boston his hockey rights for life.

Cornell, knowing this, presses on, though more like a kindly uncle than an inquisitor. "Lots of times you hear that there's lots of pressure put on youngsters to sign. What's your feeling about this?"

Carleton invokes free will, and so does Orr. "No one forces you to sign with anyone, and if you like it, you sign and you play hockey."

Cornell moves on to ask the two teenage players about their playing styles, and school, and about the upcoming playoffs. But it's the snapshot of the very young Orr, his future as one of the NHL's greatest, and most tragic, players ahead of him, that makes this interview much more than intermission filler. It's a *Hockey Night in Canada* moment revealing how clearly the show—even in its first decade—had the pulse of the hockey world in hand, and was interested in what made the hockey heart beat.

Bobby Orr appeared on *Hockey Night in Canada* as a teenager on the cusp of NHL glory.

Later that year, Orr's father would meet a young lawyer and Ontario MPP at a sports banquet. Alan Eagleson would revolutionize the world of hockey through his relationship with Bobby Orr. He would rise to the heights of power and influence, and then fall far and into prison when his crimes against the players he ostensibly protected were revealed.

And in just over three years, Bobby Orr would step onto the ice as a professional, winning the Calder Trophy as the NHL's finest rookie in 1967. He would add eight Norris Trophies as the NHL's best defenceman, two Art Ross Trophies as the NHL's leading points scorer, three Hart Memorial Trophies as the most valuable player in the league, and two Conn Smythe Trophies as the most valuable player in the Stanley Cup playoffs.

Orr would win his first Stanley Cup in 1970, and his second in 1972, scoring the winning goals in both triumphs. But it was the image of his first Cup-winning goal, of Orr flying through the air after being tripped, his arms outstretched to celebrate the win, like winged victory, that became famous. But before the decade was out, Orr was out, too. His knees were ruined, and his career was over, after ten seasons with Boston and two with Chicago. And then came his betrayal, and financial ruin, at the hands of his supposed protector, Alan Eagleson.

But on that night in February, with Cornell and Carleton—who was on the ice as a Boston Bruin, too, when Orr scored his famous Stanley Cup goal—the eye of *Hockey Night in Canada* was looking starkly at the present. There was no reason not to hope that it would be anything less than glorious.

DEATH AND DESTINY

Ward Cornell became host of *Hockey Night in Canada* because of life, and death. His low-key onscreen persona would give glimpses of the affable, and sometimes acerbic, man he could be. But Cornell carried a great burden in his job as host, a job he'd won because of death.

Cornell had nearly been killed when a plane on which he was travelling crashed near Toronto on November 3, 1959. Cornell, like CBC host Tom Foley, worked weekend football games for the network, and then would fly to Toronto to host *Hockey Night in Canada*. It was a miracle, the papers said, that no one had died on board the plane. After the crash, Cornell told Foley that as they were going down, all he could think of was how glad he was to have a load of flight insurance.

In March 1960, Foley was in an airport limousine heading into Toronto, when a car came onto the highway ramp the wrong way and hit the limo head-on. Foley was killed instantly. Flight insurance, which covered accidents on the ground, would have provided a cushion for his family, but he didn't have any. He had told Cornell after his plane crash that he didn't buy flight insurance, fearing it would bring bad luck.

From then on, CBC had two separate crews—in Toronto and Montreal—to handle *Hockey Night in Canada* broadcasts. And Ward Cornell assumed host duties for the show until 1972, when a new *Hockey Night in Canada* regime wanted to liven things up. Cornell, whose sharp, subtle interviews had fuelled *Hockey Night in Canada*'s intermissions for a generation, was suddenly too boring. So he took a job as Ontario's agent-general in London, England, where his wit and wry style won him many friends. When his successful tenure was over, he was named a Deputy Minister in the Ontario government. He remained sanguine about his time on *Hockey Night in Canada*. "Nobody does one thing forever," he said. "It would be a pretty dull life."

Hockey Night in Canada host Ward Cornell interviews Toronto Maple Leafs captain George Armstrong. After being pelted with paper cups and programs by Detroit fans when they won Game 4, the Leafs responded by winning the Stanley Cup in Game 5 at home on April 18, 1963.

Frank Selke Jr.

Thanks to Conn Smythe's belligerence toward his father, Frank Selke Jr. wound up as one of *Hockey Night in Canada*'s star hosts out of Montreal.

Frank Selke Sr. was one of the most legendary hockey minds of the twentieth century. He had helped devise the ingenious funding of Maple Leaf Gardens during the Depression, and then helped to build the team that called the Gardens home into a dynasty. It was Selke's success, however, that became Montreal's—and *Hockey Night in Canada*'s—gain.

Selke Sr. despaired of the quality of wartime hockey, whose ranks Conn Smythe depleted by demanding players get into military uniforms. Nevertheless, the Maple Leafs did well under Selke while Smythe was off fighting the Nazis, winning the Stanley Cup in 1942 and 1945. Smythe believed Selke was plotting against him to take over the Leafs. But it wasn't Selke—it was the other Gardens directors.

Frank Selke Jr. and Danny Gallivan talk hockey in the Montreal Gondola.

They found the bespectacled, mild-mannered Selke, who raised chickens as a hobby, far more agreeable than the volatile Smythe. Smythe's paranoia about his imminent overthrow got so bad that he ordered his loyal lieutenant Selke to report in to him whenever he was leaving the Gardens. Having had enough of Smythe's tyranny, Selke wrote his boss a farewell note, declaring, "Lincoln freed the slaves." Then he headed down the 401 for Montreal, an exalted franchise that had recently seen some financial turbulence. He would rebuild the Canadiens into a dynasty by creating one of the most extensive farm systems in the game.

Frank Selke Jr. grew up with professional hockey as a parent, a playmate, and eventually, an employer. With his father building Montreal into a Stanley Cup–winning machine, Selke joined the Montreal Forum (and by default,

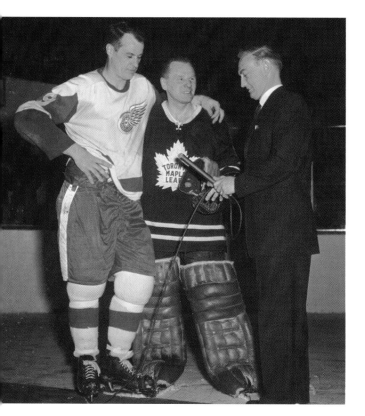

Gordie Howe and
Johnny Bower with
Hockey Night in Canada's
Frank Selke Jr.

the Canadiens) in 1951 as publicity director. He also joined *Hockey Night in Canada* as statistics man in the booth in the 1950s, and then as an intermission host and interviewer from 1960 until the 1967 NHL expansion.

A scenario that featured a team employee also broadcasting for a TV network about the team that employed him would today be smacked down as an unthinkable conflict of interest. This apparent "in-house" favouritism, however, was a necessary part of doing business in the early days of televised hockey. The connection between the game in the rink and what the viewers saw on *Hockey Night in Canada* was a far from straight line, compounded by deep rivalries between Toronto and Montreal both on and off the ice.

While the CBC broadcast *Hockey Night in Canada*, it was MacLaren Advertising that produced the show. They had to keep the show's sponsors happy, but also manage the roiling rivalries between Montreal and Toronto, both as cities and as hockey clubs. So Frank Selke was an attractive addition to the team not just for his impeccable hockey genes. He was also a kind of ambassador to an enterprise that, still dripping with bad blood from the Plains of Abraham, saw Toronto broadcasting talent as unwelcome in the Montreal Forum, and vice versa. Because Selke's father had succeeded in both places, he was more welcome in both rinks, and so he would appear on telecasts in both cities.

In 1968, another aspect of Selke's hockey pedigree surfaced, and he left his job on *Hockey Night in Canada*, as well as his vice-presidency of marketing and promotion of the Forum, to take up an even more challenging position: general manager of the Oakland Seals.

The Seals had rolled onto the rocks of the California coast with the NHL's 1967–68 expansion. Or rather, they had swum across the San Francisco Bay, a Western Hockey League team relocating to Oakland to join the NHL. The idea was to pre-empt the WHL from making a serious run at the NHL's primacy, but the move to Oakland was a failure almost from the start. The first GM, Rudy Pilous, was fired before the start of the team's first NHL season; his replacement, Bert Olmstead, quit at the end of it.

Though the Seals made the NHL playoffs for Selke's first two seasons as GM, he and the team endured multiple owners, as well as haphazard plans to relocate the Seals to Buffalo or Vancouver. And then came the arrival of one of professional sports' most flamboyant owners, Charles O. Finley.

Finley, a former Midwest insurance salesman who used to drive clients past the biggest mansion in Gary, Indiana, claiming it as his own—but off limits due to renovation—was cut from the cloth of the circus. He renamed the team the California Golden Seals, he changed their colours to match those of his Oakland A's, and he changed their skates from black to white—his baseball players wore white shoes, so why not the hockey guys? The hockey guys hated their white figure skates, and Selke couldn't work under Finley's quixotic ownership. He resigned in November 1970.

MacLaren Advertising had created the Canadian Sports Network to produce *Hockey Night in Canada*, and Selke rejoined the fold as a "troubleshooter" for CSN, which really meant picking up where he left off when he went to California, though this time he was behind the cameras. Now he had to help negotiate contracts with *Hockey Night in Canada* personalities, and keep the peace between the network, the owners, and the league. A glimpse into what he thought of it all came in the mid-1970s, when Selke was with a bunch of hockey people on the road in May, an off day for the playoffs. He suggested they go to the St. Louis Zoo, to look at the animals. No one spoke of hockey the entire day.

Toronto Maple Leafs star Dave Keon talks to Frank Selke Jr. after winning the Stanley Cup.

The Golden Age in Colour

*H*ockey Night in Canada's fifteenth season on television saw the end of one era, the beginning of another, and a huge party tucked in between. Canada was 100 years old in 1967, and what better way to celebrate than with a Stanley Cup final between the two Canadian franchises? The Toronto Maple Leafs, led by captain George Armstrong with Johnny Bower and Terry Sawchuk in net, would battle the Montreal Canadiens, starring Jean Béliveau and Henri Richard, for the old silver jug. It was a centennial gift to the nation, filled with drama.

In the spring of 1967, the Leafs and the Canadiens were meeting in the Stanley Cup final for the fifth time in NHL history. Each had won the Cup twice against the other, and this would be the tie-breaker, and perhaps much more. The series would mark the end of the "Original Six" era, as the NHL was doubling its size the following season. David Molson, of the brewing family who also now owned the Canadiens, gave voice to the unthinkable. "With the league expanding to include twelve cities next year, this could be the last time we see two Canadian teams play in the finals."

The prime movers behind the NHL's doubling were television and money. Led by New York Rangers owner William Jennings, the other NHL teams saw what rich American television deals had done for professional football and baseball. Hockey wanted a share of the wealth, and the only way to do that, the owners said, was to expand into major U.S. TV markets.

Los Angeles, Oakland, Minneapolis-St. Paul, Philadelphia, and Pittsburgh all won NHL franchises, but no team from Canada did. Vancouver had tried to get into this grand NHL expansion, but was rejected because the city wasn't seen as a bright enough TV bauble.

Canada turned 100 years old in 1967 and *Hockey Night in Canada* celebrated by broadcasting the Stanley Cup final in colour. This rare image is from a 1965 game, where colour broadcasting was being tested.

19

There was national outrage. Prime Minister Lester B. Pearson, who had won the first Spengler Cup in 1923 playing for Oxford University's hockey team, said, "The NHL decision to expand only in the U.S. impinges on the sacred principles of all Canadians."

If that wasn't enough, the NHL awarded its sixth new franchise to St. Louis, which hadn't even applied for one, because Chicago Black Hawks owner Bill Wirtz owned an arena in the "Gateway to the West." In return for the NHL's bold vote for hockey's future south of the 49th parallel, the U.S. broadcaster CBS invested $3.6 million for a three-year television contract.

So in April 1967, Canadians looked forward to a Stanley Cup series already heavy with nostalgia. This would be the end of the Original Six, an era seen through a golden prism then and now, largely because of television's power. Every week for the past fifteen years, hockey fans had watched a rotating pantheon of the Leafs, the Canadiens, Boston, Chicago, New York, and Detroit. Their players, if not gods, had become like family.

The ferocious Stanley Cup battles of the 1950s and early 1960s were born of such familiarity, and the lights shone brighter on the legendary players—Howe, Lindsay, Hull, The Rocket, Béliveau, Mahovlich, Sawchuk, Bathgate—in the toughest league to crack in the world of pro sports. It was a league that had defined pro hockey for a generation of television viewers. Now it would balloon to twice its size, the newcomers with none of the tradition, and a watered-down talent pool to go with it.

Of course, the term "Original Six" was a touch economical with the truth. With the exception of the Red Wings, who were reborn out of the Detroit Cougars in 1932, the other teams had all been founded just before or during the 1920s, with Montreal born in 1909. Even so, there had been many other NHL teams that had come and gone over the decades, through economic hardship, or managerial ineptitude, or both. But when television cast its eye upon the NHL, those six teams were the only ones left standing. And so, their "originality" became mythologized as some sanctified brotherhood from the icy mists of hockey's glorious past. No matter how you looked at it, that glory was ending.

And *Hockey Night in Canada* was looking at it in colour.

Two years earlier, on March 24, 1965, *Hockey Night in Canada* joined the colour television cosmos, televising a Wednesday game between Toronto and Montreal, with closed-circuit colour going out within Maple Leaf Gardens. The black and white telecast was broadcast as usual. Even so, there was another innovation that came out of the test.

Ted Hough, then producer of *Hockey Night in Canada* as part of his MacLaren Advertising vice-presidency, had to rent one of the few colour TV trucks then available from MGM. The colour cameras were huge, weighing 300 pounds, and when they'd been placed in their usual spots in Maple Leaf Gardens, there was one left over. Hough decided to put it on a platform, behind the goal net at the Gardens south end, the zone defended by the Leafs in the first and third periods. Late in the game, Montreal was awarded a penalty shot. And the newly placed camera was looking Yvan Cournoyer straight in the eye as he sped in on Johnny Bower—who made the save. The first incarnation of the goal camera was born.

In the colour-TV 1967 Stanley Cup final, the red, white, and blue Canadiens were heavily favoured, even after finishing the season in second place, just two points ahead of the blue and white Leafs, now sporting a new, five-pointed leaf on their jerseys. Montreal was younger, and had also come off back-to-back Cup victories.

The Leafs were getting on in hockey years, nicknamed "The Over the Hill Gang" in case anyone hadn't noticed. Defencemen Marcel Pronovost, Tim Horton, and Allan Stanley were 36, 37 and 41; centre "Red" Kelly was 39, and captain George Armstrong was 36; goalie Terry Sawchuk was 37, and his counterpart Johnny Bower was 42. When told that Johnny Bower had served in the war, 29-year-old Frank Mahovlich asked, "The Boer War?"

Expo 67 was drawing huge crowds to Montreal, and the city thought a Stanley Cup victory parade would nicely illustrate the fair's theme of "man and his world." Hope, as ever, proved no match for reality. The wily old Leafs prevailed over the young Habs in six games, their victory coming on May 2— then the latest date a Stanley Cup final had ever been played.

When Clarence Campbell presents the Cup to Leafs captain George Armstrong, he skates to the centre ice table accompanied by his proudly smiling young son, Brian. "He'll get his picture in the papers tomorrow," says Brian McFarlane, the *Hockey Night in Canada* colour analyst. And then Armstrong raises the Cup, his son helping him, in a gesture that resonates as much now with a recurring *Hockey Night in Canada* theme as it did then. Fathers, sons, and hockey.

These 1965 colour shots are prototypes. The ice was even painted blue for
testing colour broadcasting. It wasn't until 1967 that these two teams, for the
first time, would be fully broadcast in colour.

The Old
and the New

Hockey fans today can see television shows that take them inside a player's life over thirty-six hours or inside the locker room 24/7, or they can watch a team preparing for a big game, such as the NHL's Winter Classic. As popular as these contemporary shows are, and despite the temptation to think the reality-obsessed twenty-first century invented the genre, *Hockey Night in Canada* pioneered this intimate look at players' lives, deepening the connection between the viewer and the men who played the game.

Hockey Night in Canada's mid-1960s telecasts were rich with off-ice exploration. Viewers went to Gordie Howe Day in Saskatoon, riding in the car along the parade route with Howe and his young family. They saw Leafs Mike Walton and Brian Conacher slip rings on the fingers of their beautiful blonde brides. And they watched Ward Cornell carefully, kindly interview two young Swedish players who attended the Toronto Maple Leafs' training camp, their English halting as they tried to explain how much they liked Canadian-style hockey.

One of the most fascinating features the show delivered to viewers in 1967 resulted in *Hockey Night in Canada* taking a step backward in time to connect with the present. Interviewer Dan Kelly, who would later become a *Hockey Night in Canada* play-by-play man, stands on a street corner in Ottawa, talking about the curved hockey stick. Kelly displays two of them, one belonging to Bobby Hull, the "The Golden Jet" of the Chicago Black Hawks, coming off a

As *Hockey Night in Canada* discovered the power of television, the "feature" became an intermission staple: here Dan Kelly parses the history of the curved stick.

Above: Wes McKnight reminisces with Toronto's fabled "Kid Line" of the 1930s: "Gentleman" Joe Primeau, Harvey "Busher" Jackson, and Charlie "The Big Bomber" Conacher.

Right: Ward Cornell interviews two pioneering Swedish players who had come to join the Leafs' training camp.

fifty-two-goal season. The other stick, even more torqued than Hull's weapon, belongs to his teammate, Stan Mikita, who had just notched thirty-five goals.

The duo had respectively led the NHL in goal-scoring and points. They were credited with being not only the most talented players using the curved stick, but also its inventors. At this point the camera pulls back to reveal an elderly gentleman, dapper in his hat and tie, leaning on a cane. He turns out to be Hockey Hall of Fame member Cy Denneny, "the first man to use a curved stick" in the NHL. It's a wonderful moment, turning what looked to be a pump-up of two of the NHL's best players into a living history moment that not only entertains, but also reminds the viewer of the game's long arc, going all the way back to the days when television wasn't looking.

Denneny's hockey career pre-dates the NHL, and after a stint in Toronto, he played on an Ottawa Senators club that was one of the founding teams of the league. His powerful shot helped the team to win four Stanley Cups in the 1920s, and saw the left-winger top the magical twenty-goal mark eight times during his fifteen seasons in the league.

Denneny explains to Kelly that though he used a stick with about half the curve of Bobby Hull's stick, he managed to achieve a controlled, powerful shot. "Bobby Hull's shot is about 100 miles an hour," Denneny says. "Mine would be about 85."

He mentions that Hull's shot—from centre ice—had broken rink glass in a recent game, then gives a sly history lesson with an anecdote about playing in Dey's Arena, an Ottawa hockey venue (with multiple locations) from 1896 to 1920. "One night, practising in the rink, I broke two boards at the far end. I put the puck through and the boards split and Mr. Dey was manager of the rink and he said, 'Cy, you're going to have to pay $20.'" In the end, Ottawa's manager Tommy Gorman sorted out the fine.

Denneny has made his point, though, and viewers will take away the fact that hockey existed in robust curved-stick glory before television took over the story. Even so, Denneny exclaims he's a devoted fan of *Hockey Night in Canada* every Saturday, and since the 1963–64 season, of the Wednesday games on CTV. Denneny, who played his last NHL game in 1929, understands just what TV has done for enshrining hockey and its players in the national psyche. "Television," he says with a smile, "has been very good to us."

Above: Brian Conacher (left) and his brother at Brian's Upper Canada College wedding.

Right: Staunch sectarian Conn Smythe doesn't look happy about entering a Catholic church to attend Leafs Mike Walton's wedding.

US AND THEM

Another *Hockey Night in Canada* player feature in the 1967–68 season was remarkable for its portrait of the two sectarian solitudes that came together to form Toronto Maple Leafs culture. In May 1967, just after the Leafs had won the Stanley Cup, *Hockey Night in Canada* documented the weddings of Leafs forwards Mike Walton and Brian Conacher—one, a Catholic player who was born in Ontario's mining country, and then grew up in the family restaurant; the other, the son of hockey aristocracy.

While one of the criticisms of the show has been (and sometimes still is) that it is too Toronto-centric, *Hockey Night in Canada*—with just two Canadian teams until 1970—faced a tough challenge to keep its features fresh and interesting. This wedding feature worked in two ways, as a glimpse inside the private lives of hockey celebrities, but also as a document showing how the Leafs had been structured under the leadership of Conn Smythe, who grew up in a Toronto divided along Protestant and Catholic lines.

As a result, the Leafs' Catholic prospects had gone to St. Michael's College, and are out in full force at Walton's wedding: Frank Mahovlich, Tim Horton, Red Kelly, Dave Keon, and Walton himself, who was transferred to another Catholic high school when St. Mike's discontinued its program after the 1961–62 season. The wedding is in Holy Rosary church, around the corner from St. Michael's College.

By contrast, Leafs rookie Brian Conacher's wedding is at the chapel of Upper Canada College, the elite private school which he attended. Conacher's father, Lionel, was voted Canada's top athlete of the first half of the twentieth century, a multi-sport prodigy who won the Grey Cup, the Memorial Cup, and the Stanley Cup. The groom's uncle, Charlie Conacher, was a member of the Leafs' "Kid Line," and both brothers would win election to the Hockey Hall of Fame for their excellence. Lionel Conacher had died in 1954, and Charlie would die in December 1967, but he's there at the wedding, a small affair on a Monday in May. Indeed, he seems to be the only Leaf, aside from the groom, present.

In an irony that is apparent on Conn Smythe's dyspeptic face, though he's elegant in spats and tails, his granddaughter is marrying Mike Walton. And so Smythe, swallowing years of suspicion, if not blunt hostility toward Rome, has to go to the Catholic wedding. His old strategy of separating players by religion has finally come home to roost.

Former Leafs star Charlie Conacher (second from left) stands up for his nephew, Leafs rookie Brian Conacher (second from right) at his wedding.

SECOND PERIOD

In 1967, the National Hockey League made its largest expansion in its fifty-year history, placing new teams in Los Angeles, Oakland, Philadelphia, Pittsburgh, St. Louis, and Minnesota. Televised hockey, now fifteen years old, had been so successful that the league wanted to reap the riches that television was bringing to football and baseball south of the 49th parallel. The move ended the age of the Original Six, which would soon become "golden" through televisual memory as time passed. But the real gold lay ahead—both for the league's coffers and for the players' fortunes, as the men who played the game used expansion to finally gain stronger control of their contracts. *Hockey Night in Canada* was both mover of and witness to this growth, and continued to innovate in ways that other sports would borrow. And now, what had been a story told in black and white would enter the age of colour. For the first time, people who weren't actually in the rink at a game could get a clear sense of what that reality was like. Televised hockey was on its way to becoming almost better than being there.

21

The Reopening of the Montreal Forum

Hockey Night in Canada donned black tie on Saturday, November 2, 1968, to celebrate the reopening of the Montreal Forum—or rather, the re-christening of one of hockey's two Canadian temples.

The *Quebec Chronicle-Telegraph* gushed that the unveiling of the renovated Forum was like a "Hollywood premiere" with arc lights criss-crossing the heavens, limousines rolling up, and paparazzi crowding to snap photos of the famous that the limos delivered.

Inside the arena, *Hockey Night in Canada* host Ted Darling, his horn-rimmed glasses matching his tuxedo, hosted the show, flanked by potted flowers and female fans in fur coats. They were dressed for an occasion that Quebec premier Jean-Jacques Bertrand, who cut the ceremonial tricolour ribbon at centre ice, called nothing less than the "building of a new Quebec."

The Forum had undergone a $9.5 million facelift both inside and out. Sight lines were cleaned up with the removal of obstructing pillars, and seven escalators now sped the record-breaking crowd of 18,114 to their seats in the expanded arena. The Canadiens had been playing away games for the first month of the season, but now returned to face Detroit in their renewed temple, which they would eventually anoint with their sixteenth Stanley Cup in the spring of 1969.

The Forum had been home to *Hockey Night in Canada*'s French- and English-language telecasts of the Canadiens since 1952. But the irony not too loudly proclaimed on that celebratory night was that a building so associated with francophone identity was originally built for an English team. After a little arson.

> The Montreal Forum was as significant a temple as any cathedral, its crossed hockey sticks revealing the worship within.

113

When Montreal's Westmount Arena burned down on January 2, 1918, its tenants, the storied Wanderers, multiple Stanley Cup champions, were finally forced to abandon the NHL, and professional hockey. The Wanderers were in financial trouble, and their owner, Sam Lichtenhein, used the fire—which started in the Wanderers dressing room—as his reason for shutting down the franchise.

The Canadiens had been sharing the rink with the Wanderers, and were forced to move to the much smaller Jubilee Arena. In March 1922, Donat Raymond, a future Canadian senator, saw the market potential for a new anglophone team in Montreal. So did Léo Dandurand, owner of the Canadiens. He agreed to sell his territorial rights if Raymond could get someone to build a big new arena and let his team become a joint tenant. Two teams, one English, one French, with lots of seats for paying customers.

Raymond approached the president of the Canadian Pacific Railway, Sir Edward Beatty, and made his pitch. The railway company, critical in spreading and developing hockey across the country, bought it. Construction for a $1.2 million rink began in the spring of 1924, at the corner of Atwater and St. Catherine Streets. In just 159 days, the Montreal Forum was ready. Though Raymond had won an NHL franchise for an English team, the Maroons, it was the Montreal Canadiens who opened the swank new arena, on Saturday, November 29. They defeated the Toronto St. Patricks 7–1.

Nearly half a century later, the Forum had become a symbol of Québécois identity. It was more than a hockey arena, but a place invested with the hopes and dreams of a people who had long felt like second-class citizens in their own country. The Montreal Canadiens were more than a team, they were a flag planted firmly in the Forum.

It was no surprise that the Forum crowd rose in ovation when a trio of the flag's greatest bearers walked to centre ice: the Canadiens' powerful Punch Line from the 1940s made up of Toe Blake, Elmer Lach, and Maurice Richard.

Hockey Night in Canada interviewed Richard on both French and English telecasts, and Dick Irvin Jr., whose father had coached Montreal to three Stanley Cups, asked The Rocket, dapper in black-tie, which night had stood out "a little more than all the others" in a building he had lit up for eighteen seasons.

"I gotta say that the game that we played against Toronto in the playoffs [March 23, 1944], and I scored five goals in the game and we won the game 5 to 1. I asked the coach, Dick Irvin, your father—I wasn't sure if I was going to play because I had a hard time to sleep the night before the game, I didn't feel too good, I was tired—I asked him not to play me too much, but that night everything I did was perfect." Indeed, so perfect was he that *Hockey Night in Canada* awarded Richard all of the game's three stars.

Nearly thirty years after the Forum's facelift, Richard would be back at centre ice for its funeral, on March 11, 1996. This time he received the longest standing ovation in Montreal's history: sixteen minutes, or nearly the length of a full period of the game that The Rocket had redefined, under the roof of his, and the Montreal Canadiens', temple.

The Montreal Forum's reopening in November 1968 was one of the largest and most glittering events in the city's social calendar.

Anthem for a Nation

Music was an important part of *Hockey Night in Canada* even before the show had the name which has made it famous through generations. In the 1930s, Foster Hewitt would throw from his Gondola in Maple Leaf Gardens to the black-tied General Motors Orchestra back in the studio, who would play hits of the day.

When *Hockey Night in Canada* debuted on television in 1952, it commissioned noted Canadian composer and arranger Howard Cable to create a theme song. Cable's "The Saturday Game" opened *Hockey Night in Canada* TV broadcasts until 1968. That was the year that the show's corporate producers, MacLaren Advertising, had the inspired idea to hire a Vancouver woman who had never seen a professional hockey game to write them a song.

Dolores Claman had come onto the radar of Ted Hough, vice-president of MacLaren Advertising, and Ralph Mellanby, executive producer of *Hockey Night in Canada*, after writing "A Place to Stand, A Place to Grow," a song featured at the Ontario Pavilion at Expo 67 in Montreal. It not only became the unofficial provincial theme song, with its infectious refrain "Ontari-ari-ari-o," it also sold 50,000 copies.

The film of the same name in which it appeared, directed by Christopher Chapman, used the then revolutionary split screen technique, with multiple moving images, to reveal the myriad virtues of Canada's second-largest province. The world was amazed by this new technique, and more than 100 million people went to see the film. It would go on to win the 1967 Academy Award for Best Live Action Short.

Claman, along with her British husband Richard Morris, lyricist for the Ontari-ari-ari-o song, wrote ad jingles through their award-winning Toronto-

Ron MacLean and Don Cherry flank a Canadian cultural icon, Dolores Claman, who wrote the defining theme music for *Hockey Night in Canada.*

22

based company Quartet Productions. Among their many high-powered clients were General Motors, Imperial Oil, and Ford—with GM being the original sponsor of Hewitt's broadcasts from Maple Leaf Gardens, and Imperial Oil and Ford current supporters of the telecasts in 1968.

Dolores Claman was much more than a jingle writer with a knack for catchy tunes. The Vancouver born composer was a graduate of the Julliard School in New York City, one of the world's premiere music academies. When Claman auditioned for Julliard, hoping to get into their "normal" school, her adjudicators strongly suggested she apply instead for their superstar graduate program. She did, and won a scholarship.

Claman realized while at Julliard that she didn't have the temperament to put in long hours practising Bach at the piano, which a performance career demanded. She did, though, have a flair for composition. Her talents took her to England, where she met her husband and wrote songs for West End musicals. She came back to Canada, and wrote a musical about Robert Service, the Yukon poet who lyrically cremated Sam McGee and shot Dan McGrew. The 1967 CBC production starred none other than Canada's favourite gas jockey, Murray Westgate, as the poet.

The tune that would become an anthem to Canadians began life one afternoon in 1968, when Claman sat down in front of her Knabe grand piano at home in Scarborough. Outside her window she could see Lake Ontario, shimmering, and as she struck a B-flat, then a C, she didn't think of the great lake freezing over for a little imaginary pond hockey. No, she thought about Roman gladiators. On skates.

Suddenly, the tune just popped into her head. Claman put it out into the world, and it has been in the nation's head ever since. The theme not only announced *Hockey Night in Canada* on television for forty years, but also was played as a love song at weddings; as a celebration of manhood at bar mitzvahs; and as a pep rallyer at school assemblies. It was also a record setter: in 2004, 930 saxophonists converged on Toronto's Dundas Square to play the beloved theme and successfully enter the *Guinness Book of World Records*.

Claman said she wanted her tune to follow the storyline of a hockey game: the preparation at the rink, the clash of titans on ice, the glory of victory, and "a cold beer" afterward. As a well-schooled advertising veteran, Claman actually composed two pieces, knowing the lesser one would be rejected by the CBC and MacLaren. "You have to make them feel like they have a choice," she later said. "That's how the business works."

And so it did, with the CBC making the right choice. The business, however, has always been hard on the song. It began its *Hockey Night in Canada* life as the opening and closing to an advertising jingle, which resulted in a flat $800 fee for Claman. By the early 1970s, the show was using Claman's song, arranged by Jerry Toth, as theme music. She then received a music use fee, which averaged about $4,000 annually. In the early 1990s, she partnered up with a Toronto agent, John Ciccone, who got the song licensed. Claman's "Hockey Theme" earnings rose to $500 per broadcast, or about $40,000 a year.

With the rise of "new" technology, suddenly Claman's tune was everywhere—and especially on cell phone ring tones. Claman sued the CBC for improper use, and things degenerated to the point that in 2008, the CBC's offer of close to a million dollars to reach a new royalty agreement was rejected.

Canadians were outraged. The song was untouchable. When talks between Claman and the CBC hit a final impasse, the CBC announced a $100,000 prize for a new theme song.

Rival broadcaster CTV ponied up more than a million dollars, and so Claman's classic migrated networks to herald TSN's hockey nights. Still, every time it plays, anyone who heard it first on *Hockey Night in Canada* hears it there still, in their head, and most certainly in their heart.

This is what fans would have seen when they tuned in the first night Dolores Claman's unforgettable theme song was played on *Hockey Night in Canada.*

23

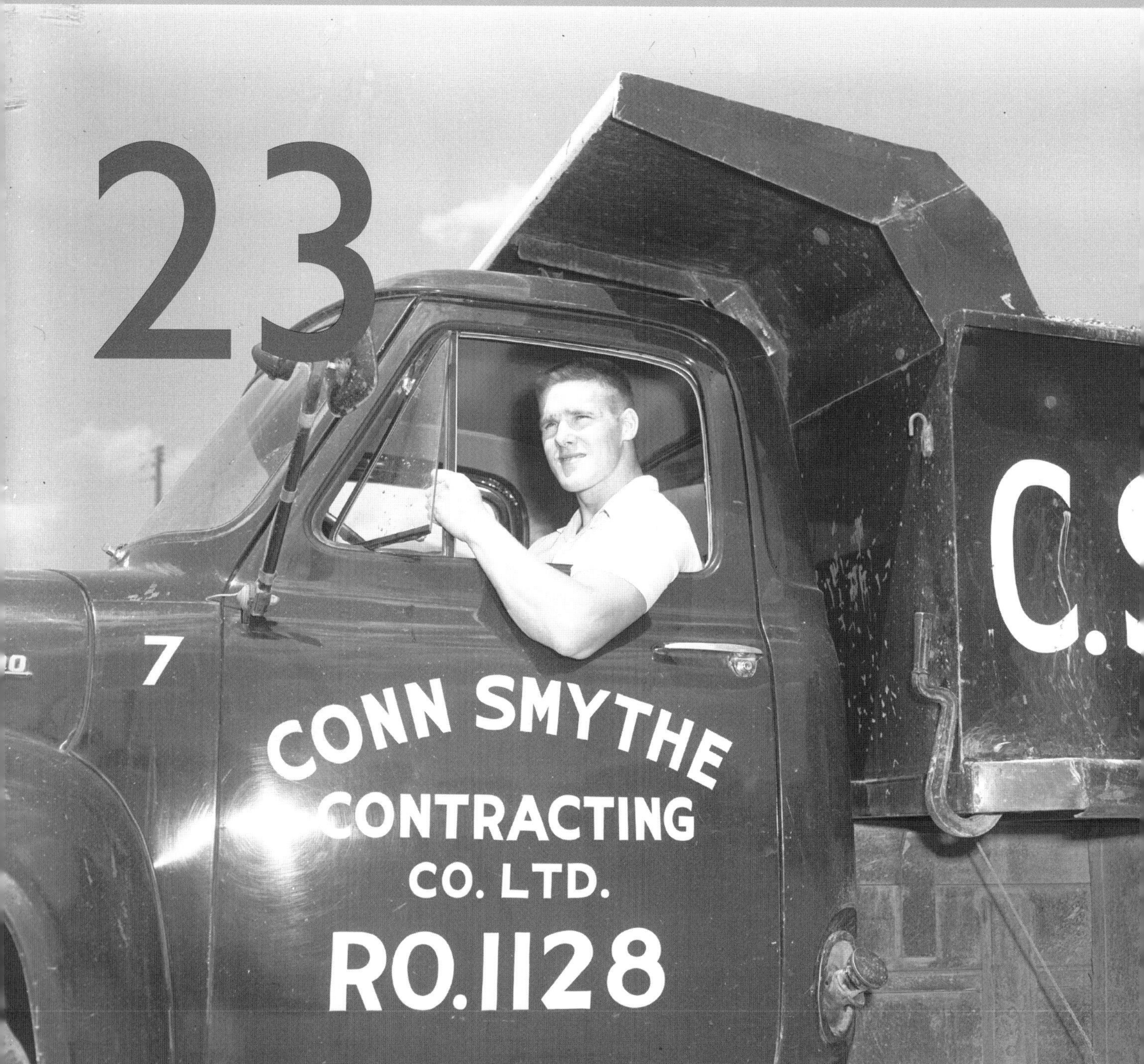

Second Period

Tim Horton's Donuts

What seemed like a routine *Hockey Night in Canada* intermission interview became a fascinating merger of one of Canada's great icons, the Leafs, with what would become one: Tim Hortons restaurants.

Of course, it was the originator of the coffee-and-donuts shop who sat opposite Ward Cornell on that Saturday night in 1968, talking hockey. Tim Horton, then in his seventeenth NHL season, had won four Stanley Cups with the Leafs and the respect of his opponents for his titanic strength. Gordie Howe, considered the strongest man in the NHL in his prime, said that Horton was the strongest man that he'd ever played against.

Nicknamed "Grim Tim," the granite-jawed defenceman came from Cochrane, a mining town in northern Ontario. His family was poor, and Horton, like many other Leafs on his team, found a way out of the mines through hockey. So desperate was he to escape, he practised on the frozen ponds for eight hours a day.

Horton caught the eye of the Leafs, and went to St. Michael's College in Toronto, their feeder school for Catholic kids. From there, he moved up to the Leafs in the 1952–53 season, and to quick success: he was an NHL all-star, and he was making $8,000 a year—a good salary at a time when average salaries in Canadian manufacturing were just over $3,000.

Television's power—and money—would soon mean that players such as Toronto defenceman Tim Horton wouldn't have to drive a truck at Conn Smythe's sand pit to make ends meet.

Ward Cornell jokes with Tim Horton about his fledgling donut "emporium" during an intermission interview in 1968. Soon, "Tim Hortons" would be that and more.

Extraordinary as it seems today, NHL players would still work alongside their fans in the off-season to top up their incomes—delivering beer, selling cars, or, if you were a Leaf, toiling at Conn Smythe's gravel company. When Horton broke his leg in 1955 and couldn't play, he recuperated there behind a desk, working the scales. The experience made it starkly clear to Horton that one career-ending hit could put him in the gravel pit for the rest of his working life. He needed to find something to support his fragile life after hockey.

After a few early business ventures failed, Horton teamed up with Ron Joyce, a former Hamilton policeman, to start a donut shop. During his interview with Cornell, Tim Horton's donut business was four years old, and he had taken some mocking for it from Toronto coach "Punch" Imlach, who told him to bring some of the donuts to practice—to use as pucks.

Today, professional athletes frequently appear in advertising, and product endorsement contracts are much sought after, as these contribute to a significant part of their wealth. In Horton's day, a player risked being seen as not fully committed to hockey if he had outside business ventures.

The then 38-year-old Horton takes the issue head on—with a smile—when Cornell asks him if he is thinking of retiring.

"Things are quite hectic these days trying to combine business with hockey and if the business that I'm involved in continues as it is, I might have to retire before I'd like to."

Cornell replies, with a touch of sarcasm, "That's the Tim Horton Donut Emporium?"

Horton, who blamed his famously hot temper for getting him sentenced too often to the penalty box early in his career, remains calm and polite. "Yes, Tim Horton Donuts, Ward, and it's very nice of you to let me get a word in about it, if I may take the opportunity I'd like to—"

Cornell interjects "No!" with a smile, but Horton plows on, the same single-mindedness that got him out of Cochrane, Ontario, on display here. "Heck, well I'm going to anyway," he laughs, and then thanks his customers in southern Ontario "for enjoying our donuts."

Cornell, wanting to move on, makes a joke: "We'd like to thank you for paying for *Hockey Night in Canada*, Tim."

And Horton replies, "It's good advertising, Ward."

It's a remarkable exchange, not only because the hockey player's donut shop has gone on to become a multinational juggernaut as Tim Hortons, but because it heralds a new era for players, who are understanding the power that television brings to them as marketers of self. Combine this with the rise of the nascent players' association, formed a year earlier, and soon the economic model will see players no longer grateful to the owners for letting them play hockey. Instead, they'll use their success at the game to get the most money out of owners, and fans, that they can during the short lifespan of an NHL career.

Tim Horton was one of the first players to understand this, and though his business would thrive, he continued to play hockey. Horton left the Leafs for New York in 1970, and then, after a season in Pittsburgh, signed with his old Toronto coach Punch Imlach, now the general manager in Buffalo.

Early in the morning of February 21, 1974, Horton was driving his De Tomasa Pantera sports car home to Buffalo after a game in Toronto.

He was going fast—a pursuing police car clocked him travelling more than 160 km/hr on the Queen Elizabeth Way—and he had twice the legal limit of alcohol in his system. He lost control of his car while negotiating a curve, smashed into a concrete culvert, and was thrown from the car. He was dead on arrival at hospital.

Horton's "donut emporium" had grown to more than forty stores, and not long after his death his partner Ron Joyce bought out Horton's widow for $1 million—a figure she tried, and failed, to have increased in a lawsuit in 1993. Two years earlier, the hockey player's smart business sideline, to serve him in an old age that never came, had opened its 500th store.

Tim Horton skates away from expansion Philadelphia Flyers forward Ed Hoekstra's impending slash during the 1967–68 season at Maple Leaf Gardens.

The Fighting Game

April 4, 1968, was a terrible day in a tumultuous year: at 6:00 P.M., Rev. Martin Luther King Jr. stepped onto the balcony at the Lorraine Motel in Memphis, Tennessee, to greet friends in the courtyard. An assassin shot one round from a rifle at the American civil rights leader, and King was dead.

Riots broke out in more than 100 cities across the United States, and dozens of people died, with thousands injured. King was eulogized hours later by Robert F. Kennedy, who was campaigning for the Democratic Party's presidential nomination. Kennedy asked his audience "to tame the savageness of man and make gentle the life of this world." He would be assassinated two months later.

Canadians were shocked by King's murder, and yet grateful that politics north of the 49th parallel were not stained in blood. Indeed, the country was transfixed that April night by the Liberal Party's leadership convention, and the rise of the country's charismatic, intellectually formidable Justice Minister, Pierre Elliott Trudeau, whose words and deeds, like King's, advocated a "just society."

CBC News was covering both the convention, and the breaking news of King's murder. *Hockey Night in Canada*'s broadcast still began in the game's second period in the spring of 1968 (it would start with the opening puck drop the next season). That night, it was delayed even further, but this allowed breathing space for the news, and for hockey fans, the anticipation of escape from the world's misery.

Fighting has been a controversial part of hockey since the first indoor game in 1875. Toronto goalie Johnny Bower catches his breath while his fellow Leafs expend theirs in a brawl against Montreal.

24

But *Hockey Night in Canada* had a problem with violence, too. This night's match featured the Montreal Canadiens at home to Boston in the first game of the Stanley Cup quarter finals. Montreal had finished first in the NHL, but had split their season series with Boston at five wins and losses apiece. Montreal had lost its last three games heading into the playoffs—and one of those losses was to Boston. If the Canadiens had any hope of advancing, they needed to send an early message to the Bruins.

Eight minutes into the game, Montreal Canadiens tough guy John Ferguson dropped the gloves with Boston defenceman "Terrible Ted" Green, whose nickname came from his tough play, and his skill with his fists. And the duo had history. Ferguson had been brought up to the Canadiens to give the team some muscle, and especially to protect superstar Jean Béliveau. He had barely stepped onto the ice his first game in the NHL, when he beat Green in a fight. But he

PART OF THE GAME

The world's first indoor hockey game, in Montreal on March 3, 1875, ended with a fight. The hockey players had commandeered a skating rink for their historic match, and when the skating club wanted their rink back, violence was the result. Ever since, fighting has been "part of the game" and a divisive reality for those who love hockey.

Opponents argue that fighting disappears almost completely in the Stanley Cup playoffs and the Olympic Games, and the hockey played there is better for it. Supporters claim that without it, players will inflict deliberate harm upon the game's "skill players," and so fighting and the "enforcers" who practise it are an effective deterrent. Even so, hockey has struggled with defining a place for something that would land you in trouble with the law if done outside the rink, and over the years hockey violence *has* wound up in court.

A case from 1905 speaks to the issue in a way that resonates still. During a game, a French-Canadian player named Alcide Laurin was killed by a stick blow to the head. Witnesses told police that 19-year-old Allan Loney had swung the stick, and he was charged with manslaughter. But when the case went to trial, the prosecutor said that Allan Loney had a co-accused: the sport itself. "Not only is the prisoner at the bar on trial, but the game of hockey itself is on trial."

Loney's lawyer argued that he'd acted in self-defence—and that Laurin's death was accidental. The jury returned in four hours, and the foreman's words reached far beyond the courtroom. "We cannot too strongly condemn the increasingly brutal methods and roughness associated with the game of hockey," he said. "We believe that unless these growing tendencies can be permanently eliminated from these games, they should be prohibited by the Legislature and put on a par with bull fights and cock-fighting."

Even so, the jury found Loney "not guilty."

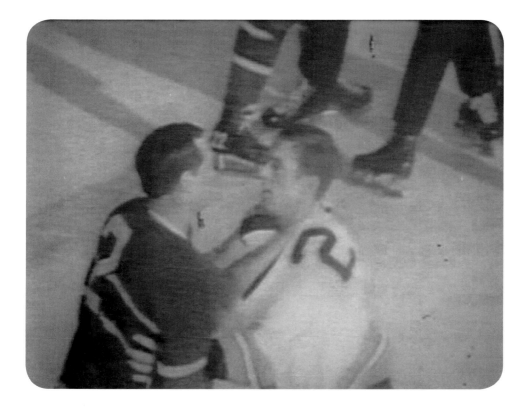

could also play, finishing first in rookie goal-scoring in the 1963–64 season and a runner-up for the Calder Trophy, which honours the NHL's best rookie.

On April 4, 1968, with the world roiling from King's assassination, Ferguson was looking for Boston bear. He'd been inflamed by the trash talk the Bruins had aimed at him before the series, and embarrassed when he'd been on the ice for their first goal four minutes into the game. His team was listless, in need of a spark, so when he came back out he was looking to detonate. And Ted Green obliged him.

Ferguson pulled Green's sweater over his head, and pounded him with uppercuts. When the linesmen broke them up, Ferguson was the clear winner. Suddenly, the Canadiens had swagger; the Bruins, suddenly, did not. The fight had become one of those game flashpoints that can change a team's momentum as much as a big goal or a big save can do. And because the game was not yet being broadcast, no one had seen it—except the people in the arena, and the *Hockey Night in Canada* crew.

Despite 1967–68 NHL expansion, old enmities from the six-team league remained strong—especially between Boston and Montreal.

Hockey Night in Canada host Dan Kelly was adamant when he collared the show's executive producer Ralph Mellanby: they had to show a replay of the fight when the broadcast went live. It was crucial to the game's story, and the one thing *Hockey Night in Canada* had learned in its thirty-seven years on radio and television was that sports matches contain as much of a story as any found in opera or theatre. The difference with sport, though, is that the outcome is unscripted. And now it looked like Montreal had just changed the plot.

Mellanby knew that Kelly was right, but he was hamstrung by tradition: *Hockey Night in Canada* didn't replay fights. Sponsors Imperial Oil and Molson forbade it. When a fight broke out on the ice in a live telecast, cameramen were instructed to swing their cameras away from the bout. This night, though, the cameras had watched the fight because they weren't yet live. And now, what the camera had seen needed to be seen again.

There was also precedent, though the crew covering that April 4 game might not have had it foremost in their minds. In 1964, *Hockey Night in Canada* used film features to help fill intermissions. Host Ed Fitkin set up the footage by describing the first goal in the fourth game of the semi-final series on April 2 between Toronto and Montreal, but didn't mention the brawl that was also included in—and ended—the highlights.

On April 4, 1967, Mellanby decided to show viewers the fight that they had missed, and to tell them about it. Dan Kelly prefaced the replay by explaining that this was not a normal *Hockey Night in Canada* replay, but that it could be a critical moment in the series.

And it was. Montreal won the first game 2–1, and went on to sweep the series with Boston. The Canadiens would lose only one game en route to their fifteenth Stanley Cup championship. *Hockey Night in Canada* saw fighting as a forbidden part of the story, but decided it, too, needed oxygen on a night when the world was in pain. Soon fighting would become the story, for within the decade bashing and brawling would define the essence of the Philadelphia Flyers, who would twice capture the Stanley Cup with violence.

This 1964 fight marked the first time a fight was replayed in its entirety during intermission. Eddie Shack is fighting Henri Richard.

25

Going West

In 1970, the Vancouver Canucks stepped onto the ice as one of the NHL's two new expansion teams. And *Hockey Night in Canada* stepped across the Prairies and over the Rockies to begin an expansion of its own. For the first time in nearly two decades, *Hockey Night in Canada* would broadcast in a different time zone from the one that had established the show as destination television. Of course, this meant that if a *Hockey Night in Canada* game aired on the national network out of Vancouver, the Canucks took to the ice at 5:00 P.M. Pacific—a time when NHLers were usually just arriving at the rink in the east.

Still, the Canucks were happy to be there at all. Their route to the NHL was fraught with so many obstacles and ironies that the superstitious, a strong constituency in the hockey world, had begun to think the franchise was cursed.

The Canucks' problems started before birth, when, in March 1965, the NHL began its first formal expansion process since 1942. The catalyst for doubling the NHL in size was a hybrid of fear and finance. The NHL worried that a rival league might set up shop on the West Coast, and that they needed to move into big U.S. markets and win a fat TV contract to stay competitive in the burgeoning pro sports market.

League President Clarence Campbell, a droll Rhodes scholar, Nazi war crimes prosecutor, and former NHL referee, harrumphed that Vancouver

Hockey visionaries Frank and Lester Patrick put Vancouver on the hockey map when they brought the city its only Stanley Cup in 1915. Here the Canucks dazzle with a multi-media pre-game show in the Rogers Arena, a constant sell-out, as fans wait for the dazzle of the city's second Cup.

Bill Good Jr. came to sports broadcasting with an impressive legacy: his father broadcast British Columbia Lions football games for CBC Radio, as well as the Brier Curling Championships. Good served as the Vancouver *Hockey Night in Canada* host for the 1970 expansion Canucks.

would be a serious candidate only when it had a serious arena. This was the cue for Toronto Maple Leafs co-owner Stafford Smythe, son of the redoubtable Conn, to step in with an offer the city couldn't refuse: he would build and operate an $8 million facility in downtown Vancouver. And he would work the owners' room so the NHL would be desperate to ice a team on Canada's Pacific coast, where the Patrick brothers had innovated so much of the game now being played.

Vancouverites weren't so lulled by the sybaritic balm of Pacific air to see Smythe's purchase of a $2.5 million piece of land for one dollar as an act of altruism. So they refused his noblesse oblige in a municipal referendum. To show they were serious, Vancouver boycotted Molson products—beer—because Molson then had *Hockey Night in Canada* broadcast rights.

Clarence Campbell took refuge in patriotism. "It would have been in the best interests of the NHL to have another Canadian franchise," he said. "It's too bad Vancouver fumbled the ball so badly in the first place."

Toronto Maple Leafs coach Punch Imlach saw a conspiracy. "Montreal and Toronto would have to share their TV with Vancouver if they had let Vancouver in," he said. "Better to split the loot two ways, I guess, instead of three."

Vancouver had won the Stanley Cup in 1915 with hockey's first superstar, Fred "Cyclone" Taylor and the Millionaires. Now, another chance at Lord Stanley's Mug was—given that fifty-year interlude—tantalizing. Within three years the city built the Pacific Coliseum, won an NHL franchise for $6 million, and then competed with the other expansion team, the Buffalo Sabres, for the top draft pick.

Bill Good. Jr. talks hockey with Walter "Babe" Pratt, a riotous star on defence with Toronto, New York and Boston, and a game analyst with *Hockey Night in Canada*'s Vancouver crew.

Incredibly, the selection took place via gambling, with management from both teams wagering the future on the spin of a roulette wheel. Vancouver would win if the wheel landed between 1 and 10; Buffalo, between 11 and 20. The Canucks management celebrated when Clarence Campbell called out "2" as, quaintly, he thought the numbers on the wheel were Roman numerals. They were not. The wheel was really on 11. And so Buffalo selected Gilbert Perreault, who would wear number 11 on his way to the Hall of Fame.

Not only did the city have a new team, made up of recycled NHLers, it had a brand new *Hockey Night in Canada* crew. A couple of the names, though, would have been familiar to eastern viewers. Ted Reynolds handled international sporting events for CBC, and now hosted the Canucks games. The boisterous Walter "Babe" Pratt had been a Hart Trophy– and Stanley Cup–winning defenceman for New York, Toronto, and Boston, and dissected the baby Canucks with his tough-talking analysis. Indeed, Pratt was known to poke his head out of the broadcast truck in the lower concourse of Pacific

Toronto Maple Leafs bench boss George "Punch" Imlach took his trademark fedora south as coach and GM of the 1970 expansion Buffalo Sabres.

Coliseum and colourfully berate Canucks players on their way to the dressing room, for poor play.

British Columbia viewers knew Bill Good Jr., just 25, as the son of a well-known Vancouver broadcaster. Good did interviews on the national *Hockey Night* and was the sometime colour man, while Jim Robson did play-by-play.

Robson had been a fixture in Vancouver sports broadcasting since 1956, calling baseball, football, and hockey. He, like so many, had grown up listening to Foster Hewitt on the radio, and then being captivated by the linguistic thrills of Danny Gallivan. Robson immediately won the affection of viewers with his crisp, accurate style, and his vast knowledge of the game, which he wore lightly. As a result, the first *Hockey Night in Canada* games out of Vancouver were, to the surprise of many, as good as those of their eastern elders.

The Vancouver Canucks played their inaugural game against the Los Angeles Kings on October 9, 1970. *Hockey Night in Canada* was there for the historic puck drop, performed by 86-year-old Cyclone Taylor, who received a standing ovation from the sell-out crowd. The rink announcer reminded everyone that "the National Hockey League is now, officially, in Vancouver," his voice dripping with irony for those inclined to hear it. And the Stanley Cup stood shimmering on a bench on the red line, its first win by the franchise still elusive forty-two years later.

Brian Spencer's Dad

In any life spanning six decades there are bound to be bad days, but December 12, 1970, was one of the worst for *Hockey Night in Canada*, a tragic twist out of a dark fable, one made real by the very power of the show.

Brian "Spinner" Spencer skated his way out of the former Hudson's Bay Company fur trading post of Fort St. James, British Columbia, and into the NHL, on a mixture of ferocious will, modest talent, and lavish myth-making. He was the fifth player taken by the Toronto Maple Leafs in the 1969 NHL entry draft, and after an injury hobbled his NHL debut season, he was recalled to the Leafs in 1970.

Spencer, a left-winger, used to entertain teammates with tales of his hillbilly boyhood in the centre of British Columbia, surrounded by spruce forest and snow. He would tell people he grew up in a dirt-floor hovel, without electricity or running water, and would have to melt snow for his bath. After he'd sorted out dinner by shooting it.

In truth, his tough, hard-drinking father Roy, a mechanic, owned 1,000 acres of land known as Spencer Ridge. The Spencer house had a generator for electricity, a hot water tank to heat the water diverted from a river nearby, and an ice rink out back, which Roy Spencer kept pristine for his son's eventual launch into the big leagues.

Brian Spencer's official NHL "rookie" season began in the first week of December 1970, and the first time he played in a *Hockey Night in Canada* game fell on December 12. Best of all, he had been picked to join Ward Cornell for an interview during intermission. For Roy Spencer, back in the bush of British Columbia, it was a dream come true.

Brian "Spinner" Spencer has his eye on the puck—and a boyhood dream—as a Toronto Maple Leaf.

26

And then it became a nightmare. The Vancouver Canucks had entered the NHL two months earlier, and *Hockey Night in Canada* thought British Columbians would want to see their new team in action against the California Golden Seals. Roy Spencer went berserk.

Riding a few drinks, 57-year-old Roy Spencer got in his truck and drove two hours to the nearest big town, Prince George, 152 kilometres south. He would fix the *Hockey Night in Canada* "mistake" in person. He would visit CKPG, the

Brian Spencer fulfills a boyhood dream: being interviewed on *Hockey Night in Canada*. Neither he, nor Ward Cornell, has any notion of the tragedy being played out between Spencer's father and the RCMP more than 3,300 kilometres to the west.

CBC affiliate, to convince them that his son's game was the one people wanted to see. And he would do it with a shotgun.

Brian Spencer's first *Hockey Night in Canada* interview is laden with pathos when viewed more than three decades later. At the time, though, viewers would have seen a clean-cut 21-year-old, whose well-spoken modesty seems the essence of all the values that Canadian hockey players are supposed to have. In the course of a routine interview, Spencer, nicknamed "Spinner" because of his manic style of play, calmly explains to Ward Cornell that he's an "emergency recall" because of an injury involving the Leafs. He has no idea of what an emergency is truly unfolding.

More than 3,300 kilometres to the west of where Brian Spencer proudly sat under the *Hockey Night in Canada* lights, his father Roy held the technicians of CKPG television at gunpoint, having forced them to air his son's game. When he had seen enough, he emerged from the station to find the Royal Canadian Mounted Police waiting for him. A firefight ensued.

When Brian Spencer came off the ice at the end of his first *Hockey Night in Canada* game, the Leafs management told him his father had been killed in a shootout with the police. The next day, Spencer insisted on playing a road game against Buffalo, scoring his first two NHL points, and getting into two fights.

He kept the names of the three RCMP officers involved in his father's death in his wallet, as he journeyed through the NHL with the Leafs, Islanders, Sabres, and Penguins. From the time he retired in 1980, Spencer descended into a rough life of booze and drugs in Florida, where he was acquitted of a death penalty murder charge in 1987. The next year, Spencer was out buying crack cocaine when he was robbed at gunpoint. He refused to hand over his wallet with the names of the three cops who had killed his father. So the robbers killed him.

Journalist Martin O'Malley wrote a book about the tragic life of Spinner Spencer, one which Atom Egoyan turned into a TV movie. There would have been no sad story to tell, though, had the power of *Hockey Night in Canada* not reached across the country, to motivate a kid from Fort St. James into the NHL. And to motivate his father to die trying to see his boy in the big league, on TV.

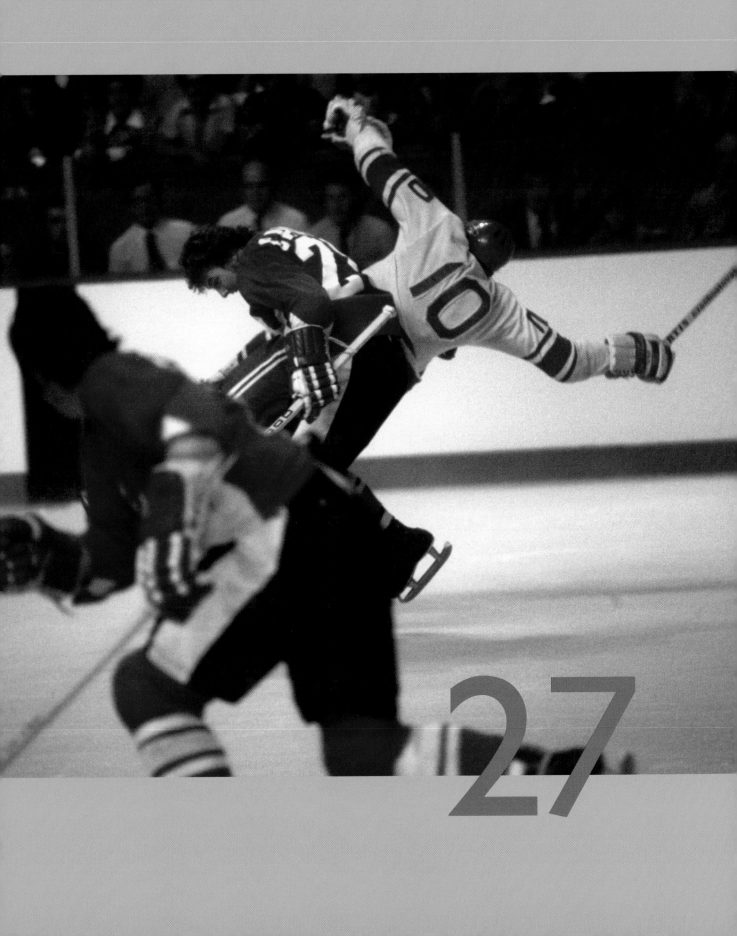

27

Second Period

The Series That Made a Nation

In September 1972, the hockey worlds of Canada and the Soviet Union were welded together by the dramatic heat of a historic series that would change not only Canada's sense of itself, but also of the game it gave to the world. Any Canadian who was sentient at the time likely remembers where they were when the eight-game series ended in ecstatic last-minute triumph for the humbled Canadians. And in that memory, the nostalgic probably see the *Hockey Night in Canada* logo intertwined with the stylized maple leaf on victorious Team Canada's jerseys. It's a forgivable trick of time, but *Hockey Night in Canada* was not the broadcaster for the series that made the nation. And yet, it was because of *Hockey Night in Canada*'s power over the national imagination that the '72 Summit Series was possible at all.

Canada had pretty much owned the Olympic hockey gold medal from 1920 to 1952, taking a silver medal just once, at the 1936 Nazi Olympics, when Canada was beaten by a team of Canadians playing for Britain. Canadian dominance was the same at the hockey World Championships, with Canada triumphant thirteen out of sixteen times between 1930 and 1961, when the Trail Smoke Eaters brought home the gold that Canadians had come to expect.

All that changed when the USSR started to dominate international hockey in the mid-1950s, shortly after *Hockey Night in Canada* came to television. Canada's rightful place at the top, achieved by teams of scrappy, talented amateurs from across the country—Smoke Eaters from Trail, Vees from Penticton, Monarchs from Winnipeg, Dunlops from Whitby—was no longer assured, now that the "robotic communists" had entered the fray. "If only," went the refrain, "Canada could send its best players to face the commies"— that is, those superstars from the galaxy of *Hockey Night in Canada*.

The Summit Series between Team Canada and the USSR was a contest between national dreams, for the Soviets loved hockey as much as Canadians did—and very nearly beat Canada at the game it gave to the world.

Dave Hodge joined *Hockey Night in Canada* in 1971, bringing journalistic integrity and a sharp wit to the show until 1987.

By April 1972, the idea had become real, thanks to an unusual all-star team. There was Gary Smith, a hockey-playing Canadian diplomat in Moscow, who shared vodka and hockey films and a "wouldn't it be nice if...?" sensibility with Russian colleagues. They, in turn, worked the idea through the bureaucrats in their hockey-mad nation.

There was Prime Minister Pierre Elliott Trudeau, not known for his hockey fandom despite his Montreal pedigree, working things with Premier Alexei Kosygin while on his first state visit to the USSR in 1971. "Both Canadians and Soviets want competition re-established between their national teams," Trudeau had said in Moscow, with hockey on his cultural agenda. "This process will take some time, but it has begun."

The deal to play the Summit Series was put together by Hockey Canada, the Canadian government's hockey program, and NHLPA boss and player agent

Alan Eagleson, who was also on the board of Hockey Canada. It was a given that *Hockey Night in Canada* would produce the series, and on June 8, 1972, Jack Miller's TV and radio column in the *Toronto Star* announced the message of victory: "September's Canada–Russia all-star series, the greatest hockey attraction ever, has been snared for TV and radio by Toronto's MacLaren Advertising Agency ... [who] will arrange coverage through its production branch—*Hockey Night in Canada*. Look for the CBC and CTV networks to be given four telecasts each, to keep peace there."

CBC and CTV had split the country's weekly hockey fix since the 1965–66 season, with *Hockey Night in Canada* airing on CBC on Saturdays, and on CTV on Wednesdays. The historic Summit Series, however, would not be a *Hockey Night in Canada* show, the *Toronto Star*'s "scoop" notwithstanding. Indeed, the fact the news had appeared in print before the deal was sealed scuppered the *Hockey Night in Canada* victory. Alan Eagleson put together a team including his superstar client Bobby Orr, and raised MacLaren's $500,000 bid for the

Foster Hewitt came out of retirement to call play-by-play for the historic 1972 series. Here he checks game notes with Brian Conacher.

series rights by another $250,000. MacLaren's hockey boss, Ted Hough, surrendered, but offered *Hockey Night in Canada*'s production services for the series.

All the series really needed in that regard was one key *Hockey Night in Canada* player (though it took more). So, Foster Hewitt, pushing 70, came out of retirement to call all eight games. In many ways, the series was happening because of Hewitt's hand in creating the *Hockey Night in Canada* nation, first through the invisible magic of radio, and then by adding pictures to words through TV. Canada had been expecting this moment for four decades, and Hewitt's presence amplified historical momentum.

Team Canada did its bit by amplifying the drama, defying all cocky predictions of their embarrassing sweep of the Russians to take the series to the very last minute of the very last game. The teams were even at three wins, and one tie. Now, with less than a minute left in the eighth and final game, and the score tied at 5–5, the USSR would win it on goals unless Canada snatched a miracle from the godless air of Moscow's Luzhniki Ice Palace.

This is how Foster Hewitt saw what happened next: "There's 1:02 left in the game. A cleared pass on far side. Liapkin rolled one to Savard. Savard clears a pass to Stapleton. He cleared to the open wing to Cournoyer. Here's a shot! Henderson made a wild stab for it and fell. Here's another shot, right in front—they score! Henderson scores for Canada!"

The celebration of that goal rocked through the team and the thousands of Canadian fans who had travelled to Moscow, then sped at light speed across Canada, as the nation gave voice to victory—and massive relief. Foster Hewitt had not saved the fate of Canadian hockey, but he had called it when Paul Henderson did. It was the biggest goal of his, and so, of *Hockey Night in Canada*'s, life.

Ken Dryden walks with his wife after visiting the Kremlin between games during the 1972 Summit Series in Moscow, Russia.

Howie Meeker

Toronto Maple Leafs
star Howie Meeker
became the team's
coach in 1956 and
tutored Leaf forward
Tod Sloan in the
art and science of
hockey. Meeker's
desire to improve
players everywhere
became his television
trademark.

*H*ockey Night in Canada has a long history of taking former NHLers—players, coaches, and referees—and using their expertise to enhance the viewers' understanding, and enjoyment, of the game. The closest thing that *Hockey Night* has to a revolutionary in that regard came by the purest of chance, when Howie Meeker subbed in for a Saturday and wound up rocking the world of *Hockey Night in Canada*—as well as that of sports broadcasting.

Howie Meeker had won a Calder Cup as rookie of the year in 1946–47, and four Stanley Cups as a feisty right winger with the Toronto Maple Leafs. The fact he was playing at all was a testament to his fierce will. Meeker had nearly lost his legs on a World War II training exercise, after a gung ho fellow soldier tossed a grenade over a wall beneath which Meeker was patrolling on manoeuvres.

During his eight NHL seasons—all of them with the Leafs—Meeker also managed to serve for two as a Progressive Conservative Member of Parliament, winning a by-election in Waterloo South in 1951. Canada's Prime Minister, Louis St. Laurent, a Quebecker, would tease Meeker in the House of Commons when the Leafs lost to Montreal. Meeker, showing the same indifference to rank that defined his TV career, would tease the PM back when Toronto beat the Habs.

Meeker retired from the Leafs at age 29, and eventually took up coaching, replacing Leafs legend Francis "King" Clancy. After a losing season behind the bench, he became Toronto's General Manager, a cup of coffee that was over before the 1957–58 season began when an argument with Leafs chairman Stafford Smythe led Meeker to respond with the rhetoric of his fist.

He went east to Newfoundland and found work with CJON, a radio and television station in St. John's. Meeker hosted a TV fitness show, and then a

bowling program, after he bought a bowling alley. He also owned a sporting goods store, and introduced the Jolly Jumper to a generation of relieved Newfoundland mothers and their bouncing babes.

When he turned up in Montreal to attend a sporting goods trade show, *Hockey Night in Canada*'s Montreal host, Ted Darling, phoned Executive Producer Ralph Mellanby with the news. "When I was a boy, I used to pretend I was Howie Meeker," Mellanby recalled. "That's what kids did when a game of hockey broke out—you'd scream your favourite player's name and it was game on."

So, Mellanby paid the fee for Red Fisher, that week's man on a rotating bench of analysts, and brought Meeker, then 44 years old, on board for a try-out, even though he had done a bit of on-camera analysis for the show in the 1960s. He stayed with *Hockey Night in Canada* for the next two decades, and former *Hockey Night* executive producer John Shannon says his influence remains today: "Nobody understood more about pizzazz and shazzam than Howie," says Shannon. "Howie found a niche, created a brand. He did what Don Cherry's done before Cherry did it."

Right from the start, Meeker didn't stand on ceremony when it came to analyzing the game. No player was safe from his acute criticisms, and when he dared to suggest that Canadiens' man-god Jean Béliveau had erred on the ice, Meeker was banned from the Montreal Forum. Such censorship was commonplace for *Hockey Night in Canada* until well after the 1967 expansion, but Meeker kept on with his "no prisoners" analysis. It was all in service to his passionate mission to teach skills to young players—done via a colloquial style that reached right through the television screen to shake some sense into the viewer.

As much as Danny Gallivan contributed to the language of hockey with his invented words, his *spinneramas* and his *cannonading drives*, Meeker contributed to the sheer joy of the game with his regular "golly gee whiz!" and "cotton pickins" as he celebrated—or tried to improve—a play and a player.

While these expressions added his voice print to the national imagination—a coarse-grade sandpaper riding an oscillating tenor—Meeker later explained his folksiness was a defence mechanism. "I spent a lot of time in the army, and

In a different era, giving a *Hockey Night in Canada* analyst a cigar on air was acceptable television. But Howie Meeker's joke cigar explodes when he lights it—and he explodes in laughter.

Howie Meeker—here with "Hap" Day—tied an NHL record for goals in one game by a rookie when he scored 5 against Chicago in 1947.

in hockey dressing rooms, so rough language is not foreign to me," he explained in one of his books. "I learned early in radio and TV that foul language has a way of popping out, especially during exciting moments such as a goal or a fight. That split second between putting my mind in action and my mouth in gear saved me a lot of embarrassment."

Or perhaps it was a nanosecond, for Meeker's mind sped along with impassioned insights into how the game should be played, whether he was analyzing the NHL or teaching young players in Newfoundland. "Howie Meeker's Hockey School" was featured over four seasons on *Hockey Night in Canada*, with the edited clips showing Meeker and his pupils practising on ice what he was preaching on camera.

When Meeker saw a magic pen that allowed analysts to highlight players and plays right on the TV screen, his development as a *Hockey Night in Canada* star was complete. Meeker and his telestrator became a fixture of the show, with Meeker hollering, "Stop it right there! Now roll it back fellas!" when he saw footage he could use to teach, by drawing a well-placed circle on the screen.

A generation of players and fans learned hockey the right way at the Meeker Academy on *Hockey Night in Canada*, entertained by his riotous love of the game. He left the show in 1987 and moved on to teach hockey on TSN, retiring in 1998. In that same year the one-time Leafs star was inducted into the Hockey Hall of Fame—as a television broadcaster. It was an appropriate honour, for Howie Meeker raised game analysis on *Hockey Night in Canada* to an all-star level, and showed those who followed the "right way" to get it done.

A HOCKEY VISIONARY

Howie Meeker was part of the broadcast team at the historic 1972 Summit Series between Canada and the USSR—and he took a lot of grief for it. Among the chorus crowning Canada as champions before the series began, Meeker stood out as someone who saw that the Soviets posed a serious challenge to Canada's default victory because they knew how to play hockey—old-time Canadian hockey, where skill and smarts trumped brawn and bullying.

Of course, the Soviets had learned old-time Canadian hockey from their Czechoslovakian satellite state, whose players learned it from Mike Buckna, a Trail, British Columbia, boy who had gone back to the homeland of his parents in the 1930s, and wound up coaching the Czech national team. Buckna taught them the game he knew, and when the Soviets decided that they'd show the superiority of communism via hockey, they learned the game from the Czechoslovaks. It was the game Meeker knew, and that he praised the Russians for playing. Meeker was berated and shunned for his view by many, who mistakenly thought his praise of how the Soviets played was unpatriotic. Meeker claimed it was quite the opposite: he proved it by devoting much of his career to teaching Canadian players how to properly play the world's other most beautiful game.

"Howie Meeker's Hockey School" became a *Hockey Night in Canada* feature. Meeker was passionate about teaching young players the proper way to play, and so became a role model for Don Cherry, who would succeed him.

29

Second Period

Hockey Night Breaks the Chromosome Barrier

*H*ockey Night in Canada is responsible for many innovations and historic firsts in the world of television. One that is often overlooked in parsing its formidable accomplishments is Helen Hutchinson, the first female broadcaster—not just on *Hockey Night in Canada*—but in the world of televised pro sports.

Hutchinson had joined CTV's morning newsmagazine *Canada AM* as co-host in 1973, one year after its launch. She already knew MacLaren Advertising's Ted Hough, but now also caught the attention of *Hockey Night in Canada*'s Executive Producer Ralph Mellanby, who had been brought on board in 1966. Mellanby, a swaggering TV commando, saw it as his mission to invigorate the show each season with new talent and features. Hough, Mellanby, and producer Bob Gordon had been thinking about bringing female talent on board, but hadn't found the right candidate. When Hutchinson won an ACTRA award as best public affairs broadcaster—male or female—she got their attention.

When Ted Hough called her up and asked her if she'd like to be on the show, Hutchinson, then on a three-year contract with CTV, had to ask permission from her boss, Murray Chercover. "He said, 'Of course!'" Hutchinson recalls with a chuckle. "It was the Wednesday night game which was shown on CTV. He was very happy. Everybody was happy."

Hutchinson had previously hosted *Matinee* on CBC Radio, which began life in 1952 as a "women's interest show." The idea was to produce a show about topics thought to be interesting to housewives—fashion, medicine, travel, housekeeping, and books—but by the time Hutchinson was hosting, the show had become a serious program investigating issues of interest to all people. Still, Hutchinson recalls one of her more light-hearted interviews being with Dolores Claman, who pulled up a bench in front of the studio piano and knocked off her *Hockey Night in Canada* theme song.

Helen Hutchinson, the first female broadcaster in sports television, enjoys the company of fellow *Hockey Night in Canada* broadcasters Dave Hodge and Brian McFarlane and Leafs captain Darryl Sittler. Helen Hutchinson was no stranger to the locker room. An accomplished athlete herself, she also endured the ups and downs of life as the wife of a CFL player.

Hutchinson grew up in Vancouver as Helen Donnelly, the only child of a sports-mad father, who often had several games playing simultaneously on the various household radios. "I was raised as a privileged boy would have been raised," Hutchinson said. "Golden Gloves, my dad and I went together. Field lacrosse, we went together. The first real hockey game I ever saw was between the Canucks and the New Westminster Royals. The reason Dad insisted I go to that—I was just a kid—was because Turk Broda was playing for New Westminster."

Hutchinson literally learned her hockey in the dining room of her family home at 28th Avenue and Dunbar Street. "There was quiet at the dinner table on Saturdays, because Foster came on at 6:00 P.M., Vancouver time," she smiles. "There would be an icing call, and I'd say, 'But they're on the ice! What's icing, Dad?' So he'd move the utensils and salt shakers around to show me. I have a good knowledge of hockey."

Hutchinson grew up playing sports, as well as watching and listening to them. "I was one helluva street soccer player, with a mean corner shot!" She was also a talented golfer, so much so that an uncle encouraged her to turn professional, but the repetitiveness of golf practice bored her, and besides, university—and real life—beckoned.

"When I was in grade school I used to think when I get to high school, that's where there'll be some real people. But when I got to high school, there were no grown-ups! So I thought, when I get to university, that's where the grown-ups are." She was disappointed to discover "they're only tall children." But the same spirit that made her take on the *Hockey Night in Canada* assignment shone through back then, when she was surrounded by her elders and betters. "I never felt that I was younger than anybody."

Hutchinson was a precocious 16-year-old when she entered UBC in 1951 to study honours English. After she got her degree—and dated Canadian journalism star-in-embryo Allan Fotheringham—she got married. She was just 20 years old, and her husband, Jack Hutchinson, was a B.C. Lions football player. So she saw first-hand the turbulent life of a professional athlete. Her husband was picked up by Winnipeg, and then a couple of years later the family—with one child, and Helen pregnant with their second, and "about $80 in the bank"—came back to Vancouver. Her husband finished his master's degree and got a job at CBC.

"I'd been waiting, a little voice inside me was saying, 'When is it my turn?'" And so, when her son started kindergarten, Hutchinson borrowed money from her father to study Canadian history and metaphysics. "I'm sorry," Hutchinson says with regret, "that I didn't know Marshall McLuhan."

Of course, McLuhan would have found her approach to sports broadcasting perfect for the cool medium. Given her athletic background and marriage to an athlete, Hutchinson saw her *Hockey Night in Canada* tenure as a serious teaching mission. "I love spending time around athletes," she said. "I find them incredibly sensitive, thinking individuals, and that's something most people, including most sportswriters, don't give them credit for."

Because of her *Canada AM* commitments, Hutchinson would go over her *Hockey Night in Canada* plan on game day, which was Wednesday. After fulfilling her *Canada AM* hosting duties, she'd figure out that night's show with her *Hockey Night in Canada* producer, either in Toronto for a home game, or on the road if the game was away. Before the game, "I'd do a pretty lengthy interview [with a player], but on *Hockey Night in Canada*, that meant about three minutes." Her interview would then air during the first intermission, and sometimes she did a second one live. But she had no interest in following the players into the locker room.

"Having been married to a professional athlete, I had no desire to go into the dressing room," she laughs. Not out of prudery, but because she respected it as a private place for those playing the game. "Guys pray in there, they throw up in there," she says. She already knew about that.

Sometimes her producers went for the joke, and Hutchinson laughed along. "The funniest interview I did was with Gary 'Suitcase' Smith," she says. "He was about 6'2" in his stockings. And when you got him on skates, he was about 6'4", or more." Hutchinson is 5'1". "The producer insisted I do the interview on the ice. So, all you get is my mike going diagonally across the screen. You get a little bit of his face, and that's it."

Hutchinson spent only a year on the show, and when she left, rumours surfaced that her male colleagues, in particular Dave Hodge, who hosted the Saturday night telecast, resented her air time. Hutchinson dismisses the notion with alarm. "Oh no, everyone was great," she says. She knew Hodge's sister, but didn't really know him, separated as they were by a few days and a network.

In the end, what killed her *Hockey Night in Canada* career was her schedule. The grind of rising at 4:00 A.M. on a Wednesday to host *Canada AM*, then travelling to cover a hockey game, and returning home—as a single mother now, to two children—was too much. "It really wiped me out. I was so tired." After Hutchinson left the show, it would be another two decades before a female voice was heard again as an interviewer on *Hockey Night in Canada*.

The Broad Street Bullies

Aggression is as much a part of hockey as skating and shooting, generating hard collisions and physical battles as ten skaters move fast in pursuit of that little black rubber disk. However, the resulting violence of that pursuit is ancillary—it comes from playing the game and is not, usually, an end in itself.

In the mid-1970s, the Philadelphia Flyers changed that reality like a punch to the head, something their players frequently applied to opponents as they bullied their way to two Stanley Cup championships, with *Hockey Night in Canada* looking on like a witness to a crime.

The Philadelphia Flyers did not invent hockey violence. It had accompanied the game from the first indoor match in Montreal on March 3, 1875. A century had passed in which hockey violence had notable flashpoints, sometimes resulting in the serious injury of players—and on at least three occasions, death—but those tragic casualties were the result of ill judgment fuelled by the heat of the game, or simply accidents.

In the early 1970s, the Philadelphia Flyers, a 1967 NHL expansion team, were always getting ice sprayed in their faces. The NHL's talent pool had been diluted by expansion, and so Flyers owner Ed Snider knew his team couldn't depend on an endless supply of skilled players to stop the humiliation. They would get to the summit with whatever it took.

This brand of "end justifying means" hockey turned out to be a type in which aggression was amped up into controlled violence, administered as part

Bobby Clarke, the kid from Flin Flon, Manitoba, was told he was too scrawny to last in hockey. He responded with a 15-season NHL career, winning two Stanley Cups and three Hart Trophies as league MVP.

30

of strategy. The results were so startling—on several levels—that the Flyers, whose rink was on Philadelphia's Broad Street, became known as the "Broad Street Bullies." It was not a term of affection.

After watching the Flyers mangle the Canucks in 1973, *Vancouver Sun* columnist Jim Taylor wrote, "There's just one thing that bothers me. The Flyers play butcher shop hockey and succeed by the only measuring stick that counts. They win. Success breeds imitators. If they make it to the Stanley Cup final, how many more goon squads can we expect next season?"

The Flyers made it to the 1973–74 Stanley Cup finals, after a regular season that saw them rack up 112 points, second best in the NHL, led by the goal-scoring talents of Bill Barber and Rick MacLeish, and the net-minding genius of Bernie Parent. They led the league with 1,740 penalty minutes—or twenty-two and a half minutes per game over a seventy-eight game season. Dave "The Hammer" Schultz accounted for 348 of those minutes, André "Moose" Dupont added another 216, and Don "Big Bird" Saleski and Bob "Hound Dog" Kelly added 131 and 130 minutes, respectively. Add captain Bobby Clarke's 113 minutes in the box and you have five players tallying more than half the team's penalty minutes.

Clarke, a diabetic kid from the rough mining town of Flin Flon, Manitoba, had fought for every scrap of ice he got on the way to the NHL. He displayed the Flyers' ethos in the 1972 Summit Series by scoring two goals and four assists, and breaking the ankle of bothersome Soviet star Valeri Kharlamov with a vicious two-handed slash—still considered a great crime in Russia, which has some impressive standards of comparison.

The fanatical win-at-all costs Bobby Clarke summed up the Flyers' strategy as obvious to anyone who cared to look: "You don't have to be a genius to figure out what we do on the ice. We take the shortest route to the puck and arrive in ill humour." Their coach, Fred "The Fog" Shero, punctuated it: "There are things I would do for my players that I wouldn't do for my sons."

The Flyers' Stanley Cup final opponent, the Boston Bruins, had finished the season with 113 points, and 960 penalty minutes. They added another 349—or more than a third of their season total—in the playoffs, just trying to respond to the Broad Street Bullies. They failed, and the Flyers won the series 4–2, and their first Stanley Cup.

The following year the Flyers were in the finals again, this time coming off a regular season tied for the league lead with 113 points and a staggering 1,953 penalty minutes. Their opponents, the Buffalo Sabres, also had 113 points, and

Red Army star Valeri Kharlamov struggles on the ice after taking a cross check to the head from the Flyers early in the first period. The Flyers are determined to batter the Soviets into retreat—which they do, leaving the ice in protest.

"IF YOU CAN'T BEAT 'EM IN THE ALLEY"

Two years after the Flyers won their first Stanley Cup with violent tactics, they found themselves in court. During a 1976 playoff series with Toronto, Ontario Attorney General Roy McMurtry had seen the Flyers cross the line between the arena and society, and laid charges against Philadelphia's Mel Bridgman and Don Saleski for possession of a dangerous weapon—a hockey stick. McMurtry also charged Flyers Joe Watson and Bob Kelly with common assault. The charges against the first two were stayed, while Watson and Kelly pleaded guilty and were fined. The violence practised by the Flyers influenced teams for more than a decade, but their style of hockey was part of an ethos that has long influenced the game. Toronto Maple Leafs founder Conn Smythe believed so deeply the nostrum "If you can't beat 'em in the alley, you can't beat 'em on the ice," that it's the title he gave to his autobiography.

had learned a lesson from the Flyers' success. They had bumped up their penalty totals from 785 in 1973–74, to 1,211 minutes. And the Flyers won the Stanley Cup again.

Hockey Night in Canada's cameras could only watch as the Flyers bashed and brawled their way to another title, almost instantly changing the NHL as they made it bleed. In the Flyers' first championship season, only four of the NHL's nineteen teams topped 1,000 penalty minutes. After seeing what the Flyers could do with deliberately rough play, fifteen teams went over the 1,000-penalty-minute mark in 1974–75.

The nadir of the Flyers' game plan came to be on *Hockey Night in Canada* in 1976. The Soviet Red Army team, along with the Soviet Wings, had come to play eight games against NHL teams in a "Super Series." The Soviets had already defeated Boston and New York, and had tied Montreal on New Year's Eve in a game of such hockey artistry by both teams that it is still considered a masterpiece.

On January 11, the Red Army entered the Spectrum to face the Flyers in the last game of the Super Series. They may as well have been stumbling unarmed into the imperial Roman Coliseum to face ravenous lions. Flyers coach Fred Shero, the son of Russian immigrants, had studied the Russian hockey system, and had even travelled to the USSR to take a closer look. He taught the Flyers basic elements of it, such as puck control and positional play, and then let their own instincts do the rest. But he told an interviewer, "If we lose, I think it will be worse than dying."

The Flyers tried to avoid that fate by hitting the Russians every chance they could. They were especially aggressive on a penalty kill early in the first period.

When Philadelphia's penalized player, Ed Van Impe, came back onto the ice, he headed straight for Red Army star Valeri Kharlamov (whose ankle Bobby Clarke had broken in 1972) and laid him flat with a cross-check to the back of the head.

With Kharlamov prone on the ice, play-by-play man Bob Cole says, "The Soviets are all standing up. They want a penalty, but I tell ya Dick, that was a solid check, and I didn't see too much wrong with it."

Colour man Dick Irvin politely disagrees. "Concerning the games I've seen, I'd have to think this is the toughest exchange…. In these last few moments we've seen more physical contact than in any of the games I've seen in person, or on the television."

When the referees don't call a penalty on Van Impe, the Red Army team does what many NHL teams had probably wanted to do when playing the Flyers: they leave the ice. "They're going home!" Bob Cole exclaims, at first in disbelief, and then again as a stunning reality.

Tournament organizer Alan Eagleson and NHL president Clarence Campbell made the Soviets an offer they couldn't refuse: both Soviet squads would forfeit their combined total of $200,000 in prize money if the Red Army team didn't return to play the game. So they did, and lost 4–1.

At the beginning of the 1976–77 season, the Broad Street Bullies met the swift, skilled Montreal Canadiens in back-to-back exhibition games. Montreal coach Scotty Bowman called up several tough guys from their minor league affiliate, put all five out on the ice, and the temporary Canadiens pummelled the Flyers tough guys.

"Sitting in the dressing room after the game, a lot of the guys were smiling," recalled Canadiens' Hall of Fame left-winger Steve Shutt. "We knew we had them. Better still, they knew it, too. And once you beat them at their style, you could impose your style on them and we knew they could never skate with us."

Montreal would defeat the Broad Street Bullies in the 1976 Stanley Cup finals by four games to none. The reign of terror wasn't over, but it had been neutralized by speed and skill. Even so, the Bullies' legacy of using violence to win was seen by a generation of hockey minds watching *Hockey Night in Canada*. As a result, their legacy played out through the 1980s in professional leagues across North America, and even today *Hockey Night in Canada* opens its weekly telecast with Canadian band Nickelback's cover of "Saturday Night's All Right for Fighting," a 1970s song written about pub violence in the U.K., used now as an exciting promise of what's about to come on the ice.

Second Period

Peter Puck

Peter Puck, a.k.a "Professor Poke-Check," was born in the United States during the bloody era of Philadelphia's "Broad Street Bullies." The chirpy and cheerful cartoon puck—about as far as one could get from the Flyers' blitzkrieg hockey—was invented to teach American children about hockey in 1973. NBC's "Game of the Week" hockey broadcast was fighting a Sunday afternoon ratings battle with the NBA on CBS, and a Sunday version of *Wide World of Sports* on ABC. The cartoon puck was designed to hook the kids into TV hockey, and so, too, their parents.

"Many of the fans we are trying to reach have never had the opportunity to experience an NHL game," said Scotty Connal, NBC's executive producer of NHL hockey. However, he saw hope in the large number of children playing hockey in the United States. "They're dedicated to the game, and they are going to become tremendous fans in a few years."

Peter Puck was the idea of NBC executive Donald Carswell, and was brought to life by the mighty Hanna-Barbera animation studios that could imagine a world including both the Flintstones and the Jetsons. More than a cartoon diversion for children, Peter Puck became both hockey guide and historian for a game which had just emerged from its so-called Golden Age into the brave new world of NHL expansion.

With his high-pitched voice (performed by actor Ronnie Schell) and indestructible optimism, the animated puck covered history, rules, equipment, and personalities in a three-minute cartoon which always began "Howdy fans, Peter Puck here to lay some facts on you about hockey—the world's fastest team sport." Much of the puck professor's content was provided by *Hockey Night*

Peter Puck, a cartoon professor of hockeyology, was created in the 1970s to teach Americans about the game for NBC's weekly hockey broadcasts.

Peter Puck, flashier and faster, returned to *Hockey Night in Canada* in 2009, after a 29-year retirement.

in Canada host Brian McFarlane, who also worked on the NBC broadcasts, and brought formidable hockey knowledge to both.

Despite the educational—and entertainment—qualities of Peter Puck, some purists derided the cartoon as a cheesy gimmick pandering to American ignorance. That prejudice ignored the fact that the NHL owed its very existence to the United States. In 1904, the hockey-playing continent tilted south, as a generation of stellar Canadian puck-chasers headed to the International Hockey League, headquartered in Houghton, Michigan.

The IHL was the first professional hockey league in the world, created by Canadian dentist Jack "Doc" Gibson and wealthy investors as part of the entertainment palette for the masses thronging to the copper-rich mining country. When his Berlin, Ontario, team shut out their archrivals Waterloo 3–0 in 1898, Berlin's mayor rewarded Gibson and his teammates—including the sons of the Seagram distillery family—with gold pieces as trophies. The Ontario Amateur Hockey Association, outraged by this act of "prostitution," suspended the entire Berlin team for the rest of the season for taking money. The experience embittered Gibson, and drove him to create a league that, in its three short years of life, would change the world of hockey forever.

Professional hockey came to Canada in 1908, morphing into the NHL in 1917. By the mid-1920s, the NHL realized it needed to tap into the champagne-fuelled bounty of the Jazz Age, and started teams in Boston, Chicago, Pittsburgh, Detroit, and New York City, which was home to both the Americans and the Rangers. The Americans and Pittsburgh franchises would fold along the way, but by 1967, the NHL was ready to head south again, in pursuit of TV money this time. Los Angeles, St. Louis, Philadelphia, Minnesota, Oakland, and Pittsburgh once again all received NHL franchises.

NBC had paid the NHL $12 million over two years to televise the NHL, but by 1975 had decided to hang up its hockey skates. Brian McFarlane eventually bought the Canadian (and then global) rights to the character, and Peter Puck headed north to *Hockey Night in Canada*. Hanna-Barbera had produced only nine episodes of Peter Puck, each costing about $200,000, so McFarlane was forced to improvise, cutting in archival footage with the cartoon to make the

Peter Puck explains the origin and colourful history of the Stanley Cup.

budget stretch. In 1980, it had stretched to the breaking point, and Peter Puck retired from *Hockey Night in Canada*.

Still, McFarlane's association with Peter Puck followed him around his long career in hockey broadcasting and publishing, with fans affectionately kidding him about the whereabouts of his "son," the precocious cartoon puck.

So, in 2009, McFarlane and the CBC brought "Son of Peter Puck" to life, with a deeper voice, and cool red skates and gloves. The new episodes, ten times shorter than in the 1970s, are more personality driven, as befitting the age. The didactic puck has explored everything from how Sidney Crosby got his shooting accuracy, to how Alexander Ovechkin celebrates a goal, to John Tortorella's famous temper. True to his roots, Peter Puck still teaches viewers a little history, even parsing the TV history of *Hockey Night in Canada* on the December 11, 2010, episode, while making history with the show: the date marked *Hockey Night in Canada*'s first television broadcast in 3D.

Imperial Oil Says "So Long"

It gave the country four decades of Happy Motoring, the three star selection, and lots of money to oil the engine of *Hockey Night in Canada*, but then in March 1976, the unthinkable happened: Imperial Oil decided to take the high road out of the rink to bid farewell to a partnership almost as old and as iconic as the show itself.

The beginning of the long story of their partnership is the stuff of myth. Imperial Oil had signed on as *Hockey Night in Canada*'s main sponsor for the 1936–37 season after General Motors decided not to renew their original five-year deal, due to the fact their new president, an American transplant, didn't think hockey would sell. And so the CBC's Charles Jennings, father of the celebrated journalist Peter, began the games by announcing, "Your Imperial Oil hockey broadcast! Bringing you … Foster Hewitt!"

To promote Imperial's "Three Star" brand of gasoline, *Hockey Night in Canada* began the tradition—now used in all North American hockey leagues—of awarding a star to each of the three best players of the game. The players chosen—first, by Foster Hewitt, and now by the home team's media—would skate out on the ice as their star number was called. They were not identified as "Imperial's first/second/third star," though, in case a reviled opponent's star brought down a chorus of boos from the fans. It wouldn't do to have the sponsor's name tarnished by association.

When *Hockey Night in Canada* debuted on television, Imperial Oil went too, and came alive as a character: the friendly, knowledgeable Esso station attendant, played for sixteen years by Murray Westgate. Esso was the brand name of Imperial Oil products, derived from the phonetic sounding of SO, the initials for John D. Rockefeller's Standard Oil, who assumed a secret majority

32

Imperial Oil schedule cards.

interest in Imperial in 1898. The Esso "Happy Motoring Song" replaced "The Saturday Game" as *Hockey Night in Canada*'s theme song in 1959, and hymned the arrival of the icemen until Dolores Claman's beloved tune replaced it in 1968.

About the same time, Esso was introducing in commercials what would become a national catch-phrase by directly playing on a primal Canadian fear: the hockey dad/coach, whose car wheezes and stalls on the way to Saturday morning's hockey game because of anaemic fuel. "Sometimes he just can't get the team started," the announcer laments, as hockey dad's engine won't turn over on a cold winter morning, and his son, in his hockey gear, looks on with Oedipal disappointment: "Some power play!"

However, it's the teammate that they pick up along the way who offers the solution: "Hey coach, put a tiger in your tank!" Dad has his epiphanic moment, fills up at Esso, and with cartoon mascot Tiger's help, the car roars, and so does the kids' hockey team. Soon "putting a tiger in the tank" will refer to everything from filling up the car, to fuelling a sluggish team, to invigorating the conjugal interests of a husband too much distracted by, say, hockey.

In 1976, Imperial Oil had seen the future, and it was enough to end the past. A *Toronto Star* business story from March 20 puts it in a kind of pyrrhic perspective by reminding readers that "*Hockey Night* ... will survive Imperial Oil's defection with a clean bill of health. But the big oil company accounted for 25 percent of $14 million a year in revenue."

The official explanation from Imperial Oil for leaving the show was that it wanted to reach a wider female audience than *Hockey Night in Canada* could provide. Of course, there was also the legacy of the oil crisis, begun in 1973 when the Organization of the Petroleum Exporting Countries conspired to raise global prices of oil and no longer ship to countries that had supported Israel after it was attacked by Egypt and Syria in the Yom Kippur war of that same year. The result for North America was an energy crisis, high oil prices, soaring inflation, and heavy losses on the major stock exchanges, consequences that lasted for several years. So, Imperial Oil realized that it didn't need to spend money on advertising to people who wouldn't buy gas anyway.

Imperial's departure was a cultural blow to the followers of *Hockey Night in Canada* and its historians, but not to the show's viability. Molson Breweries used their ownership of the Montreal Canadiens, which they bought in 1958, to increase their stake in *Hockey Night in Canada*, and by 1963 were spending the same amount as Imperial to advertise on the show. When some Canadian provinces banned alcohol advertising, Ford Motors filled the breach.

One of the significant aspects of the 1929 deal that Conn Smythe made on the golf course with Jack MacLaren regarding advertising rights to Maple Leaf Gardens included a golden clause: those rights reverted to MacLaren when a sponsor dropped out. As a result, MacLaren still had a valuable chunk of ad space to sell for a show that had become an essential part of the Canadian television diet. CBC was acutely aware of this, and took over Imperial Oil's stake. Though Imperial would come back to the *Hockey Night in Canada* fold in 1982, it was as a minority partner among many, with the show about to undergo another radical change. In 1988, MacLaren Advertising was gone too, when Molson and the CBC engineered an ouster, to complete the show's titular transformation: *Molson Hockey Night in Canada on CBC*. For viewers, it was *Hockey Night* still.

33

The Greatest Game Ever Played

On New Year's Eve 1975, the hockey game started early so spectators could make it to their parties before the year turned. By the time the game was over, all 18,975 fans in seats at the Montreal Forum, and millions more in the television arena, had already seen the glittering bauble of the evening—an exhilarating display of hockey skills between the champions of the USSR and the team that would win its nineteenth Stanley Cup later that season, the Montreal Canadiens. Where Foster Hewitt's radio legends lived in the imagination of listeners, this time viewers could watch the legend in the making, thanks to *Hockey Night in Canada*. And with each passing decade, the game got better and better, because of the way television now allows us to replay the past, and feed our nostalgia for that perfect game. But was it perfect?

The fabled New Year's Eve game was part of the Super Series featuring NHL clubs against the top two club teams from the USSR, known to North Americans as Red Army and Soviet Wings. It followed from the historic, tumultuous, and epic Summit Series in 1972 between Canada and the USSR, which had pitted democracy against communism, hockey nation against hockey nation.

The Super Series was personal: Soviet club teams had never before played NHL squads. And this time the United States was involved, with the Soviet clubs already having beaten New York and Pittsburgh. The U.S. had lost the Vietnam War in April when Saigon fell, and while Ronald Reagan and his characterization of the USSR as an "evil empire" were eight years away, the heat of conflicting Cold War ideologies was as much at play during the Super Series as it had been in 1972. "Bring on the Martians," read a sign held up by a fan in Philadelphia when the Red Army came to play, revealing where the USSR ranked in alien threats to the home of the brave.

Two champions salute each other—hockey style.

Peter Mahovlich bows—partly due to height, mainly due to respect—to Red Army star Valeri Kharlamov, who was used to much rougher treatment from NHLers.

On that chilly, dank night in Montreal, the Summit Series was much on the minds of the *Hockey Night in Canada* crew as they opened the telecast.

The atmosphere is "electric," says host Dave Reynolds, calling this the key game of the series, because "it's more than just the Montreal Canadiens versus the Soviets, it's Canada." Indeed, it's the only game of the Super Series to be played north of the 49th parallel. When Reynolds asks analyst Howie Meeker who will win, Meeker, still smarting from the criticism he took for complimenting the USSR during the Summit Series, is even more enthusiastically certain than usual.

"Well, I don't think the Russians can match Dryden in goal, Lapointe or Savard on defence, and all the fellas that play that position with them, and down centre, I think Lemaire, Mahovlich, and Riseborough give us an edge. Canada, sit back, relax, enjoy yourselves, have a ball; the Canadiens are going to win tonight!"

Up in the broadcast booth, Dick Irvin interviews former Montreal enforcer John Ferguson, who was also an assistant coach with Team Canada in 1972,

It was a tie game that earned a standing ovation, such was its display of hockey skill.

and recognizes some "familiar" Russian faces. But Irvin is more interested in what Ferguson noted during the Red Army's warm-up, revealing how their skills and drills are still unique to experienced Canadian viewers.

"Ten different exercises they did in the pre-game warm-up," Ferguson says with great seriousness. "They all move, they all handle the puck."

Irvin observes, "The way they worked the goaltenders in particular, they seem to do a little bit more of that than we do." Ferguson agrees, pointing out that the Russians practise tip ins, "one-on-ones with the goalie, and three-on-ones."

Montreal's Peter Mahovlich skates out during the introduction and pumps his stick three times to the well-dressed crowd. They go wild. And then Mahovlich punctuates that ready-for-battle gesture by singing along heartily with Roger Doucet, who performs "O Canada." In the stands, some Montrealers sing the national anthem out loud, too, while others, silent and stony faced, foreshadow the Parti Québécois victory that is less than a year away.

When the game begins, Red Army goalie Vladislav Tretiak, stellar in the Summit Series, is grateful for all the practice he had stopping shots in the pre-

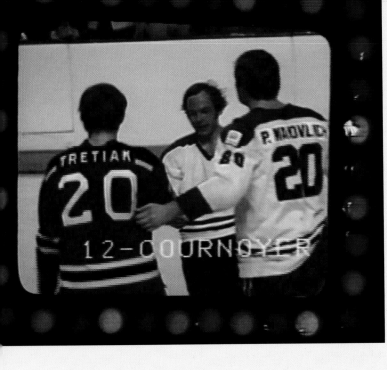

VLADISLAV TRETIAK

The 1972 Summit Series led to a series of hockey contests between NHL players—on their club teams, or wearing the colours of their nation—and Iron Curtain countries. And whenever they played the USSR, NHLers saw Vladislav Tretiak commanding the Soviet net. One of the great ironies that followed Tretiak into international competition was that he was a sieve, judged thus by Canadian scouts checking him out at a practice before the 1972 Summit Series. What they didn't know was that Tretiak had attended his stag party the night before, and was looking at pucks through a vodka-induced fog. By the time he retired in 1984, Tretiak was admired as one of the finest goalies in the history of hockey—with an asterisk. He was never tested in the NHL. Tretiak, however, longed to play in the NHL, and after the 1981 Canada Cup, mused out loud that he would like to be a Montreal Canadien. The Soviet authorities wanted to rip the epaulettes off their Red Army lieutenant for this breach of ideology. "I told them I was misquoted by western journalists," Tretiak said later. "After that I always said I belong to the Soviet people and the Red Army team. You understand I was not telling the truth. I would have loved to play in Montreal. That is my city."

Yvan Cournoyer and Peter Mahovlich congratulate Red Army goalie Vladislav Tretiak for his stellar performance against them.

game warm-up. The Canadiens come out gunning, and just three minutes and sixteen seconds into the game, Steve Shutt rifles the puck to the top corner of the short side, and the Forum erupts. Montreal's start looks just like that of Team Canada, right here four years earlier in the first game of the Summit Series. And in the cheering there is both memory of how that game turned out, and a little revenge.

When Yvon Lambert makes it 2–0 just four minutes later, the Red Army hasn't even managed a shot on Ken Dryden. The Canadiens are playing firewagon hockey—fast, skilled, creative. And everyone has raised their game a notch, for when Jacques Lemaire goes down to block a shot during a Montreal penalty kill, Dick Irvin notices: "You don't see this too often, Jacques Lemaire sprawling to block a shot."

The Red Army had clearly listened to whatever Siberian threats were levelled by coach Konstantin Loktev during the first intermission. Boris Mikhailov scores on Ken Dryden just three minutes and fifty-four seconds into the second period, and suddenly, the most dangerous lead in hockey has been cut in half.

But the Canadiens respond, and when Yvan Cournoyer scores on a power play, the Forum fans stand in joyful relief. A *Hockey Night in Canada* camera catches Brian Mulroney, then just entering the national political scene, smiling and applauding as if he willed this. Montreal has this game in the bag.

The two teams are fast, and both prefer to make a play with the puck, rather than to waste energy smashing each other up. The Russians prefer to stick check, and the Canadiens just outmuscle them to get shots on Tretiak. Howie Meeker will later tell the viewers the Russians don't play defence: "They have Tretiak."

Peter Mahovlich embraces Tretiak, who always hoped to play for the Montreal Canadiens, but because of the Cold War, never could.

A tired but exultant Peter Mahovlich enjoys a post mortem with Howie Meeker and Dave Reynolds on the greatest game ever played.

The Canadiens have Ken Dryden, who has spent the previous twenty-four hours alone in a Montreal hotel room to get focused. The solitary confinement has not helped. When the Russians score their second goal on their first shot of the second period, Danny Gallivan diplomatically points out the elephant on the ice: Ken Dryden's shaky play. Red Army are getting "maximum productivity" he says—they now have two goals on seven shots. "Two out of seven, you don't do much better than that."

Red Army ties the game four minutes into the third period and Tretiak bolts shut his net, holding off waves of Canadiens and "glittering" scoring chances for the rest of the game. The Russians nearly win it when they ring one off the Montreal crossbar, but the Canadiens hit a goal post as well, in the second period, so the hockey gods are playing fair.

Tretiak makes two point-blank saves on Jacques Lemaire in the last minute of the game, to the shrieks of the Forum crowd, and when the siren sounds to end the game, the fans rise in ovation for a 3–3 tie. Really, though, they're applauding the efforts of their Canadiens against the game's first star: Vladislav Tretiak.

"I don't think we're being anything but fair to say that the Soviets were completely outplayed tonight," says Dick Irvin, referring to the 38–13 shot total in favour of Montreal. "But we've just seen one of the greatest displays of goaltending that you could ever see."

Peter Mahovlich, the sweat dripping off his face, appears in the broadcast booth for the post-game interview and, after wishing all the viewers a happy New Year, makes a speech oddly reminiscent of one Phil Esposito made in Vancouver in 1972, after Team Canada was booed off the ice during a loss to the Soviets. "We tried our best," Mahovlich says. "On behalf of the Montreal Canadiens I apologize we didn't win."

His apology startles Dave Reynolds and Howie Meeker. "Peter, I don't think you really have to apologize one bit," Reynolds says. "I think you played the finest game, the team has played the finest game I've seen it play in years."

Meeker invokes the Cold War idea that the Russians are robotic masters of the game. "I think you punched holes in the theory that they're supermen, that they're better hockey players than we are, and they're more skilled than we are."

Mahovlich graciously listens, but it's what he says next that sums up why the game was so beautiful, and why its memory has been enshrined as a timeless example of perfection—it's because it was about a time Mahovlich and all players have enshrined for themselves: when they were kids. "The way they played, it brings back memories of the way we used to play it on the pond," he says. "You used to be able to take a puck and get your head up and not worry about a stick across your ears. And I love to play that way."

Darryl Sittler's Ten-Point Night

On February 7, 1976, *Hockey Night in Canada* would have had to point its camera at the rafters of Maple Leaf Gardens to miss Darryl Sittler's miracle on the ice. His was the kind of performance that catapults a player and a game into the Hall of Fame of memory—largely because we can see it again and again, thanks to *Hockey Night in Canada* seeing it first.

Darryl Sittler, then in his sixth season with Toronto, had been named captain of the Leafs for the 1975–76 campaign, when Dave Keon had departed for the World Hockey Association after contract talks with team owner Harold Ballard went the way so much did with Ballard—his way.

Sittler's opponents that night were the Boston Bruins, coached by Don Cherry, who would win Coach of the Year that season. On that Saturday night in February, however, Cherry and the Bruins were in a tough position. Their goalie, Gilles Gilbert, was injured. Their former all-star goalie, Gerry Cheevers, had just returned to Boston from the WHA as a free agent, and was playing backup.

So the Bruins went with rookie Dave Reece in goal. In the thirteen games he'd started for the team, Reece had notched seven wins—two of them shutouts—and the team in front of him came into Maple Leaf Gardens riding a seven-game winning streak.

That streak would begin to end in record-breaking fashion six minutes into the game. Darryl Sittler blocked a Bruins shot with his stick, and fed a quick break-out pass to Lanny McDonald. Down the right wing he went, and blasted

Darryl Sittler would spend a lot of time seeing pucks that he had touched fished out of the Boston goal on his ten-point night.

34

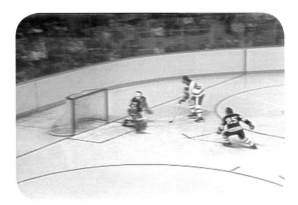

Boston goalie Dave Reece saw far too much of Darryl Sittler on this night. Reece would never play another NHL game.

the puck from the top of the face-off circle past goalie Reece and inside the far post. Play-by-play man Bill Hewitt called it "a perfect shot." Colour man Brian McFarlane added, "There's a very disconsolate Dave Reece, the goaltender down there, hoping as a rookie would, to get off to a good start."

Hope was all Reece would have that night. Less than a minute later, Toronto's Errol Thompson intercepted a Bruins pass, fed it to Sittler, who fed it to Ian Turnbull, streaking down the left wing. And Turnbull, at the top of the face-off circle, blasted the puck at Reece—who had come far out of his net, at the bottom of the circle—and into the net.

"We may see Gerry Cheevers yet tonight," Brian McFarlane said, more as a strategic move on Boston's part to focus the team, than as a comment on Reece's play. But as Don Cherry later explained, Cheevers was not an option. "He had just come back from the WHA; he didn't even have a practice with us."

The Bruins scored late in the first period, and went into the intermission down a goal, thinking they had a chance. Darryl Sittler drove a nail into that idea 2:56 into the second period, picking a deflected pass out of the air and swatting it past Reece. A *Hockey Night* camera caught Sittler, smiling in slight disbelief on the bench, as he demonstrated to an amused Lanny McDonald how high the puck was in the air when he made contact.

Thirty-seven seconds later, they were smiling again when Sittler won a face-off in Boston's zone, backhanding the puck to defenceman Borje Salming at the blueline. Salming let rip with a slapshot, and the Leafs were up 4–1.

By the end of the period, Sittler had added two more goals, one of them a solo rush from his own end, and another assist. "We better get out the record book," said McFarlane, "as this is a night of agony for the goalie, Dave Reece.

He hasn't been getting much help, and the Leafs have been scoring from every angle."

In the third period, in case anyone had missed the point, Sittler scored another goal just forty-four seconds in. "He just tied Rocket Richard's record of eight points in a game," said McFarlane, as the crowd rose in a standing ovation for the Leafs captain. But Sittler wasn't done.

When he scored his next goal, McFarlane reminded viewers that Sittler had just smashed a record that had stood since 1944, and Hewitt added that when Richard had his record-setting night, he was named all three stars for the game. "That's not a bad idea," McFarlane replies. The camera catches Leafs owner Harold Ballard, impassive in his box, doubtless pondering the contract implications for the captain whom he will—within five years—drive out of town.

Sittler's final goal, and second hat-trick, of the game is one which must have proven to Reece that the hockey gods had a malicious sense of humour. Sittler was trying to pass the puck out from behind the Boston net when it banked off a Bruins defenceman and into the net. "As long as he lives he'll remember this evening," Brian McFarlane said, as Sittler skated out to acknowledge the roar of the crowd.

After the game, host Dave Hodge interviewed the first star, who hadn't lost his perspective despite his record-setting night. "Jim Gregory [Toronto's general manager] just congratulated you," Hodge told the viewers, "and said they want the stick for the Hall of Fame and you said?"

Darryl Sittler replied: "I need to keep the stick for the next few games as we need the wins."

Boston would have its revenge on Detroit the next night, shutting them out 7–0, with Gerry Cheevers in goal. Dave Reece, who had been told he'd be sent back to the minors when Cheevers arrived, was out of the NHL forever. And Darryl Sittler would go on to become the first Leaf to score 100 points, which he accomplished in that season thanks to his extraordinary night.

BOSTON 4, TORONTO 11

FIRST PERIOD

Toronto, 1—McDonald (Sittler) 6:19; 2—Turnbull (Sittler, Thompson) 7:01; Boston, 3—Ratelle (Schmautz) 16:54. Penalties: Sims, Boutette (minors, majors) 13:00.

SECOND PERIOD

Toronto 4—Sittler (Salming, McDonald) 2:56. 5—Salming (Sittler) 3:33. Boston 6—Schmautz (Bucyk, Ratelle) 5:19. Toronto 7—Sittler 8:10; 8—Sittler (Valiquette, Ferguson) 10:27. Boston, 9—Bucyk (Ratelle, Schmautz) 11:06. Toronto, 10—Ferguson (Hammarstrom, Garland) 11:40. 11—Salming (McDonald, Sittler) 13:57. Boston' 12—Ratelle (Schmautz, Gibson) 14:35.
Penalties — Park 3:29; Sheppard 8:45; Ferguson 16:27; Forbes 19:44.

THIRD PERIOD

Toronto, 13—Sittler (Salming, Thompson) 0:44. 14—Sittler (Thompson) 9:27. 15—Sittler (McDonald) 16:35.
Penalties — Salming 3:46; Edestrand 9:50.
Shots' Thomas (Tor.).........................11 9 12—32
        Reece (Bos.)......................... 9 21 10—40
ATTENDANCE: 16,385

The score sheet tells the story: Darryl Sittler defeats the Boston Bruins.

Showdown

Ozne of *Hockey Night in Canada*'s most popular intermission features not only entertained viewers, but also would come to influence the NHL, and the show itself, by introducing the shootout to NHL games, and the net camera to broadcasts. And it may well have sent the Toronto Maple Leafs into decades of misery.

This "showdown" between a shooter and a goalie first appeared on television in the 1950s, on the American network CBS, which broadcast NHL games on Saturday afternoons. One keen viewer of the CBS show was future Hall of Fame goalie Ken Dryden, who paid particular attention to this penalty shot contest between a goalie and an NHL sniper.

Except, in the first incarnation of the idea, the goalie wasn't an NHL player. "The goalie they used each week was an assistant trainer for the Detroit Red Wings, named Julian Klymkiw," Dryden recalled in *The Game*, his essential story of a life in hockey. Klymkiw had played goal for the Brandon Wheat Kings as a junior, and had even strapped on the pads for fifty-seven games as a "roving goaltender" for the Eastern Hockey League. Klymkiw also served as the practice goalie for Detroit, in an era when teams carried only one game goaltender. So, on the CBS show, in order to protect the game talent, Klymkiw was drafted into stopping NHLers.

"Short and left-handed, Klimkiw wore a clear Plexiglas that arched in front of his face like a shield," Dryden remembered. "None of us had ever heard of him, and his unlikely name made us a little doubtful at first. But it turned out he was quite good, and most weeks he stopped the great majority of shots taken at him."

Julian Klymkiw, an assistant trainer and practice goalie for the Detroit Red Wings, was the backstopper in the original CBS version of "Showdown."

The NHL's best players tested their skills against each other weekly in "Showdown."

This penalty-shot feature appeared on NBC's telecasts in the 1970s. Now sixteen NHL shooters would test their skills against four NHL goalies. When NBC ended its hockey experiment in 1975, "Showdown" migrated to *Hockey Night in Canada*, and became a popular and innovative intermission feature.

Hosted by Brian McFarlane and "Professor" Howie Meeker, *Hockey Night in Canada*'s "Showdown" pitted two players against each other, and both against a goalie. Meeker would analyze the chances the shooters had, and then comment on their form as they engaged in a "skills competition," the forerunner of what would become a highlight of the NHL's All-Star Weekend.

A "Showdown" contestant—vying for a $15,000 top prize by 1980—would take the puck behind his "own" goal, and with a stopwatch running, would skate around a series of pylons, pass the puck to mannequin players along the way, and then shoot on a live NHL goalie. Then players engaged in a "shooting for accuracy test." An earlier format for this competition saw four automated targets attached to the net. They would swing out at random on a player as they skated in, and a cameraman crouched behind the net would capture the shot in the first incarnation of what would become *Hockey Night in Canada*'s "net cam."

The competition would culminate in the "breakaway" segment, with skaters going one-on-one with the goalie. The shooters would have five pucks laid out along the blue line closest to the goalie, and have to skate, shoot, and retrieve the next puck before their thirty-five-second time limit expired.

"Showdown" featured the NHL's stars of the day, but when George "Punch" Imlach returned as Toronto's general manager in 1979, he saw the show as a threat to team integrity—and to his own authority. Imlach didn't like the NHL Players' Association, and the fact the NHLPA supported "Showdown" was a direct challenge. He even went to court to try to obtain an injunction that would prevent Leafs stars Darryl Sittler and goalie Mike Palmateer from appearing on "Showdown." When that failed, the Leafs' eccentric owner Harold Ballard phoned *Hockey Night in Canada*'s executive producer Ralph Mellanby, and forbade him to produce "Showdown." If he disobeyed, he would be banned from Maple Leaf Gardens.

The show went on, and Mellanby wasn't banned from the Gardens, though *Hockey Night in Canada* wasn't allowed to broadcast "Showdown" in Ontario that season if Leafs players were featured in it. That reality hurt the show in its largest Canadian hockey market, and "Showdown" was over that season. The NHL and international competitions would reconfigure the "penalty shot contest" as the shootout, and the net cam would become an essential *Hockey Night in Canada* camera.

As for the Toronto Maple Leafs, Ralph Mellanby figures that Imlach's showdown with "Showdown" created the toxic mindset that saw him get rid of supreme hockey talents Lanny McDonald and Darryl Sittler, in the name of restoring his order. For the next twelve seasons after "Showdown" ended, the Leafs would not post a winning record.

Harold Ballard celebrates with Eddie Shack after Toronto wins the Stanley Cup against the Detroit Red Wings, April 18, 1963.

Gordie Howe's Last Hurrah

When Gordie Howe entered the NHL as a 6'1", 200-pound teenager, the Nuremberg Trials were revealing the extent of Nazi war crimes in World War II, during which Foster Hewitt had consoled homesick Canadian troops with weekly *Hockey Night in Canada* highlights transmitted via the BBC to Occupied Europe.

Howe had grown up during the war years in Saskatoon, Saskatchewan, listening to Hewitt's voice crackle through prairie winter cold—Howe told *Sports Illustrated* that "if you stuck your head out of the door at night, you could hear a guy walking two blocks away." He dreamed of one day being as famous as the heroes—and villains—that the even more famous Hewitt chronicled for the nation. Little did he or anyone know that once *Hockey Night in Canada* got its sight, six years down the road, the show would be celebrating him on TV screens across Canada and the northern United States for the next twenty-eight years.

Howe played professional hockey for thirty-two seasons—twenty-six of them in the NHL, and six in the World Hockey Association. When he hung up his skates almost for good (he'd play a shift for the Detroit Vipers of the International Hockey League in 1997), his name was attached to a long list of hockey superlatives: six Art Ross trophies as the NHL's top scorer; six Hart Memorial trophies as the NHL's most valuable player; four Stanley Cup championships; two Avco World trophies in the WHA, as well as that league's 1974 most valuable player award, which was renamed after him the following season.

He also had won the Lionel Conacher Award as Canada's male athlete of the year in 1963, the year he broke Maurice Richard's record of 544 regular

36

Wayne Gretzky poses with his idol Gordie Howe after having just
beaten Howe's seemingly insurmountable NHL points total.

season goals—something Richard never thought possible: "He is a great hockey player," Richard said in 1957. "If I had to make any comment about the guy it would be that he doesn't seem to go all out every time he's out there. If he did, there's no telling what he might do to the record book."

The last laugh would be Howe's, whose long skating stride and superhero strength made every shot—and he could shoot with both hands—look like a casual afterthought. He had always been knocked as being all lazy brawn and no brain, but the truth was quite the opposite: he could see the ice as well as Wayne Gretzky, the genius kid who would idolize him. Howe was able to see where a play (or player) was going to be before it happened, and take advantage.

He also had an easy, sharp wit, as seen in his many appearances on *Hockey Night in Canada*. In 1964 host Ward Cornell shows a golden puck given to Howe by the Toronto Maple Leafs to commemorate his 545th goal—breaking The Rocket's record, in Montreal, no less. "If I'd knew things were that good," Howe smiles, admiring the golden puck, "I'd have hurried up and gotten it sooner."

In 1967, he appears in shirt and tie and a Red Wings jacket at centre ice of Maple Leaf Gardens with *Hockey Night in Canada*'s Brian McFarlane and Toronto Maple Leafs winger Brit Selby. They're surrounded by 600 pucks scattered within the centre ice circle to commemorate Howe's 600th NHL goal. "Brit was six months old when you scored your first NHL goal," McFarlane says. "How does that make you feel?"

"A little older," Howe replies with a smile. Then comes the punchline: "I think I was in grade school when Johnny Bower was in the league."

Howe and the Maple Leafs goalie were great friends who would fish together in the summers in Saskatchewan, and appear together for interviews on *Hockey Night in Canada* when Detroit was in Toronto. In a ten-minute joint interview in 1963, notable for its relaxed bonhomie (imagine a goalie and a scoring prodigy from opposite teams chatting in the studio between periods today), Howe, Bower, and Cornell talk about everything from hockey, to golfing, to fishing. *Hockey Night* posts a photo of Howe taking a penalty shot on Bower, and Cornell asks if the puck went in. Bower thinks it did, and Howe confirms it, adding, "That don't happen too often."

Of course, it did happen often—there were 801 times that Gordie Howe found the back of the net in the NHL's regular season, and another 174 in the WHA. When Howe, nearly 52 years old, skates out on February 5, 1980, for his twenty-third All-Star Game, the crowd in Detroit's Joe Louis Arena rises

Gordie Howe played in 23 All-Star games during his long career. This appearance would be his last.

in ovation as the rink announcer says, "And from the Hartford Whalers, representing all of hockey with great distinction for five decades, Number 9." There is no need to say his name: the crowd chants "Gordie! Gordie!" for more than two minutes as Howe bashfully acknowledges the tribute to his extraordinary hockey life.

Also playing, in his first NHL All-Star Game and representing the western Campbell Conference, is a 19-year-old Wayne Gretzky, who will go on to shatter Howe's records over his own long career. On that night at the Joe, the crowd doesn't know (and it wouldn't care), sending out all of its energy to Howe each time he steps on the ice. As the game draws to a close, Howe, seemingly without effort, comes up with the puck in the corner, glides behind the net, then threads a pass out to Real Cloutier, who beats goalie Pete Peeters with a low shot along the ice. It's an assist for Howe, but the fans in the Joe who have loved him since 1946 cheer as if he's just won them the Cup.

Gordie Howe, Mr. Hockey in Hockeytown, acknowledges his long-standing ovation from Detroit fans at the 1980 NHL All-Star Game.

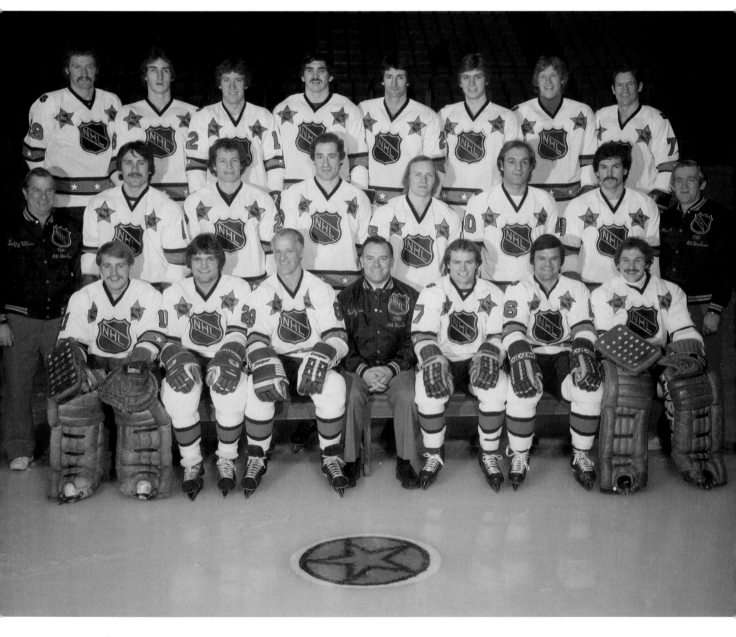

Gordie Howe has a front row seat befitting his status as hockey's best
ever in this team photo. But Wayne Gretzky will soon take his place.

37

Coach's Corner, Part 1

It is a segment that has run, astonishingly, for more than half the life-span of *Hockey Night in Canada*, but when it began during the 1980 playoffs, it was a one-off intermission filler starring an NHL coach who had some free time because his team had come nowhere near the playoffs. And *Hockey Night*'s host Dave Hodge introduced it with a slash of mockery, calling it "a special Stanley Cup feature, with Don Cherry, who vowed he would make the Stanley Cup playoffs this year—and he did, not with the Colorado Rockies, but with *Hockey Night in Canada*."

Enter Don Cherry, then a 46-year-old NHL coach fresh from a dreadful season in Denver, where his Rockies finished in a tie for last place in the twenty-one-team NHL. Or as Cherry put it with beer parlour wit: "I could show the fans both hands and both feet and I still needed to pull my pants down to show them where we stood."

Cherry had won the affection of fans and media—if not management—during his coaching tours, thanks to the paradoxical combination of his blunt, Legion Hall-style oratory and his dandyish attire. And he had won success as well. He was voted coach of the year as bench boss and later general manager of the AHL's Rochester Americans. He won the Jack Adams Award as the NHL's outstanding coach for helming the Boston Bruins to a first-place finish in the Adams Division in 1976. The Bruins had made it to the Stanley Cup finals twice under Cherry's guidance, but were beaten both times by Montreal.

It was in the 1979 Stanley Cup semi-finals that Cherry's unrepentant showman was captured by *Hockey Night in Canada*'s eye, and the footage would become an iconic part of his television image. The Bruins were leading by a goal with two minutes left in Game 7 of the Wales Conference final

Don Cherry learned how to coach the hard way—by toughing it out in the minor leagues for all but one game of his hockey career. His blunt style reflected his path to the NHL.

Don Cherry, always a fan favourite for his coaching theatrics, plays to the crowd.

against their fierce rivals, the Canadiens, when they received a bench penalty for too many men on the ice—a penalty for which Cherry took the blame. The Canadiens tied the game, won it in overtime, and went on to win the Stanley Cup. That was the end of Cherry's tenure with the Bruins.

The image of Cherry, standing up on the bench, mockingly accepting the derision of the Forum crowd as if it were great praise for the "too many men" penalty is one that defines the opening Coach's Corner montage today. However, it was also present at the very beginning, defining the sharp-dressed people's pundit, and accompanied by a trumpet fanfare as Cherry began what would become one of the longest-running careers in television.

At the time, neither he nor Dave Hodge were thinking of his appearance on the show as anything more than a short-term gig. Indeed, the journalist Hodge presses the dapper Cherry—his grey pin-striped three-piece suit more stylish banker than bordello boss—about recent headlines suggesting his coaching career in Denver is over.

"Eye of the hurricane again, I don't know what's goin' on," Cherry begins in response to Hodge's query, his sometime spaghetti-junction syntax in evidence from the beginning. "They make a million dollars, $960,000, what more do they want? We got everybody's attention this year, next year we make the playoffs. You don't make a million bucks and they still get mad, I don't understand it, but I'll be back there, no problem."

Hodge pokes him: "You don't put any credence to what you're reading?"

And Cherry shows a flash of swagger: "Listen, it's Colorado's loss and someone else's gain. In about ten minutes."

Hodge laughs, then tries again: "You're confident you'd get another job?"

Cherry calmly replies, "Absolutely. Absolutely."

Hodge then gets down to business, and wants Cherry to talk about the series that viewers are watching, a first-round playoff between Toronto, coached by mid-season replacement Joe Crozier, and the Minnesota North Stars, coached by Glen Sonmor. It's immediately clear that Cherry has keen insight into the game, and a broad sense of hockey history, much of it personal.

Don Cherry with Paul Romanuk and Joel Darling as "runners" for *Hockey Night in Canada*. Many broadcasters and media people started off as runners for the show.

"They're both different, they're exact opposites. Glen, he's effervescent, he's jumping around, he's yellin' and hollerin', I played for him in Springfield. And Crow is a calm, cool guy back there, ya know, fundamentals and all that stuff. Two opposite guys, but I'll tell ya, that Crow, we won four championships under him and he's a heckuva coach, I'll tell ya."

Cherry's colloquial language—the dropped *g*'s, the *tell ya*'s—adds credibility to his thoughts, giving him the voice of a man who has been through the hockey wars, and, as he reminds us, has won a few championships. He's not yelling at Hodge with brimstone bombast in the way he'll come to do regularly at Ron MacLean, but he's well-modulated, and confident in the worth of what he has to say.

Hodge suggests that Joe Crozier is a little too calm, and Cherry smiles to himself at the wrongness of that idea. He reveals what he finds amusing which instantly burnishes his bona fides, and turns the joke on himself. "Well,

I remember one time we were going with six defencemen and I went up and I told him, I says, 'Crow we can't go with six defencemen, we gotta go with four defencemen,' and I never played another game for sixty games."

When Hodge asks him, "What sort of things are you going to be looking at in this series?" Cherry is quick to proclaim, "I think Minnesota's going to win it" (he's right), but Hodge interjects, "In your own particular series I'm talking about, the Coach's Corner?"

And Cherry, thinking quickly, delivers the template that is going to make him "must-see TV" for hockey fans for the next three decades. "What we're going to do, we're going to take game situations, two-on-ones, we're going to point out things, what loses games, I've had a lot of experience this year on that"—Hodge is laughing—"and what wins games, I've had a lot of experience with [that in] Boston. I'm really excited. I'm gonna have a good time and we're gonna look at all the films, and it's gonna be for the kids, and all the fans, it's gonna be good."

And it turned out Cherry was right when he said early in the interview that he'd get another job. When no one hired him to coach an NHL team, the CBC's press release for *Hockey Night in Canada*'s twenty-ninth season announced three new members to the team, one of whom was an "ex- and probably future coach...." The ex-coach is, of course, the colourful Don Cherry, most recently fired by the Colorado Rockies. No one knew it at the time, but Cherry had already found his perfect team to coach: *Hockey Night in Canada*'s viewing audience.

Don Cherry always projects a tough confidence, if not downright swagger, but he worried on many occasions that he had gone too far, and his *Hockey Night in Canada* career was done.

Alan Eagleson and Darryl Sittler

Alan Eagleson was once the most powerful man in professional hockey. He had made his reputation as a fearless protector of players, which derived from his success at organizing the NHL Players' Association, and from his representation of many NHLers as their agent—including superstars such as Bobby Orr. He'd wrapped it all in the Canadian flag as the prime mover behind the 1972 Summit Series, a defining national moment played out with high drama on the ice between Team Canada's NHLers and the Soviets. So when Eagleson appears on *Hockey Night in Canada* on December 12, 1981, he is at the apex of his power. And in the post-game interview after Toronto had lost to Montreal, he expertly uses the show to reveal just how powerful he is.

The government of Prime Minister Pierre Trudeau, reeling from a severe recession, made changes to how high-income Canadians were taxed. So Alan Eagleson used that event to conduct the business of his client Darryl Sittler in public, under the guise of protesting the government's budget.

With a graphic proclaiming "Special Report: Budget Repercussions," Eagleson, also a former Conservative MPP and a vigorous fund-raiser for Canada's Progressive Conservative Party, explains to interviewer Dave Hodge how the proposed tax changes will essentially impoverish Canadian players. Not only that, it will speed them south to the more generous tax laws of the United States (in the way Canadian players had voted with their wallets by swarming to the U.S. upon the advent of the world's first professional hockey league in 1904).

Eagleson breaks it down starkly: a player earning $100,000 in Buffalo would take home $47,000, while a player earning the same amount in Toronto would take home $22,000 after taxes, and a Montreal Canadien would see $13,000.

38

The final score of Darryl Sittler's last game as a Toronto Maple Leaf.

Later, he mentions jokingly that they also can't deduct their lawyer's fee—which causes him concern—but he doesn't mention how much he's already taken off their earnings with his agency fees (and what he will embezzle from the players, for which he will serve six months in prison in 1998).

Hodge reminds him that "we don't want to sound like accountants here," and while Eagleson laughs, he presses on with his agenda, explaining how the old tax rules let players sock away money for their retirement. It's a strategy Eagleson claims he's been trying to teach the players, and now the government is undoing all of his altruistic pedagogy.

And then he does something brilliant. He uses Toronto Maple Leafs captain Darryl Sittler—an Eagleson client—as an example of how the new tax law will punish players. Interviewer Hodge seizes on the mention of Sittler to ask his agent about whether the rumours of Sittler leaving Toronto have any substance.

It becomes apparent that this is what Eagleson wanted to discuss, and the interview becomes a fascinating damnation of the Leafs' eccentric owner Harold Ballard. Eagleson explains that while Sittler has several hundred reasons why he'd want out of Toronto, it's "the Boschman incident that has bothered Daryl Sittler more than anything that's happened to him in the last two years."

Laurie Boschman was drafted ninth overall by Toronto and joined the club in 1979. Darryl Sittler kept an eye out for the rookie. "Boschman reveres Darryl Sittler," Eagleson explains, and calmly lays out his air-tight case to the television jury. "Sittler's the captain. Boschman goes to him and says, 'What am I supposed to do, I have certain beliefs, I believe in Christ as my saviour, I'm a born again Christian. Is that bad?' And Darryl has taken that position forward to management and he's been shrugged off. He's very disappointed, very disillusioned. I think Darryl Sittler is closer now—not for tax reasons—to leaving Toronto than he's ever been before. I underline the Boschman incident as more crucial because of the type of man Darryl Sittler is."

Dave Hodge interviews player agent Alan Eagleson, who represents Darryl Sittler—and most of the NHL's star players.

Of course "management" was code for Harold Ballard, who dismissed Boschman's religious renewal as another reason the vaunted player had gone soft. Eagleson, a profane and pugilistic street-fighter, here assumes the piety of a choirboy, casting Sittler in a Christ-like role: Boschman "reveres" him. Management by contrast is clearly unchristian, and by default, evil.

It is a brilliant set-up to what follows, when Hodge asks just how close Sittler is to leaving Toronto. "It wouldn't surprise me if we've seen Darryl Sittler for the last time in a Leafs uniform."

Eagleson ends the interview reminding viewers that no one cheers louder for Canada than he does, but he'd have to tell players, in light of the punitive tax laws, that "Buffalo isn't that bad."

What viewers didn't know was that Eagleson was already negotiating with other NHL clubs for Sittler, and so Eagleson's sorrowful prediction was, in fact, just an act. Sittler was already gone—and had even added not-so-bad Buffalo to his list of acceptable trade destinations. The trading of the captain of the Leafs took several weeks to sort out, and on January 5 Sittler walked out on his team, citing depression. Later that month he was traded to Philadelphia, and Leafs fans had another massive grievance to lay at the feet of Harold Ballard. Alan Eagleson had triumphed in one of his many propaganda battles thanks to his powerful pulpit on *Hockey Night in Canada*.

39

Roger Neilson Invents Towel Power

The power of *Hockey Night in Canada* displayed itself in one of the most unusual ways on April 29, 1982, at Chicago Stadium, the NHL's version of a gladiator pit. Vancouver had won the first game of the Campbell Conference final in double overtime, but the second game couldn't end soon enough for the Canucks, who felt like they were being sacrificed to the lions—or rather, to the zebras. Referee Bob Myers seemed to have tilted the ice in Chicago's favour in the second and third periods, where a string of judicial calls went against the Canucks. When Denis Savard put the Black Hawks up 4–1 with less than four minutes left in the game, Canucks coach Roger Neilson had seen enough. Rather than erupt in a pantomime of profane fury, Neilson, his dignity as obvious as the white towel on the butt end of the hockey stick in his hand, simply surrendered.

Hockey Night in Canada's cameras catch the Chicago fans noticing Neilson first, pointing and laughing at something we can't see. And then when we do: there's the curly-haired Canucks coach standing in silent protest with the white towel aloft, Neilson's great, ironic gesture.

Play-by-play man Don Wittman then notices what the camera is showing, and says in disbelief, "He's waving the white flag. I've never seen that before, not in a hockey rink anyway."

Roger Neilson was no stranger to the unusual. He had coached the Toronto Maple Leafs from 1977 to '79 and endured the whims of mercurial owner Harold Ballard. When Ballard fired Neilson, the howls of protest

Towel Power was invented as a protest in 1982, but soon became—and still remains—a symbol of fan support across the NHL.

Roger Neilson waved a towel on a stick in surrender to mock bad refereeing against his Vancouver Canucks. The referees managed to see that infraction and ejected him from the game.

from players, public, and press were so loud that even the tone deaf Ballard had to hear them. So he rehired Neilson, but wanted him to show up at the next Leafs game as a "mystery coach"—by wearing a paper bag over his head. Neilson refused, and coached the next game as if his firing and re-hiring had all happened only in the mysterious mind of Harold Ballard. After a season coaching in Buffalo, Neilson joined the Sabres' 1970 NHL expansion twins, the Vancouver Canucks, as an assistant. He was elevated to head coach after Harry Neale was suspended for ten games following a fight with a Nordiques fan who attacked the Canucks' bench in the aftermath of a brawl in Quebec.

The Canucks, hitherto unknown for their winning ways, went on a 6–0–3 streak to finish the regular season. Neale, who had given posterity and losing coaches everywhere a gem of analysis of the Canucks—"Last season we couldn't win at home. This season we can't win on the road. My failure as a coach is I can't think of any place else to play"—was as surprised as anyone. He let Neilson stay behind the bench, and removed himself to a box seat to observe in wonder.

The Canucks had finished the season with thirty wins, thirty-three losses, and seventeen ties, for seventy-seven points—good enough to put them second in the weak Smythe division, despite their .481 record. And despite one of the ugliest uniforms in the history of sport, with a V-shaped logo cleaving a dog's breakfast of yellow, orange-red, and black that would have dispirited any team, the Canucks knocked off Calgary and Los Angeles—who had stunned Wayne Gretzky and the Oilers in round one. All that stood between them and their first-ever Stanley Cup final was Chicago, a team that finished the season with an even worse record than the Canucks.

Roger Neilson was hockey's lonely genius, pioneering the use of video—and the use of irony— to motivate his teams.

When Neilson raised the white towel, his players followed suit, and soon there were three, then four sticks raising the improvised white flag. With no small irony, the Canucks had to send an emissary to referee Myers, to point his eyes in the direction of their surrender. Myers responded by ejecting Neilson from the game, and into history.

The coach apologized to the team after the game, but the gesture had caught the imagination of long-suffering Canucks fans, who knew how Neilson felt after watching their team set a standard for underachievement through its first decade and onward into its second. When *Hockey Night in Canada* broadcast Game 3 of that series on Saturday, May 1, the 15,713 Canucks fans made Vancouver's Pacific Coliseum look like a giant rally—not of surrender, but of triumph. White towels fluttered in every hand, to cheer on the Canucks and their inspired coach.

Vancouver won the next three games to defeat Chicago and take on the mighty New York Islanders, then playing for their fourth straight Stanley Cup title. Towel power wasn't enough to win the Cup for the Canucks, but Neilson's ironic, sarcastic gesture had taken root. The white towel would rocket through the hockey world via *Hockey Night in Canada*, and then onward to become a global phenomenon symbolizing not fan discontent, but power.

Jim Robson

To those who followed the Vancouver Canucks from their NHL debut in 1970 until his retirement in 1999, Jim Robson was their voice no less than Foster Hewitt was the voice for Toronto or Danny Gallivan was for Montreal. Like those other two *Hockey Night in Canada* icons, Robson was as scrupulously impartial as it's possible to be when you love the team you cover. Unlike the teams covered by Hewitt and Gallivan, the Canucks did not reward with a Stanley Cup the man who made them come alive for a generation. Even so, Jim Robson always called their games as if they just might.

Robson was born in Prince Albert, Saskatchewan, and moved to British Columbia when he was 8 years old. When his Grade 11 class at Maple Ridge Secondary School made a professional-day field trip to radio station CKNW, then based in the Vancouver suburb of New Westminster, Robson heard the radio waves call his name.

Like many Hall of Fame broadcasters, Robson began his career calling games in the minors, doing play-by-play for baseball and lacrosse on Vancouver Island. In 1956, Robson landed a job with CKWX in Vancouver, honing his talent by calling games for the British Columbia Lions, the Vancouver Mounties baseball team, and the Western Hockey League's Vancouver Canucks.

Had the Seattle Pilots baseball team been less parochial and willing to hire a Canadian, Robson could have become their voice in 1968, but when the NHL came to Vancouver in 1970, Robson was calling hockey games on CKNW. MacLaren Advertising VP Ted Hough suggested to *Hockey Night in Canada*'s executive producer Ralph Mellanby that Robson was their man. So Mellanby checked out his tapes. He wanted to make the show truly coast to coast, and parachuting in talent from Toronto or Montreal to call Vancouver games wasn't

the answer. And when he heard Robson's work, he knew he had found his Vancouver voice.

Even so, Danny Gallivan was the voice calling the play-by-play when the Canucks stepped onto the NHL ice on October 9, 1970—though he was doing it on CKNW radio, as the station had let Jim Robson moonlight from his regular Canucks radio gig to call the game for *Hockey Night in Canada*.

Robson's voice was crisp and cool, not one to soar on the whims of the crowd, but full of understated professional authority—if it was worth seeing and reporting, then Robson saw it and said so. When the Canucks scored their first-ever NHL goal, Robson said: "Two–nothing for the Kings, Lunde passes to Wilkins, getting set, is he going to shoot it? Here he goes … he scores!"

The action on the ice accompanying the call is a little more showbiz, with Vancouver's Barry Wilkins doing what Gallivan might have called a "Wilkinsian Whirligig," spinning with the puck and putting the LA defenceman on the ice, sitting on his jock. Then he catches Kings goalie Denis DeJordy moving to his left, and so backhands the puck to DeJordy's right, and into the net.

The next time Robson speaks is after the replay, when the rink announcer Tom Peacock delivers the particulars of this historic moment. Robson says: "Barry Wilkins getting the first goal for the Vancouver Canucks in the NHL." It's a significant moment for *Hockey Night in Canada*. Foster Hewitt moved radio to television, and described what viewers could see as if they couldn't see it; Robson let the viewer do some of the work, and provided context: everyone could see Wilkins' bravura moves with the puck, but was he going to put it on goal or not?

Robson saw his job as that of a reporter/interpreter, later decrying the pyrotechnics that colour so much of professional sports broadcasting. "I was more interested in the traditional, paint the picture style of broadcasting," he said, adding that some play-by-play guys today "get frantic just describing the national anthem."

Robson's picture painting always included a greeting to "hospital patients and shut-ins, people who can't get out to the game," a gesture that seems quaint today when getting to a game is more a problem of being able to afford (and find) tickets, not mobility. Yet quaint also was the fact that every time he did a national television broadcast on *Hockey Night in Canada*, he had to pay for his own replacement on CKNW radio.

As a result of his having two masters, Robson wasn't seen on national *Hockey Night in Canada* telecasts as much as Ralph Mellanby would have liked. But Robson was there for the 1975 and 1980 Stanley Cup finals, as well as the Canucks' biggest moments: their improbable run into the 1982 Stanley Cup finals, and their epic heavyweight bout with the New York Rangers in 1994, where they were vanquished by the Rangers (or the Rangers' Curse) in seven games.

Robson had left *Hockey Night in Canada* after the 1984–85 season, so the 1994 Stanley Cup call was a radio gig, following the team he had defined in so many ways as they came their closest yet to achieving that elusive silver jug. As testament to how good he was, Robson's Vancouver role was taken on by another B.C. boy who had apprenticed in the minors, and went on to become the national voice of *Hockey Night in Canada*: Jim Hughson.

Jim Robson analyzes game action with former Philadelphia Flyer Gary Dornhoefer.

THIRD
PERIOD

In the late 1980s, *Hockey Night in Canada* would undergo a revolution when the game's most singular player, perhaps ever, left Canada to sell the game, once again, in the United States. Wayne Gretzky's departure from Edmonton to Los Angeles went from being unthinkable to being an opportunity for innovation. *Hockey Night in Canada* would show doubleheader matches to catch Gretzky's games in the Pacific time zone, feeding the nation's need to see their lost national treasure. The innovation was a gain, in the end, for it not only expanded the *Hockey Night in Canada* talent pool, but the sense of what was possible. Along would come tripleheaders, the Heritage Classic, the Winter Classic, and *Hockey Day in Canada*. And with the arrival of the internet, the game that once upon a time allowed the eye of the *Hockey Night* cameras to look in only at the beginning of the second period became a 24-hour affair.

41

Us and Them

In English, it's known as the Good Friday Massacre. In French, as *la bataille du vendredi saint*. It was ugly in either language, and once upon a time, Catholic Quebeckers would have been appalled at the sacrilege of going to a hockey game—let alone a brawl—on the day Christians solemnly commemorate the crucifixion of Jesus. But on this Good Friday, April 20, 1984, the Montreal Forum was the church and *Hockey Night in Canada* provided the homily as the passions of the Quebec Nordiques and the Montreal Canadiens shed blood on the ice in the name of the other provincial religion: hockey.

The Quebec Nordiques had moved to the NHL from the WHA in 1979—exactly sixty years after the city's first NHL franchise, the Bulldogs, had bid adieu. Where the WHA had made some hockey purists feel like second-class citizens—echoing a larger cultural issue in Quebec—the return of the NHL was, for them, a return to the "true church." And it was a chance to stick it to "les glorieux" in Montreal, who were no longer the only hockey salvation available to Quebec.

The first season was tough for the Nordiques, who finished in last place. The following season, Czechoslovakian star Peter Stastny donned the fleur-de-lys jersey as a saviour. He had been snatched from behind the Iron Curtain in action-adventure style by owner Marcel Aubut, and won the Calder Trophy as rookie of the year. His 109 points helped to lead the Nordiques to the playoffs. In 1982, the Nordiques stunned the Canadiens by eliminating them from the playoffs in five games. Suddenly, the Nordiques were second-class no more.

The Good Friday Massacre was one of hockey's ugliest brawls, fuelled by intense rivalry between Quebec and Montreal.

Even the goalies fought (right), while the man who inflamed the Canadiens by injuring their teammate, Quebec's Peter Stastny (below), leaves the ice.

Families and friendships were cleaved by conflicting loyalties, and the two teams played each other like feuding family—with intimate hostility. By the time the series reached Game 6, the Canadiens were one win away from a place in the conference final. And at the end of the second period, they were on the wrong end of the 2–0 score.

Play-by-play man Bob Cole and colour analyst Mickey Redmond, the former Montreal and Detroit right winger, probably thought they were going to make it safely out of the period, when Montreal's Chris Chelios has his shot blocked and the siren sounds. Then the *Hockey Night* camera catches a Nordique on top of a Canadien, and suddenly Cole says, "And a fight's started to the left of [Nordiques goalie] Bouchard."

Redmond interrupts to say, "Look at this. They got both clubs coming on the ice. Look out!" And Cole punctuates that observation with drama. "This. Is. Bad." And it's going to get worse. Almost all the players from both teams are on the ice, fighting. Even the back-up goalies Richard Sevigny and Clint Malarchuk are throwing punches. The camera catches Nordiques Dale Hunter and Anton Stastny standing at the Quebec bench, restrained by the idea, as Redmond points out, that they could be suspended if they join the brawl. The Quebec trainer is taking the reasonable side by holding them back. "There are fourteen fights, or nearly fights, going on at this one time," Cole says, helping out the viewers. The cameras can't possibly take them all in.

As the Forum organist plays a tango, the players gather in a giant scrum, pausing in the brawl, and then suddenly the camera catches a Montreal player

lying on the ice. Trainer Gaetan Lefebvre hovers over Jean Hamel, as if administering last rites. Then the Montreal players notice, and skate over to see what's wrong with their fallen teammate. The club doctor arrives as well to take a look at Hamel, who isn't moving.

Meanwhile, the crew in the *Hockey Night in Canada* truck are looking for the smoking blow that knocked Hamel out. Fifty-eight seconds after the camera first spots Hamel on the ice, the replay comes up to explain what happened: Hamel is being pulled back by teammate Mario Tremblay, who thinks he's helping the linesman John D'Amico break up a fight with Quebec's Louis Sleigher. As Hamel releases his grip on Sleigher, the Nordique lands a left-hand sucker punch to Hamel's head, dropping him. "I wouldn't be surprised if he's out cold," Redmond says. "He has not moved yet."

Redmond explains that Hamel thought the fight was over, and so does Mario Tremblay, to Montreal coach Jacques Lemaire, as he heads to the dressing room. Calm has returned to the Montreal Forum, but it's the kind of pause in a battle when casualties are assessed and counter-attacks are plotted.

To make a bad situation worse, there has been miscommunication by the officials to the teams about the game misconducts. Players who should be watching the rest of the game on the dressing-room TV are back on the ice to start the third period. And all the Canadiens have heard just what Sleigher did to Hamel, and Sleigher—who also had a game misconduct—is back on the ice, too.

So the brawl begins again. "This is bad blood!" Cole exclaims, and Redmond explains, "They're after Louis Sleigher." As fights and skirmishes break out, the Montreal PA announcer surreally "continues his duties," Cole says, reciting the penalties incurred in the second period as more are being racked up before viewers as he speaks.

The director in the truck has started to select master shots of the Forum to give the viewers a sense of the carnage within: gloves and sticks and grappling players cover the length of the ice. Yet when the game can finally resume, the cheap-shot attack on Jean Hamel has fired up the Canadiens. They score five goals to win the game, and the series, but Bob Cole sums up the mood: "I'm sure the hockey fan does not relish what they see here now on the Forum ice." Yet the doubleheader brawl was as much a part of the story as the game was. The Good Friday Massacre goes into the books as one of the more shameful displays seen by the eye of *Hockey Night in Canada,* but one which it had to watch.

Quebec's tough guy Louis Sleigher tries to escape custody to resume the brawl.

Dave Hodge

"Take Ward Cornell. He'd been around too long." The speaker is not some mob boss explaining the whacking of the thirteen-year *Hockey Night in Canada* host, but Ted Hough, president of MacLaren Advertising's subsidiary Canadian Sports Network, formed for tax reasons to produce *Hockey Night in Canada*. "When we gave him the word, he warned us: 'Your ratings are going to drop. My fans won't put up with it.'"

Hough chuckled as he wheeled his yellow Cadillac through the streets of Toronto in 1972, talking to journalist Brian McKenna about "software"—or the talent in front of *Hockey Night*'s cameras, all of whom were employed by MacLaren first, and then CSN. "We eased Cornell out slowly. Now we've got a kid, Dave Hodge, who has made people forget all about Ward Cornell. And we didn't get one letter."

On the surface, as hosts, Cornell and Hodge were as different as the beginning of training camp is to the Stanley Cup final. The portly, avuncular Cornell's relaxed, laconic style belied a sharp, well-read mind, whose focused questions were designed to draw out the subject. Hodge's sleek, tightly controlled manner and equally sharp, educated mind also led to probing interviews and to surprises—when he broke the serious mode with a laugh. Of course, his sharp asides and gimlet-eyed simmers kept everyone on edge, and made his hosting all the more effective for its unpredictability.

Dave Hodge was a precocious talent who parlayed his Radio and Television Arts degree from Toronto's Ryerson Polytechnic Institute into a triple play in Chatham, Ontario: writing sports for the newspaper, serving as sports director for a radio station, and calling games for Chatham's junior hockey team, the Maroons. His success led to a radio play-by-play gig for the Buffalo Sabres

during their first NHL season in 1970–71. Hodge was 25 years old.

In 1971 he was invited to audition for *Hockey Night in Canada* as part of Executive Producer Ralph Mellanby's drive to shake up the show with new talent and sexy features. The young, handsome Hodge, with his hockey player helmet of hair, seemed the perfect candidate. Despite his experience behind the mike, Hodge had to audition for the big leagues, and he was nervous. Bob Gordon, a talented *Hockey Night in Canada* producer himself, was running the auditions. He saw Hodge's evident gifts, took him aside, calmed him down, and let him do his shaky audition interview again. Imperial Oil and Ralph Mellanby liked what they saw, and so Dave Hodge became the new guy in the blue *Hockey Night in Canada* jacket, handling the hosting duties in Toronto on Saturday for CBC, and on *Hockey Night*'s Wednesday games.

Dave Hodge flips his pen in disgust after being pre-empted by the news. The "pen toss" incident would become the stuff of legend and end Hodge's *Hockey Night* career.

Hodge's studio style was masterful. With his sports experience (he also broadcast Toronto Argonauts football games for CFRB radio) and his interest in social affairs, he had easy command of both interviewees and the camera. He liked to interview guests "cold"—without doing a pre-interview—as he felt that led to more genuine drama. He even got the best out of Don Cherry, serving as the interlocutor for the first six years of Coach's Corner, speaking to Cherry as an equal, which resulted in a compelling conversation.

To be sure, Cherry's own style was different then. His suits were sharp, but not shouting, and neither was he. When Hodge disagreed with him, it provoked either debate or a switch to the next topic, and Hodge was more than adept at parrying Cherry's swagger with wit. In a 1984 segment, the duo speak of Scotty Bowman setting the record for coaching wins when he achieved 691, after his Sabres defeated Chicago 6–3 on December 19.

"Does this make him the greatest coach in history?" Hodge asks Cherry. "Who is that do you think?"

"You mean after me," Cherry responds, half-joking.

Hodge enjoys a joke with former Leafs captain George Armstrong.

Dave Hodge's skill
as an interviewer
meant players
such as Gordie
Howe—who had
been interviewed
hundreds of
times—were
keen to speak to
him.

Hodge steps in with a stomp and a kick. "No, be modest enough to let somebody else nominate you. You ask me the question."

Cherry obeys. "Alright then. Who's the best?"

And without a pause Hodge replies, "Toe Blake."

It was Hodge's direct approach that eventually led to his departure from *Hockey Night in Canada* in an incident that time and tales have magnified into a full-blown rant against television bosses à la Howard Beale's classic outburst in the 1976 film *Network*. But in truth, Hodge was just saying what many viewers—and network executives—thought.

On Saturday, March 14, 1987, the CBC was broadcasting the Canadian curling championships in the afternoon. Some of the *Hockey Night in Canada* crew, including Hodge and Bob Cole, were watching the semi-final between Newfoundland and British Columbia in the guest lounge at Maple Leaf Gardens. With three rocks left in a tight game, CBC decided to cut away at 6:00 P.M. Eastern time to show the New Democratic Party convention in

Montreal. If a viewer was lucky to be living in Edmonton, then curling drama gave way to a *Star Trek* episode instead.

Hodge and the others were stunned. The seemingly arbitrary decision, made with no apparent understanding of the drama inherent in sport, added another arrow to Hodge's quiver of hostility toward CBC's executives. He had long tussled with the network over his ideas of journalistic integrity versus theirs, and over money. The last thing Hodge wanted was to give the network anything for free, and he resented how the network had been flexing its muscles after its ousting, the previous year, of the Canadian Sports Network as *Hockey Night in Canada*'s producer.

That night, the Toronto game against Calgary ended at 10:35 with a 6–4 Leafs win, and the network switched to the game between Montreal and Philadelphia. With less than a minute to go, Scott Mellanby, son of *Hockey Night in Canada*'s now former executive producer, tied the game for Philadelphia. The show cut for a commercial, with the clock ticking close to 11:00, the sacrosanct time for broadcast of CBC's flagship news show *The National*.

During the commercial, Hodge heard bad news in his earpiece. And now he had to tell the viewers, with no preparation or chance to form his words. There was just the shock of his own feelings combined with the curling indignity earlier in the day.

"Are we able to go there?" Hodge asks the voice on the other end of his earpiece, then opens his hands in exasperated supplication to the broadcast gods. "We are *not* able to go there," he says, his eyes hot as he looks into the camera. "That's the way things go today in sports at this network. And the Flyers and Canadiens have us in suspense and we'll remain that way until we can find out somehow who won this game. Or, who's responsible for the way we do things here. Good night for *Hockey Night in Canada*." Then, with the irritation of someone who has cracked a tough math problem and is then told their right answer is wrong, he flicks his pen—a couple of inches—into the air.

"It was about as small a misdemeanour as I could imagine," Hodge said later, when he was a successful analyst for TSN. "I mean, I didn't swear, I didn't call anybody a name. Had the network managed to find another way to leave the air without making me explain it, I probably wouldn't have exploded. But because live television is 'cue, the red light's on, 30 seconds to go to say goodbye,' and I wasn't in a position a) to agree with it or b) to know how to explain it, I chose my own way of showing my frustration and the rest is history. And so was I."

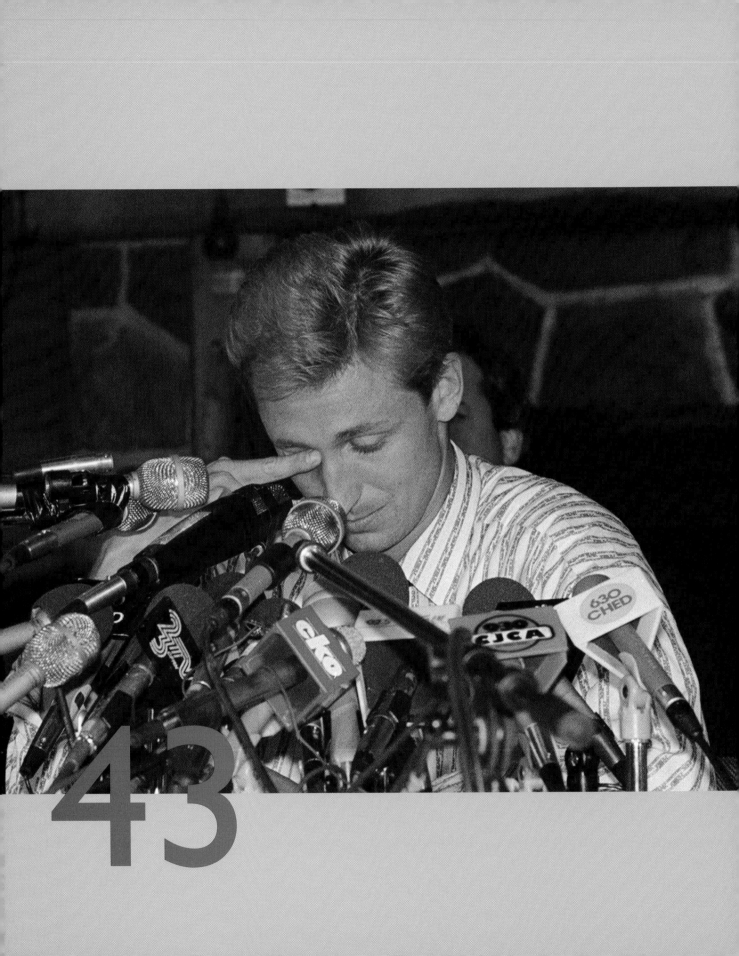

43

The Doubleheader

It took a bittersweet event to get hockey fans a double dose of their *Hockey Night in Canada* fix, but when the country lost Wayne Gretzky to Los Angeles in 1988 CBC had to expand its vision to keep an eye on Canada's favourite hockey son.

It's fitting that Gretzky, who wrote a whole new NHL record book for himself, would also be the catalyst for changing an institution. When he was shipped to the LA Kings in the summer of 1988, national feeling ran so high that the social implications of his trade for Canadians were debated in playgrounds, pizza parlours, and Parliament.

New Democratic Party House Leader Nelson Riis, who had already spearheaded legislation to make hockey Canada's official winter sport, implored fellow Parliamentarians to do something to stop Gretzky from leaving. "Wayne Gretzky is a national symbol, like the beaver. How can we allow the sale of our national symbols?" Riis lamented, not without a sense of humour. "The Edmonton Oilers without Wayne Gretzky is like apple pie without ice cream, like winter without snow, like the *Wheel of Fortune* without Vanna White—it's quite simply unthinkable...."

Indeed, it was unthinkable. Only months earlier, Gretzky had sipped champagne on May 26 with his fellow Edmonton Oilers after winning their fourth Stanley Cup in five seasons. He had promised a locker room full of friends, family, and reporters that "we're going to be even better next year." Less than two months later, on July 16, Gretzky starred in Canada's version of a Royal Wedding, as ten thousand people lined Edmonton's Jasper Avenue to watch The Great One proceed to St. Joseph's Basilica for his marriage to American actress Janet Jones.

Wayne Gretzky weeps at his press conference announcing his trade to Los Angeles from Edmonton. The nation wept, too.

Inside the basilica, Wayne's idol Gordie Howe, Soviet star goalie Vladislav Tretiak, and many of the Oilers watched the current king of hockey and his fairy-tale princess make their vows about happily ever after. And then, on August 9, the man on whose slender shoulders and hockey genius the Edmonton Oilers were built was another kind of king—the kind who played hockey in Los Angeles.

A weeping Gretzky told a press conference that it was his decision to go south, but in the days following the trade, shock would turn to anger. People pointed one finger of blame at Oilers owner Peter Pocklington, and another at Gretzky's wife Janet Jones, who was vilified as a Jezebel, or as the "Yoko Ono of the Oilers."

For *Hockey Night in Canada*, any finger pointing was done at a gaping hole in the Saturday schedule. The greatest player in hockey was now playing for an American team in a time zone that saw his games starting when the games in Toronto and Montreal were ending. It was a eureka moment for *Hockey Night in Canada*. If he wasn't coming all that often to Canada, then Canada would go to him.

The first *Hockey Night in Canada* doubleheader featured Gretzky's old team against his new one when the Oilers took on the Kings in Los Angeles on Saturday, October 7, 1988. Eight days later, *Hockey Night in Canada* was in Edmonton to watch Gretzky do another unthinkable thing: climb past Gordie Howe's seemingly insurmountable 1,850 points.

"Wayne Gretzky just signed the stick that's going to the Hockey Hall of Fame," says colour analyst Harry Neale as Gretzky autographs the stick that he used to backhand the puck past Bill Ranford. The replay of the goal then starts, and Neale says, "Thousands of his fans will be able to remember this goal, right here, as everybody around the world will be watching this tonight and tomorrow on all the newscasts. Aren't we lucky that we saw it here in person?"

It quickly became apparent that Gretzky's trade to Los Angeles had been a good thing for the balance sheet of the Kings, and for the NHL. The 1989–90 season would see the Kings turn a profit for the first time in their 22-year history. Advance ticket sales were up $4 million, and the team had twenty-four home sell-outs in the previous season, three times more than ever before.

Hockey Night in Los Angeles as the show follows The Great Gretzky to SoCal.

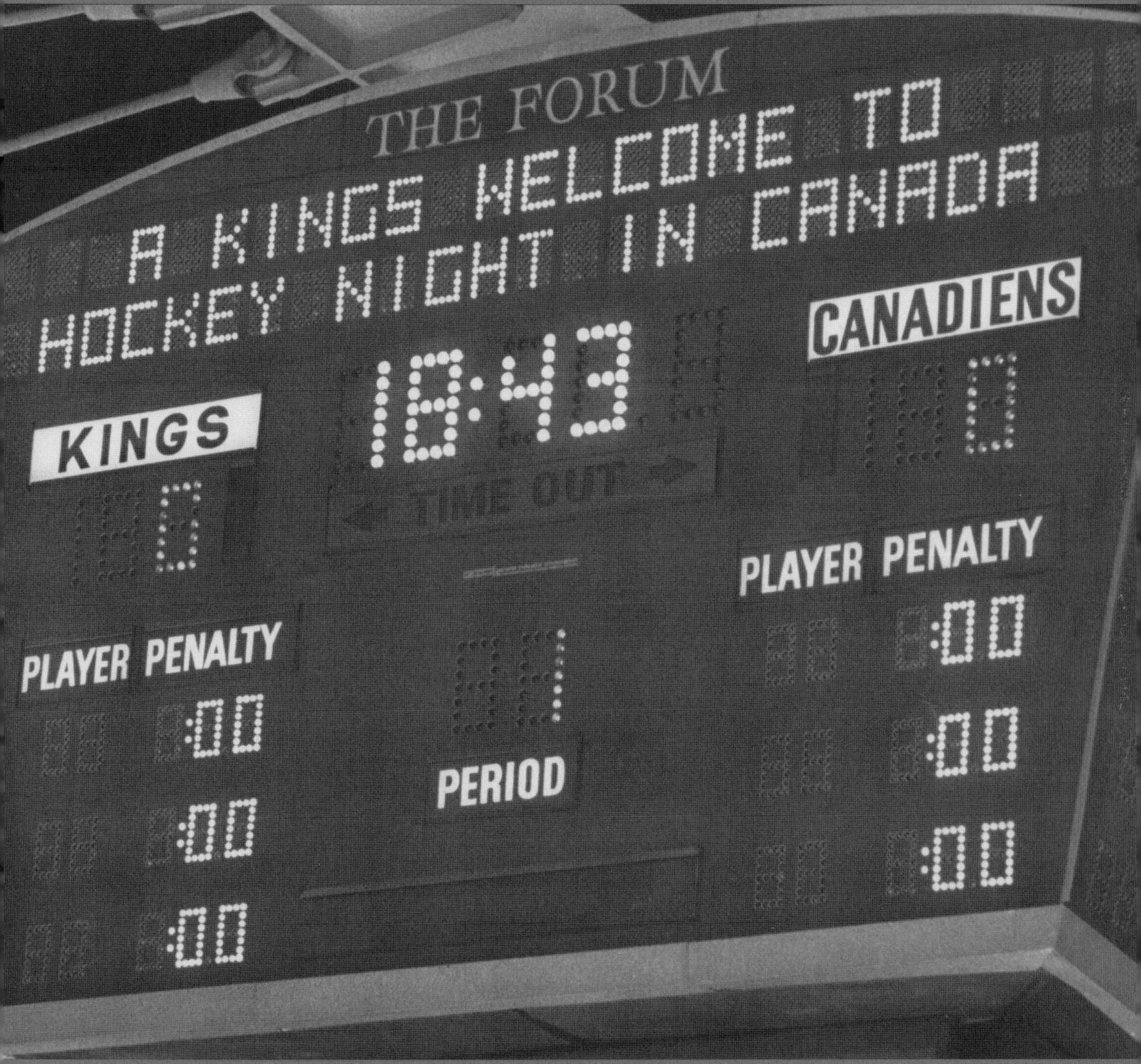
THE FORUM
A KINGS WELCOME TO
HOCKEY NIGHT IN CANADA
KINGS
CANADIENS
18:43
TIME OUT
PLAYER PENALTY
:00
:00
:00
PERIOD
PLAYER PENALTY
:00
:00
:00

The Vancouver Canucks saw attendance for four home games against the Kings in 1988–89 rise 92 percent over the season before—adding more than $750,000 to the team coffers. Winnipeg saw a 33 percent rise and an additional $400,000. Minnesota, which had the lowest attendance in the NHL in 1988–89, put 32 percent more fans in their seats because of Gretzky and the Kings, who played thirty sold-out road games in 1988–89, and none the year before.

Hockey Night in Canada saw viewers enthusiastically respond to more hockey on Saturday—first because of Wayne Gretzky, and then because viewers in Pacific and Mountain time zones could see more of their teams at home, and not have to wait for them to make a rare appearance in Toronto or Montreal on a Saturday night.

In the 1995–96 season, *Hockey Night in Canada* doubleheaders became a regular part of the schedule, with each game starting at 7:30 P.M. in Eastern and Pacific time zones. In 1998, the start time was moved up by thirty minutes. It had taken a singular player to open *Hockey Night*'s eyes wider and later, but the nation had such a hearty appetite for more of the show that by the beginning of the twenty-first century, *Hockey Night* would become supplemented by a daytime celebration of the game that made the nation.

Mark Messier and Wayne Gretzky, two legends who won four Stanley Cups together, now greet each other as opponents. Messier congratulates Gretzky on beating Howe's record. Gordie Howe is also there for the occasion.

Game Seven
and a Curse

It was one game, winner take all. On June 14, 1994, in Madison Square Garden, the Vancouver Canucks took on the New York Rangers in the last game of a series that had been as dramatic as any thriller. "We'll see who wants it the most," says Ron MacLean in a voiceover as the cameras show raucous, laser-lit-up Madison Square Garden. "They built the building in New York expressly for heavyweight title fights; they've got a doozy this evening."

The CBC has cameras in Vancouver's Pacific Coliseum, jammed to its exposed rafters with face-painted, fist-pumping Canucks fans, thrilled that their Cinderella team is still playing, and willing to pay to be, by satellite proxy, in a hockey rink for a Stanley Cup final Game 7. "If you're not in either rink," says MacLean to the nearly five million Canadian viewers—then a CBC sports ratings record—"you're lucky enough to have a *Hockey Night in Canada* ticket."

The last time the Rangers had been to the final was in 1979. The last time they'd been to a Game 7 was in 1950, when they lost 4–3 to Detroit—in the first Stanley Cup Game 7 to go to overtime. And the last time they'd won the Stanley Cup was in 1940, the same year they earned The Curse that said they'd never win it again.

There are many stories that explain the origin of the Rangers' Curse, but the most likely one in the superstitious world of pro hockey has to do with the holy of holies, the Stanley Cup. Though the silver jug has endured many indignities in its long life, having been used as everything from the greatest champagne vessel ever conceived to a latrine, the ultimate blasphemy came when Rangers president John Hammond burned the paid up mortgage to Madison Square

Mark Messier promised that the Rangers would defeat New Jersey to make the 1994 Stanley Cup final, and he delivered with a hat trick.

44

Garden in the bowl of the Cup in 1940. The desecration of hockey's Grail with the grubby cinders of commerce was too much for the hockey gods, and the Rangers were punished for it for more than half a century.

At this Game 7 in 1994, the *Hockey Night in Canada* camera catches a female fan in a Rangers jersey holding up a sign that reads "The Curse Ends 2Nite." And that was certainly the expectation at the beginning of the playoffs for the best team in the NHL.

The Rangers had led the NHL wire-to-wire in the 1993–94 season, finishing top of the league with 112 points in 84 games. They swept their suburban rivals, the Islanders; defeated Washington in five games; and then went to the seventh-game wall with New Jersey. It was there that captain Mark Messier, who had come to the Rangers in 1991 as part of an Edmonton Oilers exodus, cemented his reputation as a steely-eyed leader of men.

Messier, in response to the baying for Rangers blood if the Blueshirts lost to their rivals from the swamp, promised a Game 6 win in New Jersey. Then he

The Rangers and the Canucks took the 1994 Stanley Cup final to the wire in seven exciting games.

delivered a miraculous hat trick to win it 4–3 for New York. Stéphane Matteau won Game 7 for the Rangers in overtime.

The Canucks, on the other hand, were barely over .500, and squeaked into the playoffs in fourteenth place. It took a miracle save from goalie Kirk McLean's toe in Game 7 of Round 1 overtime against Calgary, and a subsequent game-winner by the Russian Rocket, Pavel Bure, to send them on their increasingly magical run through the playoffs. After knocking off favoured Calgary, the Canucks beat Dallas in five games, did the same to Toronto, and then took the first game of the Stanley Cup final with an overtime win. And then it stopped.

The Canucks lost the next three games, and the Rangers looked to win their first Stanley Cup in fifty-four years at home, in Game 5. Phil Pritchard, famous now as the keeper of the Stanley Cup for the Hockey Hall of Fame, had spent the afternoon polishing The Jug for its all-but-certain presentation later that evening.

And then something odd happened. Rangers team officials came into the sanctum where the Cup was resting, a challenge to superstition to be sure. Then they fondled it, posed for photos with it, and generally spoiled Pritchard's polishing job. Pritchard knew that all NHL players believed that touching the Cup before you won it was very bad karma. This transgression would be called to account.

And so it seemed that it would, with the Canucks up 3–0, going into the third minute of the third period. And then the karma seemed to suddenly get reversed. The Rangers tied the game mid-way through the period. Pritchard wheeled the Cup in its coffin-like case out onto a concourse at MSG. As soon as he opened the case, the Canucks scored. And then again, and again, to win by a convincing six goals to three. It looked to Pritchard, and to Rangers fans, that The Curse was very much alive. Pritchard was spooked.

The Canucks followed up that win with another in Game 6 in Vancouver, sending the Rangers home on the wrong end of a 4–1 result. So the showdown in Game 7 was filled with the tumult of this see-saw battle between the Goliath from Gotham and the now not-so-accidental tourists from Vancouver.

Just before puck drop, viewers hear Sinatra singing "New York, New York" and colour man Dick Irvin says to Bob Cole, a fan of Ol' Blue Eyes, "They're hauling out all the artillery just for you. Sinatra! Before the opening face-off. It can't get any better than that from an excitement standpoint."

Despite Vancouver captain Trevor Linden attempting a Messier-like miracle of his own with two goals, the Canucks heard the echo of their own curse when Nathan Lafayette rang the possible tying goal off the Rangers' post with five minutes left. There were three face-offs in the Rangers' zone in the final thirty-seven seconds, the last coming with 1.6 seconds on the clock. "A lot has happened in fifty-four years," Bob Cole reminds listeners, "but for New York hockey fans, nothing better than this."

And then Mark Messier is jumping around like a little kid, despite the fact this win will put a sixth Stanley Cup ring on his fingers. "To accomplish great deeds, one must dream as well as act," says analyst Harry Neale, "and many, many dreams have come true, here, at Madison Square Garden for the Ranger players, former players, and fans."

Meanwhile, in Vancouver, a nightmare was just beginning. Before sunset over the Pacific, the air downtown would sting with pepper spray and tear gas, as hooligans took over the streets and launched a running battle with the police. Seventeen years later, they'd riot again, when Vancouver lost Game 7 of the Stanley Cup final to Boston. One curse had ended, and another had begun.

Top: The New York Rangers celebrate their victory over Vancouver in Game 7 and their first Stanley Cup since 1940.

Bottom: Mark Messier wins his sixth Stanley Cup as a New York Ranger and ends the team's 54-year-old curse.

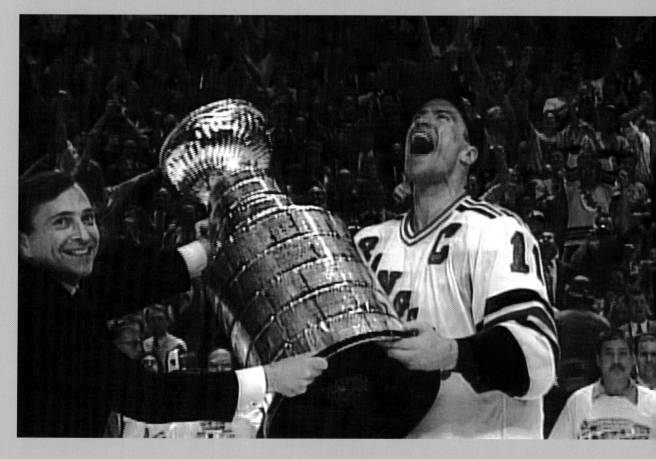

45

CBC Takes Over
Hockey Night in Canada

*H*ockey Night in Canada's long life, on both radio and television, has been inseparable from the CBC (once the CBC was born, in 1936), and today is the network's most successful "brand" show: synonymous with the CBC, and provider of a generous revenue stream to support other network projects. The most surprising detail about *Hockey Night* is that until 1994, the CBC was a guest at its own party, providing the venue and most of the production personnel, but not in full command of the bar.

In the beginning, Conn Smythe's handshake with advertising executive Jack MacLaren on a golf course in the summer of 1929 enshrined the rights to what would become *Hockey Night in Canada* in a gilded cage for the next six decades.

MacLaren Advertising produced the show and sold its sponsorship rights as it journeyed from radio to television. By the mid-1970s, MacLaren had created the Canadian Sports Network as its *Hockey Night in Canada* production arm, in partnership with the CBC. Still, CSN controlled the show until 1986, when sponsor Molson Breweries made a Godfatheresque offer. Molson told CSN that they'd take over the show and the personnel for free—after all, as the main sponsor of *Hockey Night in Canada*, they were already effectively paying to run the show.

Molstar Communications, in collaboration with the CBC, subsequently partnered up to produce *Hockey Night in Canada*, but by the time the epic 1994 Stanley Cup final between Vancouver and New York was over, the CBC had seen enough.

"Alan Clark [then head of CBC Sports] felt the brewery was having too much influence in the show's presentation," said John Shannon. "In one game they did a Molson shoot-out on the ice, which drove the CBC people nuts.

Hockey Night in Canada, a CBC flagship for six decades, finally became the network's own show in 1994.

237

There was always a clause in the contract, never invoked, that the CBC could hire their own Executive Producer."

So they hired John Shannon in 1994. Shannon's résumé was that of a prodigy: as a 21-year-old Ryerson Polytechnical Institute student in 1977, Shannon wanted to do an audio-visual project on *Hockey Night in Canada*. The show's producer, Canadian Sports Network, said sure, but they wanted to see it when it was done. Shannon showed them, and they offered him a job. "I started in the fall of '77 as a gofer for $10 a game and a blue jacket."

From there, his rise was swift. He started by making note cards for Brian McFarlane each Saturday morning, because he saw that "no one was doing any research." Then Dave Hodge wanted the note cards, which Shannon had paid for out of his own pocket. And then, by the time Shannon was 23, he was producing the Stanley Cup final.

Shannon was a B.C. boy, and *Hockey Night in Canada*, feeling the heat of anti-eastern sentiment, wanted to expand its production base. So they asked him to head west to produce the Canucks–Flames–Oilers–Jets games out of Calgary.

In 1994, CBC invoked its right to produce *Hockey Night in Canada*, and Shannon, by then fresh from producing the Lillehammer Winter Olympic Games for CTV, went back to where he started—though he wasn't exactly wooed. "They offered Doug Beeforth the job, and he turned it down," Shannon recalled. "So Alan Clark agreed to do an interview with me. I sat for three hours without any papers in front of me, with Doug Sellars, Phyllis Platt, and Alan as the board. And I think they were shocked that I could talk about every aspect of the show, the history of the show, the commentators, without any paper in front of me."

He got the job the next day. Shannon's six-year tenure at *Hockey Night in Canada* became a mini golden age, seeing many innovations that define the modern show: the doubleheader, *Hockey Day in Canada*, and the Satellite Hot Stove.

Shannon gives Alan Clark a lot of credit for the shape of the modern show, but he's particularly proud of the resurrection of the Hot Stove, which was fuelled by the need to compete in the sports TV marketplace. "We needed to be more technologically savvy," Shannon says. "Other shows, particularly the NFL, were talking more gossipy stuff."

Shannon was a fan of *Boston Globe* sports writer Kevin Paul Dupont's Sunday hockey gossip column, and wanted to transfer that sense of insider intimacy to television, while staying true to *Hockey Night*'s broad national vision. "The original Hot Stove was always reflecting three different regions of hockey in North America," Shannon says. "Jim Hughson represented the west; John Davidson represented the United States. And then the third body represented wherever the host show was from, either Montreal or Toronto. So that's how we ended up with Red Fisher, Yvon Pedneault, Scott Morrison, Al Strachan, and a few other guys in Toronto."

The idea driving the segment was to keep viewers glued to their televisions during the second period the way Coach's Corner did in

Elliotte Friedman gets the goods from Sidney Crosby between periods. When John Shannon joined the *Hockey Night* team, his innovations led to a series of new traditions, such as rinkside interviews and expert panels, which would soon become a huge part of the broadcast and the game.

the first. "It was what we needed to do to make sure the second intermission had the same vitality and newsiness," Shannon explains, "That 'I can't afford to turn away from the game or go get a beer.'"

Shannon sees the success of the Satellite Hot Stove as a seminal cultural moment in sports broadcasting. "I think the Hot Stove—more than anything else—spawned a whole industry. It spawned Bob McKenzie and the guys at TSN, it spawned Elliotte Friedman, it spawned us at Sportsnet, it spawned everything. And now everybody does it every night."

The intensity of the competition and the demands for "new and better" is a fact that *Hockey Night in Canada* has to meet head on, Shannon says, while at the same time preserving the "tradition" that has seen the show last sixty years. "Just like every other business that thrived in the '60s, '70s, and '80s, *Hockey Night* has to evolve or die," he says. "You don't get brownie points for just staying the same. You have to make changes all the time."

Maple Leaf Gardens Closes

The Leafs' last hurrah in Maple Leaf Gardens was their 1967 Stanley Cup championship.

Foster Hewitt was back from the grave, a black and white ghost in the Gondola telling the 15,700 souls in Maple Leaf Gardens that they were gathered for the end: of the house that Conn Smythe built, of the game that he gave voice to, and of the building that hockey—and *Hockey Night in Canada*—had turned into a temple.

Of course, the return of the long-dead Hewitt on February 13, 1999, was digital magic unavailable to the technicians helping him to open Maple Leaf Gardens nearly sixty-eight years earlier, when the Toronto Maple Leafs played their first game in the swank new building that had risen from the ashes of the Great Depression in an astonishing 196 days.

Conn Smythe, who built both the Leafs and the Gardens, astute to hockey's dramatic firepower equalling—or besting—anything on the silver stage, wanted to create a building where people could go as if to the opera. So he charged $3 for a top ticket at a time when $2.50 would get you the best seat at the Royal Alexandra Theatre to see Sir James Barrie's play *Dear Brutus* direct from London. Smythe's reasoning was simple: if he attracted high society to the Gardens, everyone else would follow.

For almost seven decades, pretty much everyone did. Queen Elizabeth made a visit, as did Elvis, Sinatra, the Beatles, and countless concerts and cultural events. Muhammad Ali fought there, taking on Canadian heavyweight George Chuvalo, the toughest man that Ali said he'd ever faced.

There were also historic firsts beneath the venerable rafters of the Grand Old Lady on Carlton. The Gardens saw the first goal lights, first flood lights, first plexiglas, and first All-Star Game, the latter which grew out of the charity game for Toronto's badly injured "Ace" Bailey, in 1934.

Topping the building's rich history there were the Leafs themselves, and their years of glory and despair. By the time the last game came to the Gardens, eleven Stanley Cup banners hung above the ice. And yet *Hockey Night in Canada*'s "last game" montage showed 1980s footage of the destructively capricious Harold Ballard sitting in his box, as the anthemic song accompanying the video reminded everyone, "Through good times and hard years we've made a sacrifice."

The Chicago Black Hawks were the first team to play the Leafs in their new building, and they were there to close it. The ceremonial face-off featured two players who were on the ice on November 12, 1931, the Leafs defenceman and captain George "Red" Horner and Chicago's Harold "Mush" March. It was March who scored the first goal in the Gardens at 2:30 of the opening period of the very first game in the building, one which Chicago won 2–1. The Leafs would atone for this lapse and anoint the temple by winning their first Stanley Cup in the Gardens at the end of their first season.

Horner and Marsh, then 89 and 90 years old, saw the decades fall away as they met at centre ice of the Gardens one last time. And with the very puck that Marsh had put past Toronto's goalie Lorne Chabot nearly sixty-eight years earlier, they began the countdown to the end.

Bob Cole and Harry Neale, the premier *Hockey Night in Canada* crew, called the last game at the Gardens. The building had been the birthplace of *Hockey Night in Canada*'s radio broadcasts, and its English telecasts. By 1999, it had become the mothership to all other broadcasts that originated across the country: from Vancouver, Calgary, Edmonton, Winnipeg (until 1996), Ottawa, and anglophone Montreal.

On this hockey night, as on the nights of yore, the show went on as usual, but with a special sense of occasion. Don Cherry, looking retro in a black pinstripe suit and black fedora, did his Coach's Corner live from rinkside in the Gardens, while peewee Timbits players engaged in intermission play on the same ice where Tim Horton, the founder of their sponsor, created his own legend.

Cherry had only "seen" the Gardens through the voice of Foster Hewitt when he first played there in 1948 as a 14-year-old. "I skated out on the ice and I thought I was in heaven," he said, then explained his fedora was not zoot-suit style from that era but a tribute to Major Conn Smythe.

"All the coaches in the old days used to wear fedoras," Cherry said. "We should all thank Major Conn Smythe because if it hadn't been for him we

Leafs captain Mats Sundin greets Red Horner, one of the many surviving Leafs who helped close Maple Leaf Gardens.

wouldn't be standing here today. He doesn't get enough praise. That's it. I just want to say, Major Conn Smythe, we're all sad, but we have to leave...."

The end of the Gardens had come because of money: in the bold new NHL at the turn of the twenty-first century, teams needed luxurious amenities to satisfy the sophisticated palates of their corporate customers—and to pay the salaries of the millionaires on the ice. Maple Leaf Gardens might have become the country's premier spiritual temple, but the teams needed a physical one.

So, in a week's time, the Leafs would move downtown and closer to the bankers of Bay Street to take up tenancy of the Air Canada Centre, with 115 luxury boxes. Coach Pat Quinn, himself a former Leaf, was under no illusions when asked if he feared losing the blue-collar fan. "We've already lost the blue-collar fan," he said, knowing how much a family of four would have to spend to attend an NHL game. "I'm worried about the white-collar fan."

During the second intermission, the Hot Stove segment, now prefaced by "Satellite" because two of its panellists, Montreal journalist Red Fisher and New York Rangers colour analyst John Davidson, were linked in to Ron MacLean and journalist Al Strachan via outer space, spoke of hockey issues of the day. Strachan, in black tie "because Conn Smythe would have dressed this way on opening night," lamented the fact that Cliff Fletcher, President and GM of the Leafs from 1991 to 1997, had not been invited to the party due to bad blood between him and management, a traditional Leafs affliction over the years.

"Harold Ballard pretty well destroyed everything with respect to [the team's] grandeur and its heritage," Strachan said. "Cliff brought all that back; he's responsible for most of the team that's out there tonight. I think to not invite him is disgraceful."

The team on the ice that night clearly had a respect for history, too, losing to Chicago as they had done in 1931, though by a score of 6–2 this time. After the game, Ron MacLean hosted the farewell, with a parade of 105 former Leafs, and the 48th Highlanders, and Anne Murray singing "The Maple Leaf Forever" to a video montage of the team's forever—so far.

But the person who gave voice to how everyone felt was Paul Morris, the public address announcer for the Gardens. The invisible man with the neutral, nasal monotone was now spotlit at centre ice, in the building where his father had worked as an electrician, and where the son had announced the goals and penalties and the last minute of play since 1961.

"I feel like I'm leaving my home, the family home that we've been in all our lives," Morris tells the fans on their feet in the Gardens and the millions of viewers across the country. "And I think most Canadians feel the same way, even if they didn't live here the way I did—they lived here in their dreams."

Ron MacLean, appropriately in black, stands outside Maple Leaf Gardens on the night of February 13, 1999, before the last NHL game is played in the fabled old ice palace.

Dick Irvin

When Maple Leaf Gardens closed in 1999, *Hockey Night in Canada* celebrated sixty-eight years of history by featuring a 67-year-old who had lived much of his life right in the middle—as a gleam in his father's eye, as a boy, and as the longest-serving player on *Hockey Night*'s on-air team.

"My main memories and thoughts of Maple Leaf Gardens go way back, even to before I was born, you might say," Dick Irvin Jr. told viewers on that historic night for an arena he was genetically a part of. "My dad took over as coach of the Leafs a few games into the season, and the first game they won—a game in the building—was the first night he was behind the bench as the team's new coach."

"They won the Stanley Cup a few months later just after I was born [in 1932], and that was his first Stanley Cup in Toronto, and I saw my first NHL game at the Gardens, the second game of the 1938 Stanley Cup final between the Leafs and the Chicago Black Hawks."

In the 1939–40 season, when Irvin was eight years old, during his father's last year in Toronto, his parents let him go to the Saturday night games at Maple Leaf Gardens, the ones that *Hockey Night in Canada* was broadcasting on the radio. "I remember the thrill I had watching Syl Apps play—he was my hero, and also the thrill I had when before the game, sitting with my mother, I'd see Foster Hewitt walking around at the bottom of the Garden on his way up to the gondola. Little did I know that someday I'd be going up in the same area to do the odd hockey broadcast. So, despite what some Toronto fans may feel, there's a bit of blue and white blood coursing through my veins because of all of that. And it still does."

Dick Irvin interviews Montreal Canadiens enforcer John Ferguson, who, like many of hockey's tough guys, had something of value to say about the game.

It was a stunning moment, reminding viewers that the guy who'd been the elegant, erudite colour analyst and host all these years on *Hockey Night in Canada*'s Montreal broadcasts was a Toronto hockey aristocrat of the first order. Irvin's self-deprecating remark about the colour of his blood was a beautiful riposte to those Leafs fans who had accused him of being a Montreal "homer."

And of course he was that, too. Irvin could have presented a similarly exalted account of his life with the Montreal Canadiens, for that's where his father, Dick Irvin Sr., went to coach after he left Toronto. Irvin celebrated three Stanley Cups with the Montreal Canadiens between 1940 and 1955, featuring hockey legends such as Elmer Lach, Toe Blake, Doug Harvey, and Maurice "The Rocket" Richard.

Dick Irvin Jr. came to *Hockey Night in Canada* in 1966 as a McGill commerce graduate who'd spent a few years working in accounting. He wanted to get into television, and despite misgivings about his "thin" voice, broke into the medium with CFCF, eventually rising to sports director.

Hockey Night in Canada's sponsor Molson also complained about Irvin's voice—an odd objection considering the nasal tenor template of Foster Hewitt—but Ralph Mellanby was his champion. He liked Irvin's creativity, his work ethic, his team play, and his pedigree. He also liked Irvin's "straight arrow" qualities, and regretted tormenting the teetotal Irvin by sending him into the Montreal dressing room to interview champagne-spraying Habs after yet another Montreal Stanley Cup win—of which there were eight between 1968 and 1979.

Paired with play-by-play man Danny Gallivan, Irvin provided intelligent, insightful commentary as both counterpoint and grounding-pole to Gallivan's soaring, operatic play-calling. The duo starred in Montreal until Gallivan retired in 1984, and the versatile Irvin remained, doing hosting and reporting at a level that saw him join his father in the Hockey Hall of Fame in 1988 as a broadcaster.

Irvin's stature in the *Hockey Night in Canada* community is such that only Ron MacLean and Don Cherry were worthy to interview him on May 4, 2010, during the second intermission of Game 2 between Montreal and Pittsburgh in the second round of the Stanley Cup playoffs. And once again, pedigree takes the day.

"Who's your favourite Canadien?" Cherry asks him.

"Well, if you want to go way back to when I first started being associated with this team at eight years of age I'd say Elmer Lach. Then medium far back,

Dick Irvin brought an impeccable hockey pedigree and professional polish to *Hockey Night in Canada* for more than three decades.

Jean Béliveau. Then after Béliveau, through the '80s, '90s, Mats Naslund. But, for all you Rocket Richard fans, now don't get mad at me, I always say The Rocket was the most exciting player I ever saw, and Guy Lafleur the most exciting played I ever broadcast. I think I covered everything."

To which Cherry humbly injects a bit of his own history, which, in its way, speaks for how a generation of *Hockey Night in Canada* viewers felt about Irvin's connection to them and the game: "You know, Dick, I never told you this but when I was in the minors in Three Rivers, Quebec, and knocking around and everything and I used to hear you two guys and I was the lowest of low you could get, one of the biggest thrills I ever had in my life is the first time I sat down with you and Danny and I helped do the colour and I said, 'Maybe I have arrived and I'm not a failure, just being with you guys.'"

Wayne Gretzky's Last Game

On November 7, 2009, *Hockey Night in Canada* aired a segment that revealed just how much Gretzky had influenced the culture of a game, and a country. In it, the cartoon character Peter Puck explains how the man who scored 894 goals and 1,963 assists in 1,486 regular-season games would often set up a goal from an area behind the opponent's net that became known as Wayne Gretzky's "office." The fact that Peter Puck is speaking Punjabi, and the segment is airing a full decade after Gretzky has retired from the NHL, reveals the astonishing potency of his career, and its legacy.

When he finally called it a career on April 18, 1999, *Hockey Night in Canada* had to be there to bear witness to an epoch-defining player whom it had covered for nearly half of its television life. Gretzky, who had also defined the Edmonton Oilers dynasty in the 1980s, and then shocked the country as he became the NHL's brightest star in Hollywood, ended his superlative-defying career on Broadway, as a 38-year-old New York Ranger.

Though the Rangers would finish in eighteenth place that season and would not make the playoffs, Gretzky led the team with sixty-two points—nine goals and fifty-three assists in seventy games. The Art Ross Trophy winner that season was Jaromir Jagr, whose Pittsburgh Penguins were Gretzky's opponents on that Sunday afternoon game. When the camera isolates Jagr on the bench, analyst Harry Neale heaps praises on the 27-year-old Penguins captain, but says, as another camera catches a girl holding a sign reading "Hockey's Greatest, #99": "But to replace this guy is an impossible assignment."

When Gretzky assists on the Rangers' goal to tie the game at 1–1 late in the second period, Madison Square Garden explodes, as if Gretzky has scored the Stanley Cup–winning goal. The Rangers applaud. Mario Lemieux, the

Even legends must take their leave. Wayne Gretzky waves farewell after more than twenty years spent rewriting the NHL record books.

48

The Great One's season-long farewell to the league he helped build culminated in a night at Madison Square Gardens that hockey fans will not soon forget.

Penguins' owner and Gretzky's teammate on national team campaigns, stands and applauds. Gretzky's wife, Janet Jones, and his kids and his parents Walter and Phyllis applaud. Even the Penguins on the bench applaud—Harry Neale catches them. Everyone knows they are saying goodbye to much more than genius. They are bidding farewell to their own time and place in the Gretzky Legend, and saying hello to nostalgia.

In the second intermission, Ron MacLean sets up a feature that attempts to parse the legend of Gretzky.

"When he was 6 years old, he says it was the only time he was ever overmatched. He started in Novice Triple A with 11-year-olds, and scored one goal. By the time he was 11 he had 378. And we all know when he became 'the kid' in the NHL, nobody could match him."

The "Legend of 99" feature takes the viewer deep into the hero's creation myth. There he is as a toddler playing hockey on a frozen river near his grandmother's house; there he is indoors, playing floor hockey with Grandma, who's seated on her couch, playing goal. In a nice bit of postmodern criticism, Gretzky sits on a stool, watching and commenting on the footage he sees of himself as a legend in the making onscreen. He's quick here, as he has done elsewhere, to take much of the mystery out of his success.

"I can't tell you how many hours I've spent…" he begins, looking at his two-and-a-half-year-old self skating on the river. "I tell my boys, now … when I was your age, I'd skate seven, eight hours a day. And they're 'Oh Dad, you didn't skate that much.' And I don't know why, I don't know what possessed me to do that, it wasn't like somebody saying you'd better get out there and skate, you'd better get out there and practise. My life, that's what I enjoy doing."

Gretzky, as a kid, practised until it was dark, and then his father Walter put flood lights out so he could keep going. Gretzky credits his father's drills and hockey smarts with honing his own natural talent. But his father also gave him the drive to succeed that even now, after unimagined success, pushes him on.

"What do you hate the most about hockey?" Gretzky repeats the interviewer's question. "I would say the winning and losing.… We were groomed and taught that there was nothing other than winning. So you learn that winning becomes everything, and when you lose, it's gut-wrenching. And to this day, I'll go home after a loss, and lie in bed 'til 3, 4 in the morning and think about what happened, and wonder why you lost, and what went wrong and what you could

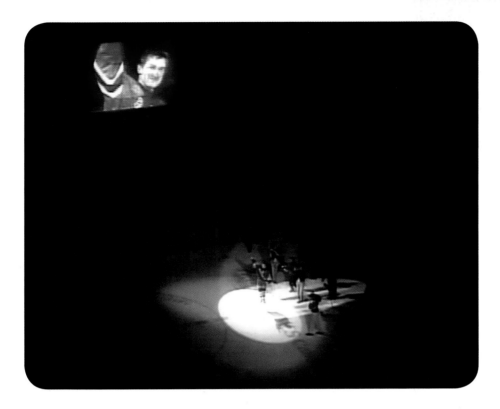

Wayne Gretzky stands under the spotlight one last time on April 18, 1999.

have done, and at this point in my life it hurts me more to lose than it did when I was 24 years old."

But even though he can explain his game, he still acknowledges the mystery of his immense talent. "I don't know why I have it and why I was chosen. I don't know why I love it so much. This has been my life, and I love it."

The feature ends by scrolling Gretzky's records—sixty-one of them, when he retired—down the screen. The speed with which they pass, and the astonishing number of trophies—nine Hart as MVP, ten Art Ross as top scorer, five Lady Byng for sportsmanship, two Conn Smythe as playoff MVP—seems an editorial comment on how fast his career has gone by.

And then it's over. At 1:22 into an overtime that no one wants to end, Jaromir Jagr puts the puck past New York's goalie, Mike Richter. Gretzky exits to the roar for a hero, but something in the second intermission feature on his legend stays with us, something that he said about the life to come:

"The truth is that I expected to play professional hockey 'til 30 or 31…. But I can also say I used to always think in my mind what is going to give me the high, and the fun and the energy of hockey? What is going to replace hockey? And I still haven't found that."

Hockey Day in Canada

Early in the new century, *Hockey Night in Canada* decided to make the most of the country's four time zones by broadcasting a show that would see daylight from coast to coast to coast. As *Hockey Night in Canada* approached its fiftieth birthday, its cultural influence on the country had become so dominant that the idea of a thirteen-hour broadcast devoted to hockey not only was possible, but was nominated as being a worthy dead-of-winter public holiday.

"It doesn't get much more hockey than this. It doesn't get much more Canadian than this," wrote Peter Goddard in the *Toronto Star* in response to the approaching first *Hockey Day in Canada*, after a lament that the United States had three winter public holidays, and Canada had none. "And we'll never have a better reason for a holiday than this. Let hockey be the reason, *Hockey Day in Canada* an annual event, and a day off the result. All we need is a name."

The name was there already, and, as Goddard hoped, the day celebrating the nation's love affair with hockey has become an annual event with the feel of a public holiday, even if it falls on hockey's holy day, Saturday. The first day-long celebration, on February 19, 2000, was conceived by *Hockey Night in Canada*'s executive producer John Shannon and his team as a special event at the traditional low point of the NHL season. The idea, though, would be to weave the NHL into the day, but not make it the sole focus of the party. The eye of the camera would be on the people *at* the party—one that began two centuries earlier, on the frozen ponds of Nova Scotia and the indoor rinks of Montreal.

"It's grassroots hockey," Shannon explained before the event. "It's players, coaches, parents, volunteers. It's the love that this country has for this game." Shannon and Alan Clark, CBC's Head of Sports, had been working on an even

The new millennium saw *Hockey Night in Canada* seize the day—literally—with the invention of *Hockey Day in Canada*, a day-long celebration of the national sport.

Hockey Day in Canada sees the team move across the country to produce reports from communities off the NHL grid. Here, Ron MacLean reports from ice level in the company of future stars.

grander vision of the day, one that would involve a women's game, between Canada and the USA, then matches featuring Canada's six NHL teams.

The problem, however, was that TSN had a contract with Hockey Canada to broadcast the Canadian women's team, and wouldn't release the rights. The other problem was that Shannon had won air time for four hockey games from the CBC and needed to fill it.

"I said to Alan Clark, don't give the time back. We'll do a four hour pre-game show," Shannon recalled. "I was a hockey father at that point, so I was really in tune with what was going on at minor hockey rinks and how many people worked their tails off. So the first *Hockey Day in Canada* was designed to be a celebration of the game and to celebrate what the game has done for the country."

That first *Hockey Day in Canada* was anchored in Toronto, with remote crews stationed in all ten provinces and the territories. It featured segments on the birth of hockey, female players on Baffin Island, an arena manager in Fox Valley, Saskatchewan, and kids playing games from Newfoundland to the Yukon. All was built around three NHL games on the slate that day, featuring Canada's six NHL teams—Vancouver against Ottawa, Toronto against Montreal, and Calgary against Edmonton.

There were also two panel discussions on the state of hockey, then plagued by clutching, grabbing, mugging, and violence which today is noteworthy for the harsh reaction against it. In 2000, some saw it as "old time" hockey. Sports media critic Chris Zelkovich, reviewing the day's events the following Monday, called out *Hockey Night in Canada* analyst Kelly Hrudey for previewing *Hockey Day*'s Calgary–Edmonton match by using clips of a Calgary player trying to take out Edmonton captain Doug Weight's knee, and Weight responding with a slash and a cross-check. Hrudey used them as examples of "passion," to which Zelkovich responded, "Passion is not synonymous with senseless violence."

Despite the argument about how the game should be played—one that evolved with *Hockey Day in Canada*—the success of the first *Hockey Day* wasn't enough to keep its producers from expanding the vision. Instead of a studio-based program, the show went on the road, to Red Deer, Alberta. Host Ron MacLean went back to the town where he'd once been a TV weatherman, while the *Hockey Night in Canada* on-air crew spread out to do features on what the game means to communities across the country.

Since then, *Hockey Day in Canada* has traversed the world's second-largest country with singular ambition, producing shows in Windsor, Nova Scotia; Iqaluit, Nunavut; Shaunavon, Saskatchewan; Stephenville, Newfoundland; Nelson, British Columbia; Winkler, Manitoba; Campbellton, New Brunswick; Stratford, Ontario; Whitehorse, Yukon; and in 2012, Prince Edward Island— picking up Scotiabank as its titular sponsor along the way.

In 2007, the show went multi-cultural, making live online broadcasts of the day's NHL games available online in languages reflecting the audience's diversity. The Detroit Red Wings and Toronto Maple Leafs game could be heard in Mandarin; Montreal and Ottawa's game, in Hindi; and the Colorado and Vancouver late game, in Cantonese.

For the 2012 edition of *Hockey Day*, CBC's operation looked like a military campaign: The network had satellite trucks in Charlottetown, Prince Edward Island; Windsor, Nova Scotia; Verdun, Quebec; Thunder Bay, Ontario; Winnipeg, Manitoba; Prince Albert, Saskatchewan; and Richmond, British Columbia to show community events, junior hockey games, and volunteer profiles. While CBC's Toronto studio handled the NHL games, Joel Darling, the network's Director of Production, estimated that 90 percent of *Hockey Day* was run out of Summerside, Prince Edward Island, with a crew of fifty spread throughout the province, and about 275 spread across the country (and in Pittsburgh for an interview with Sidney Crosby, recovering from a concussion) to weave the stories of hockey and Canada into one seamless winter quilt.

"It has really become a national holiday and a key date on the schedule for us," Darling said, echoing the hopes expressed twelve years earlier by a prescient journalist, and a happy reality for the national network: an audience of 11.4 million, or more than a third of the country, tuning in to watch a show that, through the power of *Hockey Night in Canada*, had become a giant national party for itself.

Mario Lemieux Comes Back Again

Once, they had been stars conjured by the imagination from the cold dark of the radio waves. But when *Hockey Night in Canada* aimed its TV lights upon them, they had to shine brighter than any who had gone before. Viewers could see the truth of their talents for themselves, and demanded more. So when stars fell, they fell farther and harder because we could see them fall. And Mario Lemieux was a star who had fallen from the greatest of heights.

As soon as he played in his first competitive league as a kid, Lemieux's name became a literal description of his talent: the best. Players tried to stop him as he rolled over the blue line and flicked the puck into another net. But he was too strong, too good, and the records piled up. Their parents tried to stop him with every underhanded tactic in the Bad Hockey Parent Playbook, complaining about his ice time, harassing him and his family, even spitting at him—as if a little spew of venom would diminish his star.

Lemieux responded by scoring points—247 goals and 315 assists in the Quebec Major Junior Hockey League, and then on his first shot in his first game in the NHL. Six Art Ross Trophies as the NHL's top scorer would follow, as would three Hart Trophies and the league's most valuable player award, and two Stanley Cups with Pittsburgh, in 1991 and 1992.

Yet he was shadowed by the kind of mortality that Achilles would have understood. His chronic back problems had ravaged him with pain so crippling that sometimes he was unable to bend to tie his skates. When it was at its worst, he couldn't even play.

In December 1992, he went to see the doctor. He had a lump on his neck and a sore throat that wouldn't go away. The doctors told him he had Hodgkin's disease—a type of cancer.

Mario Lemieux was a hockey magician, coming back from cancer, and then from retirement, to pull on #66 for the team he now owned. "He's a suit-wearing executive by day," said a Penguins team executive. "At night he puts on his cape and plays."

Lemieux knew cancer up close: he had two uncles who had died of it. He had also served as honorary chairman of the Pittsburgh Cancer Institute, not just glad-handing the star-struck at charity golf tournaments, but visiting sick children who could only dream of the odds Lemieux had been given: he had a 95 percent chance of being cured.

On March 2, 1993, after taking his final radiation treatment—four weeks of daily blasts—and with the radiation burn marks still fresh on his neck, Lemieux flew to Philadelphia to rejoin the Penguins. After a ninety-second ovation from Philadelphia fans not known for their kindness to strangers, he celebrated his return by scoring a goal and adding an assist. But the grind of the game, the residual fatigue from radiation therapy, the clutching and grabbing, and more surgery on his damaged back all conspired to make him want to leave it.

So Lemieux retired at age 31 in 1997, punctuating his farewell by scoring on his last shift of his last game. The Hockey Hall of Fame shelved its three-year waiting period for mortals, and admitted him to the pantheon that autumn. But that elevation couldn't stop him from being pulled down by the financial woes

Mario Lemieux scored a goal and added an assist in a 5–0 Penguins win over the Leafs. He had not played an NHL game for nearly four years.

of the team he had defined. The Penguins could not pay him the outstanding $33 million remaining on the $42 million contract he had signed in 1992.

After failing to remedy the matter in the courts, Lemieux did something that no other professional sports player had yet done: he bought his old team as part of an ownership group. And in order to raise the value of the franchise—after a forty-four-month retirement—he did something extraordinary. He pulled his Number 66 jersey down from the rafters, where it had been retired, and over his head. Then he went back on the ice.

Lemieux's return to the NHL came on Wednesday, December 27, 2000, and *Hockey Night in Canada* was there to bear witness to a fallen star rising again. There's a thundering ovation for Number 66 as he skates out onto home ice. A shot of a banner draped over an upper deck expresses how Pittsburgh fans feel about this unexpected gift: "Hey Santa, Thanks!"

Pittsburgh fans— and hockey fans everywhere— welcome Mario Lemieux back to the game.

The Toronto Maple Leafs, the Penguins' opponent that night, did not share the sentiment. Though Lemieux was now 35 years old, and he hadn't played in the NHL for nearly four years, he answered any doubters just thirty-three seconds into the game against Toronto, by setting up a goal.

Midway through the second period, the young Czech wizard Jaromir Jagr— whose first name is, amazingly, an anagram of Mario Jr—was revived by the return of his mentor. Jagr burst into the Leaf zone on the right wing, curled in an arc, and found Lemieux in the slot. And Lemieux found the back of the net. "Mario Lemieux gets a goal!" play-by-play man Bob Cole shouts over the roar. "Ohhhhh, baby! Is this a movie, or what?"

The Penguins shut out the Leafs 5–0. Mario Lemieux had defied time and chance to shine as a star in the NHL firmament once more, a movie plot come true.

51

Salt Lake City Gold

It was about revenge, for losses both recent and those that were decades old. At the 2002 Winter Olympic Games in Salt Lake City, the men and women on Canada's Olympic hockey teams promised to avenge Canada's reputation as the best hockey nation on the planet.

The promise, however, looked to be on thin ice. Canada's women came into the gold medal game on February 21, 2002, as clear underdogs, having lost eight straight pre-Olympic matches to the USA. Canada's women had also lost the gold medal to the Americans at the 1998 Winter Olympics in Nagano, Japan, and now they were playing the United States on home ice.

Or trying to kill penalties, for it seemed to the Canadians that the American referee, Stacey Livingston, wasn't wearing the black and white stripes of an impartial judge, but the stars and stripes of a homer. "It was almost like she had a U.S. jersey on," said Cassie Campbell, today a *Hockey Night in Canada* reporter, but then the captain of Team Canada.

Team USA finally ties the game at 1–1 on their fifth straight power play. "Five power plays, and they get a power play goal," said CBC play-by-play man Mark Lee, his professionalism straining to contain his disdain. The referee would call thirteen penalties against Canada—eight in a row—and only six against Team USA. Cassie Campbell, her frustration evident, skates in close to the referee to give her a piece of her mind before Hayley Wickenheiser directs her to calmer ice.

Wickenheiser then scores to put Canada in the lead early in the second, but the Americans seem to tie it on another power play four minutes later. "It was in and out?" Mark Lee asks. "No!" he shouts. "They're waving it off!" And sure enough, the puck went through the crease, bounced off the inside of the post,

The 2002 Winter Olympics was Canada's moment to prove to the planet that it owned the game it gave the world.

and came out. "That was close," Lee says, adding that the U.S. player who just missed swatting the puck into the net "can't buy a goal in this tournament."

At least, not with the money buried beneath the ice. The Salt Lake City Olympics premier hockey venue was the "E" Center—and it was 15 feet wider than an NHL arena. Since the Salt Lake logo on the ice had no centre ice mark, Olympic icemaker Trent Evans, the wizard behind the celebrated ice for the Edmonton Oilers, had to find a way to gauge the measurements of the bigger arena to ensure that the nets and other markings were in the right place. First he used a silver dime to fix a point at centre ice; then he used a golden loonie.

The loonie had come into being in 1987, when the Royal Canadian Mint began replacing one dollar bills with the gold-coloured coin. On one side is the image of Queen Elizabeth II, and on the other, a loon, an indigenous Canadian waterfowl. The new dollar quickly became known as the "loonie"— affectionately mocking the humble coin, and a government that saw this duck-like bird as the most fitting one to imprint on a new currency. Now, it was buried beneath Olympic ice as a golden talisman.

Hayley Wickenheiser dominated women's hockey in the 2002 Winter Olympics and would be named MVP of the tournament.

Hayley Wickenheiser
7 goals - 3 assists in tournament

With one second left in the second period, a streaking Jayna Hefford scoops up a long pass, beats a poke check by the U.S. goalie, and puts Canada up by two. The Americans score on yet another power play late in the third period, but Canada's women hold on to win their first Olympic gold medal ever, cheered on by the Canadian men's team that the camera catches in the stands: Iginla, Fleury, Lemieux, as happy as kids at their countrywomen's triumph.

Three days later, it was the Canadian men's turn to keep their end of the promise. The fact they were in the gold medal final at all was a combination of pluck and luck. After losing their opening match 5–2 to the formidable Swedes, the Canadians were as startled—and relieved—as the rest of the country when a fluke goal sent Belarus past the favoured Swedes to meet Canada in the semi-final. And get thumped 7–2.

The eyes of the nation—or nearly eleven million pairs of them—were on the gold medal game against Team USA. The *Hockey Night in Canada* dream team of Harry Neale and play-by-play man Bob Cole didn't need to remind viewers that the last Canadian team to win Olympic gold was the Edmonton Mercurys in 1952. It was a championship drought that was older than the flag.

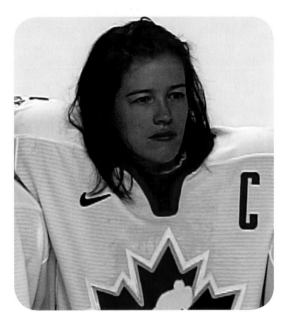

The USA strikes first, and Cole's voice deflates when he has to confirm that Tony Amonte has put the puck past Martin Brodeur. But he's chipper again when Paul Kariya scores for Canada, after a brilliant feint by Mario Lemieux, who lets the puck go through his legs and on to the stick of the better-placed Kariya.

Top: Hayley Wickenheiser grew up watching Don Cherry on *Hockey Night in Canada*, kissing his heroes. Now she's one, too.
Bottom: Cassie Campbell, Team Canada's captain, listens with pride to her national anthem as Canada's women win their first ever hockey gold medal.

When Joe Sakic puts Canada in the lead, Cole's voice is now triumphant. "It's Canada *two*, USA *one*." This is not a regular NHL game, where the play-by-play man must aim for the impartial. This is the gold medal game, and Cole is a Canadian calling the game for CBC. Any pretense of neutrality would be as transparently phony as, say, the officiating in the women's gold medal game.

Team USA ties the game on a power play during an exciting, chance-filled second period, but when Joe Sakic scores again, Cole is ecstatic. So, too, are team boss Wayne Gretzky and assistant Steve Tambellini, whom the camera catches rising to their feet to applaud—and exhale.

Jarome Iginla demonstrates the meaning of power forward as he wills the puck into the USA net.

Midway through the third period, with the U.S. pressing and Canadian players sprawling and diving to block or clear pucks, Cole sees what we see: "Canada is just barely hanging on." And when Jarome Iginla bashes the puck into the net for Canada with just under four minutes left, Cole is so caught up in the moment that he calls out "Gore!"—a mash-up of "goal" and "score." Or a prediction of what Canadians will do to their team should they blow it now.

When Joe Sakic scores again on a breakaway, he's mobbed on the ice by teammates as if the game is over. Gretzky and his team hug in the stands, and viewers celebrate in TV rooms across the nation. "And that makes it 5–2 Canada!" Cole hollers over the roar in the rink. "Surely, that's gotta be it!"

"Or good enough," says Harry Neale. And it was good enough, a cathartic moment for a country that had been waiting for this since the year *Hockey Night in Canada* first broadcast on television. And now, the show that had stoked that hope and expectation was there to deliver it. "It's time for Canada to stand up and cheer," Cole says. "Stand up and cheer everybody! The Olympics, Salt Lake City, 2002, men's ice hockey, gold medal: Canada!"

Opposite top and above: With Canada trailing the USA 1–0 in the first period, Mario Lemieux lets the puck pass between his skates and onto the stick of Paul Kariya. His fake works and Kariya ties the game.

Scotty Bowman Retires

It was one of those moments that was both spontaneous and calculated. On June 13, 2002, the Detroit Red Wings had just defeated the Carolina Hurricanes 3–1 in Game 5 of the Stanley Cup finals. Scotty Bowman, the Wings' coaching legend, had just achieved the kind of record that may take a few generations to eclipse: his ninth Stanley Cup as bench boss. He'd quickly laced on his skates to take a turn on the ice with his victorious team, and *Hockey Night in Canada* reporter Scott Russell caught up with the famously enigmatic Bowman—rather, Bowman caught up with him.

"You said something to me just a moment ago, Scotty," Russell said, grinning as if he could scarcely believe his luck. "What's up?"

Bowman, smiling and relaxed, in startling counterpoint to his jut-jawed *froideur* behind the bench, had the kind of scoop reporters dream of. "Well, it's my last game as a coach. I've been thinking about it, I made up my mind on the break, the Olympic break [for the 2002 Winter Olympics], we got lucky again and I had a little bit of a rest, but I'm happy to go out now."

And there was Bowman the retiree, his face open in childlike delight, hoisting the Cup, and sprawling on the ice with his players, all of whom were as surprised as everyone else. Steve Shutt, who won five Stanley Cups playing for Bowman in Montreal, once said that players loathed Bowman for 364 days a year before putting on their Stanley Cup championship ring on day number 365.

Scotty Bowman's attention to detail as a coach was legendary—he would even measure the distance between rink glass and stanchions to get an advantage. And so he did, retiring as the "winningest" coach in NHL history, with 1,244 regular season victories and 223 more in the playoffs.

52

Scotty Bowman brought his coaching genius to *Hockey Night in Canada* from 1987 to 1990 as an analyst.

Of course, Scotty Bowman hadn't won all those Stanley Cups by accident, and as he told Russell, he had decided to retire in February, during the Winter Olympics. He just waited until the perfect moment, the night when he beat a record seemingly etched into the granite of legend: the eight coaching Cups won by Montreal's Hector "Toe" Blake.

Blake, though, had also won three Stanley Cups playing left wing for Montreal's Maroons and Canadiens. So deft at making the goal light shine, he was nicknamed the "Old Lamplighter" as part of the Habs' fabled Punch Line, also starring Elmer Lach and Maurice "Rocket" Richard.

And Bowman wasn't finished either, eventually beating Blake's eleven by adding three more Cups as a behind-the-scenes player, winning his twelfth Cup as a *consigliere* to his son Stanley, who was General Manager of Chicago when they won the prize after which he is named in 2010.

Bowman had wanted to play in the NHL, too, but a slash to the head by Jean-Guy Talbot in minor hockey fractured his skull, and was one of the things that ended his career. Ironically, Bowman later coached Talbot when both were with the St. Louis Blues in the late 1960s.

Rumours followed Bowman that the metal plate put in his head after the fracture accounted for his eccentric behaviour—micromanaging every detail in the rink including the thickness of the plexiglas, and yet refusing to speak directly to his own players, using an assistant coach, or, on occasion, a bullhorn.

In 1996, Marc Crawford, then the volatile coach of the Colorado Avalanche who defeated the Wings in the Western Conference final, said Bowman's oddness was due to radio signals he received through the plate in his head. Bowman replied that he had never had a plate in his head.

He just saw the ice—and the world—differently, the way Wayne Gretzky saw it, able to envision what others could not. He had speed in Montreal, so he used speed to win five Cups. He had Mario Lemieux and Jaromir Jagr in Pittsburgh,

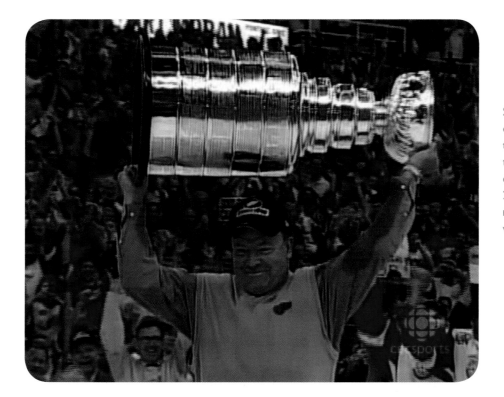

Scotty Bowman laced on his skates to take a turn around the ice with the Jug after Detroit defeated Carolina in 2002. It was Bowman's ninth Stanley Cup victory.

so he used their mighty talents. In 1997, when Philadelphia sent its steamrolling Legion of Doom at the Wings, Bowman countered with defencemen who could quickly move the puck. His Wings swept the Flyers to win their first Cup in forty-two years. And then, too, Bowman put on his skates to take a turn around the ice with the Cup.

"I always wanted to be a player in the NHL and skate with the Cup," Bowman said at the time. "It is pretty heavy, but it is pretty light, too. I have always dreamt about doing it, like to be a player, but couldn't play."

And away he skated then, seeing, as only he could, that he would be doing this again, on the night when he hung up his skates for good.

53

Cassie Campbell Joins the Crew

"We welcome Cassie Campbell, two-time Olympic gold medallist, to sit alongside me, here, in the booth. I'm honoured."

That's how Bob Cole introduced *Hockey Night in Canada* history on October 14, 2006, when a star of Canadian women's hockey, Cassie Campbell, took over the colour analyst's job from Harry Neale, Cole's celebrated sidekick. Neale was stuck in his Buffalo home-base due to an early snowstorm, and Campbell, who had signed on as a rink reporter, got a hasty trial-by-blizzard.

"And welcome, Cassie!" Cole says at the first break in play, a minute into the game.

"Well thanks Bob, for having me here," Campbell replies, as coolly as if Cole has welcomed her to his house for a beer, and not into the broadcast booth as his analyst for the national *Hockey Night in Canada* telecast between Toronto and Calgary, the first time in the show's fifty-four-year history that a woman has filled the position. "Truly it is an honour to be with the legend, Bob Cole, on *Hockey Night in Canada*," Campbell continues, then steps right in with a pithy analysis of Calgary goalie Miikka Kiprusoff.

In the meantime, a camera at ice level captures Campbell high up in the Foster Hewitt Media Gondola, alongside Cole, in case the viewers need proof that they're not imagining this. "Say hello to everybody," Cole says, as he spots the shot on the monitor, and Campbell laughs, and says hello, as if she's been up there all her life.

Campbell's hockey pedigree had put her in some hot spots before, but she has always displayed the type of team-play character that saw her emerge triumphant. Campbell is the only captain of a Canadian Olympic hockey team, male or female, to lead her team to two Olympic gold medals: in Salt Lake City

Cassie Campbell interviews Bruins goalie Tim Thomas, April 9, 2011. Campbell made the jump to broadcasting almost seamlessly, no doubt because of her in-depth knowledge of the game.

273

in 2002, and in Turin in 2006. She also won a silver medal playing left wing for Canada at the 1998 Nagano Olympics.

Campbell has also won six world championships for Canada, and has played professionally in Calgary, Toronto, and Mississauga. Even so, she had only been on the job as a *Hockey Night in Canada* rinkside reporter for a week when she got the news that she was skating in the big leagues.

"That morning I showed up at the rink," she recalled, "and I thought my producers were playing a rookie joke on me. They pulled me to one side of the rink, and they said, 'Cass we have a bit of an issue tonight....'"

When she realized that the show's producers were serious about putting her next to Cole, her first concern was not for herself, but for the women's game she had worked so hard to build. "It was about potentially embarrassing

BRENDA IRVING

Nearly two decades after Helen Hutchinson became the first female broadcasting face on *Hockey Night in Canada*, Brenda Irving arrived in 2001 to add a female dimension to the show, along with Martine Gaillard. Hired to do rinkside reporting, Irving brought an impressive background to the telecast, having been a news journalist for seven years before switching careers as soon as she noticed there were more women in sports.

Appropriately, she got her love of the game from her mother. "Growing up in Cambridge, it was my mom. Hockey would be on all the time whenever there was a game." As the nearby Kitchener Rangers were also the farm team for the New York Rangers, Irving had a crush on New York's goalie Eddie Giacomin. "I used to write songs about him," she laughs, but found herself mortified when she went to Maple Leaf Gardens as a 12-year-old with her friends, and they found themselves sitting right next to the Rangers bench. "And Bobby Rousseau was at the end of the bench and one of my girlfriends said, 'Oh, she's written a song about the Rangers and Eddie Giacomin.' And he says, 'Oh, you've gotta sing it for Eddie.' At the end of the game he brought him out and I burst into tears. I couldn't even look at him." Irving didn't have a regular spot on the show, as she was covering other sports at the time, too, which made life tougher for her "because you didn't have the familiarity with the players and with having your face on TV." Irving stayed with the show until 2006, when Cassie Campbell came on as a reporter, and moved to covering the Summer Olympics and soccer's World Cup.

women's hockey because that's how people think," she said, explaining how her lack of on-camera experience might be damaging. Then she took a Stanley Cup finals kind of attitude. "But I'd do it, knowing maybe I'd never get another opportunity again."

Even so, the pressures built up over the course of the day, as Campbell had time to think about what lay ahead. "I was worried about what Bob Cole would think, and he accepted it right away. But it was one of the most stressful days for the crew. They were taking a chance, so they totally over prepared in case I bombed!"

And she wasn't thinking about making history. "I didn't realize at the time—it didn't even cross my mind—that I was going to be the first woman to do colour on *Hockey Night*. That didn't even enter my mind, until the next day...."

On that night, Campbell showed that she could play, when eight minutes into the first period, Toronto scored. "It was a Darcy Tucker power play goal," Campbell laughs, recalling how she had just predicted it. "About five seconds before, I went through what to look for with Bob, and one of the things was Darcy Tucker, far post. And five seconds later that's exactly what happened."

It was a little longer than five seconds, but Campbell's analysis of what the Leafs would try to do was now up as proof, on the score sheet. She had done colour for women's games before, "so I knew what I should look for, what I should prepare for."

She also had a fortunate bounce. "The funny thing was I had sat with Darryl Sutter, the general manager of the Flames, and he had given me a ton of stuff, and I knew the Leafs like the back of my hand, so I couldn't have lucked out any more."

Luck continued when Maple Leafs captain Mats Sundin scored the overtime winner—shorthanded—to give him a hat trick and his 500th NHL goal, becoming the first Swedish player to reach the milestone.

"Nice going, Cassie. It was great having you aboard for this historic evening," Cole says, while the Air Canada Centre fans give Sundin a standing ovation as the game's first star.

It wasn't Campbell's last turn in the colour seat, either, for *Hockey Night in Canada*'s leap of faith propelled her into a broadcast role she is passionate about. "I've done about thirty games since, in the last six years," Campbell said. "Anyone who has been a player before would love colour. Colour is *the* job... you basically get to talk hockey and get paid for it."

The First Heritage Classic

Edmonton goalie Ty Conklin still feels the pain of letting in a goal even when playing outdoors on a frozen pond—though one with more than 57,000 people watching in the stadium and 2.7 million more on TV.

When James Creighton moved hockey from the outdoors into Montreal's Victoria rink on the night of March 3, 1875, he put a roof on winter that allowed the game to develop—a set of rules, an illustrious trophy, and then professional leagues. The fact that hockey had become an indoor game is what allowed it to flourish. But in November of 2003, the game went back out into the cold wrapped in such a rich history that it could call its very first incarnation a "Heritage Classic."

The days of great hockey played on frozen ponds ended in 1961, when the Trail Smoke Eaters won the world championship playing four of their games outdoors in Lausanne, Switzerland. To be sure, some impoverished European teams still played in roofless rinks, but when a record hockey crowd of 74,554 crammed into Michigan State's Spartan Stadium in October 2001 to watch State play to a 3–3 draw against the University of Michigan, some hockey brains got thinking again of hockey on frozen ponds.

So, on the eighty-sixth anniversary of the founding of the NHL, their "What if?" led to the league's first Heritage Classic, between the Edmonton Oilers and the Montreal Canadiens on November 22, 2003. But it was more than just a regular-season outdoor game—it was a doubleheader, with the first game starring alumni from Edmonton and Montreal. For the 57,167 in Edmonton's Commonwealth Stadium, braving temperatures of close to –18°C (–30°C with wind chill) and the 2.7 million viewers watching on TV, it was the chance to time travel. There on the ice for the alumni game were the legends made on *Hockey Night in Canada* over the previous three decades, playing as if the clock had been turned back. Playing in what host Ron MacLean calls "shinny night in Canada."

54

Montreal goalie José Theodore responds to −30°C temperatures with a Canadian winter classic: the toque.

THIS SEASON
JOSE THEODORE

RECORD	GAA	SAVE PCT.
7-9-0	2.31	.916

Two hockey titans—former Oiler Wayne Gretzky and former Canadiens Guy Lafleur—drop the ceremonial puck for the first Heritage Classic.

There are other milestones marking this day—the twenty-fifth anniversary of the Edmonton Oilers joining the NHL in 1979; the twentieth of their first Stanley Cup win in 1984. And this edition of *Hockey Night in Canada* marks the first NHL game broadcast in HD on CBC. The show references itself in the making of the legend, opening with glory clips of Guy Lafleur and Steve Shutt and the mighty Montreal Canadiens riding four straight Stanley Cup wins, then making their first visit to Edmonton to play the Oilers on December 14, 1979. There is Wayne Gretzky and Mark Messier, just kids about to create their own dynasties. On a later clip they both score on the Canadiens to lead their team to a victory that has them celebrating as if they already won the Cup. "And the crowd is going absolutely wild," shouts Howie Meeker.

Then we fast forward to the present. Reporter Steve Armitage stands in the Oilers' locker room with Gretzky and Messier before the 2003 game. Gretzky retired in 1999, but Messier, then 42, was still playing for the New York Rangers and got special dispensation from Rangers boss Glen Sather—the Oilers coach during their triumphant years. "Gentlemen," says Armitage, "we're looking forward to history, Moose and Number 99, on the ice, one more time."

The Ford MegaStars game featured players from both teams who had won Stanley Cups (with a couple of exceptions), but it was more like a conference of the Hockey Hall of Fame: Grant Fuhr, Guy Lapointe, Larry Robinson, Paul Coffey, Jari Kurri, Steve Shutt, Guy Lafleur, and Messier and Gretzky all pulled on their Heritage Classic jerseys and toques and skated the years away under the winter sun.

"This is going back to shinny hockey," said Shutt, who lit up the NHL with his blazing speed and shot on a line with Guy Lafleur. "No glitz. No glamour. With all the things going on in pro hockey—now, for one day, people get a chance to watch guys get on the ice and just play."

The Oilers won the first oldtimers game 2–0, on goals not from Gretzky and Messier, but from Ken "The Rat" Linseman and enforcer Marty McSorley. The Canadiens won the official game, 4–3. But *Hockey Night in Canada* was the ultimate winner, for the Heritage Classic was able to draw so many people to it only because of the heritage created through the lens of the show imprinted on the national imagination for more than half a century.

55

Third Period

Harry Neale

During Harry Neale's first season coaching the Vancouver Canucks, he was told the struggling Canucks didn't like his practices. "That makes us even," Neale replied, "because I don't like their games."

The spring of 1978 saw Harry Neale introduced in a swank suite at the city's waterfront Bayshore Inn Hotel—where Howard Hughes had lived for nearly six months earlier in the decade on the final leg of his sad, mad journey. Neale, introduced as the coach whose teams had never missed the playoffs, liked everything about that day until the Canucks unveiled their new uniforms, which they had paid a San Francisco marketing firm $100,000 to design.

"I don't want to say we were horrified, but we were certainly surprised," Neale recalled, upon seeing the black, orange-red, and yellow jerseys, with a V running from the shoulders to the stomach. "It was my first year there and I remember we warmed up in the old Canuck uniforms and then took them off after the warm-up and came out in those."

Neale said the team took a lot of abuse, especially when they played on the road. "We played Halloween night in New York and we were the costume (contest) winners." But although they were hampered by an embarrassment of a uniform, Neale managed to get his Canucks into the playoffs that season as advertised, despite their twenty-five wins in an eighty-game schedule.

After playing two years of junior hockey with the Toronto Marlboroughs, Neale worked his way through the coaching ranks, moving from high school to college to the World Hockey Association's Minnesota Fighting Saints, and then to the league's Hartford Whalers. From there he became coach and eventual General Manager of the NHL's Canucks, before moving on for a season to coach Detroit.

Harry Neale's famous wit was evident both as a coach and a broadcaster. As bench boss of the losing Canucks, he lamented that his real problem was finding a place to play, as his team couldn't win at home or on the road.

Neale had been fired by the Red Wings on New Year's Eve, 1985, after his team was sitting at eight wins, twenty-three losses, four ties, and so he joined *Hockey Night in Canada* as an analyst. Don Wallace, the eventual successor to Ralph Mellanby as the show's executive producer, hired Neale despite Mellanby thinking Neale wouldn't last long in television. "I was convinced he'd soon return to the NHL as general manager or president of a team."

Neale turned out to be a natural, able to work with anyone on the *Hockey Night in Canada* crew, but showing special chemistry with play-by-play man Bob Cole. With their combination of Cole's Gallivanesque flourishes and Neale's sharp wit—and even sharper analysis—the duo soon wound up as the marquee team covering the prime games each Saturday night, and on into the playoffs. Together Cole and Neale covered twenty Stanley Cup final series, until Neale left the *Hockey Night* broadcasts after the 2006–07 season to take a job as colour analyst for his hometown Buffalo Sabres.

In Neale's final season with *Hockey Night in Canada*, he gave typically pithy advice to the Ottawa Senators before their third game against Anaheim in the 2007 Stanley Cup final, advice that sums up his laconic broadcasting style. "Don't try and do more," he said. "Do less, better. You'll get the results you're looking for if you try that."

Harry Neale spent twenty years in the booth with Bob Cole, bringing a sharp eye for the game—and a sharp tongue, as well—to help make the duo *Hockey Night in Canada*'s premier broadcast team.

Bob Cole

Over its long life *Hockey Night in Canada* has unearthed many treasures, but Bob Cole, the show's Hall of Fame play-by-play man, had to make *Hockey Night in Canada* notice him. Nearly five decades later, Cole's musical, agile voice still calls the hockey action on Saturday night, defying time and infusing the viewers with nostalgic affection for the last of the show's crew members from its golden age.

It was touch and go when Ralph Mellanby received a phone call in 1968, two years into his role as the executive producer of *Hockey Night in Canada*. Mellanby didn't know who Cole was, despite the fact Cole was working for the CBC in his home province of Newfoundland, reporting on sports and hosting a quiz show.

One of the things Mellanby was tasked with—and wanted to do—was to expand the show's vision both onscreen and with the talent it chose from across the country. It was, as he says, *Hockey Night in Canada* and not *Hockey Night in Toronto* (though the show's nerve centre lies there). So he took Cole's call.

Cole told him that the head of CBC Sports had suggested he audition for *Hockey Night in Canada*. Mellanby, impressed by Cole's nerve, said sure. Then he upped the stakes in a way that would have terrified lesser voices. He invited

Bob Cole convinced *Hockey Night in Canada* to hire him, but his rhapsodic play-by-play made the Newfoundlander the show's rock for more than 30 years—and an honoured member of the Hockey Hall of Fame. Bob Cole made history in 2002 when he announced Canada's first Olympic men's hockey gold medal in 50 years.

56

Cole to pay his way to Montreal and do an audition tape right away, during the Stanley Cup finals against Boston.

Knowing the production pressures for *Hockey Night in Canada* during the Stanley Cup playoffs—and keeping his allies close—Bob Cole brought his own crew from Newfoundland to Montreal, and did his audition tape. His timing was perfect. *Hockey Night in Canada* had lost play-by-play man Dan Kelly to the United States, and Danny Gallivan was about to abandon his radio slot for TV, so Cole eventually had a gig as radio play-by-play man for Montreal games, before moving to television in 1973.

Cole's legend had been defined by television, and it's easy to forget radio history: he was the radio voice who had called Paul Henderson's nation-saving goal in the 1972 Summit Series.

"One minute left to go, a 5–5 tie, this is the tie breaking game, you couldn't get it any closer," Cole says, his voice sharp, cutting through the tension of the listeners, and yet he's edgy, too. Team Canada moves the puck down the ice, and Cole's voice stays steady, following it into the Soviets' corner. And then it's classic Cole.

"Vasiliev goes back of the net. Cournoyer steals it! A pass in front, Henderson! ... was upended as he tried to shoot it. HERE'S ANOTHER SHOT, HENDERSON RIGHT IN, HE SCORES! HENDERSON!"

Team Canada piles over the boards to congratulate Henderson, and Cole marvels as Ken Dryden skates the length of the ice to join in. "HENDERSON HAS GOTTA BE THE HERO OF THE ENTIRE NATION NOW!" Cole shouts above the noise. And thirty-four seconds later when the game ends, he is.

The clip is also revealing because it illustrates a Cole quirk: he hates his colour analyst to talk when he's talking, and that happens when he spots Dryden on the move. Fred Sgambati starts to enthusiastically join in, and Cole just raises his voice and effectively silences him.

He also doesn't like to be touched while doing play-by-play, an obvious way to get his attention when the colour man or other personnel in the booth aren't able to speak into his ear. If anyone transgressed, Cole would whip his headset off and straighten them out—touching distracted his professional comportment, and the game, and his view of the game was paramount.

Of course, he had his props and rituals to aid his artistry. In his smoking days, he'd light up a cigarette—in a holder, no less—the tobacco giving tang to his voice. He also liked to undo his belt buckle and expand his diaphragm. It led to a comic result—at least once—when calling a game in the tight broadcast

The Bob Cole Media Centre in Mile One Stadium in St. John's. Like all great artists, Bob Cole has his eccentricities. He's known by broadcast colleagues for his Heisman move—a stiff arm to anyone who tries to interfere with his play-by-play.

space at Quebec's Le Colisée. Cole, whose intensity level is high no matter what happens on the ice, jumped up when a goal was scored. He banged his head on plumbing pipes directly above him, sending debris down to the floor, along with his unbuckled trousers. His colour analyst Mickey Redmond was laughing so hard that he couldn't respond to the desperate pleas from the broadcast truck for someone to say something over the replay, now on screen. Cole, too busy holding his head, and his trousers, couldn't respond either.

From 1980 through 2008 Cole called the Stanley Cup final, and Harry Neale sat next to him as his colour man for twenty of those broadcasts. Despite Cole's quirks, Neale found a way to make him laugh, and the duo became the premier act in *Hockey Night in Canada*'s formidable on-air crew. On the rare occasion when Neale talked into Cole's play-by-play, he received "The Heisman"—Cole's arm shooting out as if to stiff-arm a football tackler, just like the statue on the Heisman Trophy.

Though Cole joined the so-called second unit of *Hockey Night in Canada* broadcasters in 2008, calling games out of Montreal, his voice is going strong even in his mid-70s. He, too, plays on the rhythms around him: the game, the crowd, and his own response to a play. His longevity in the booth, combined with his versatile baritone—rising into joyful tenor, sinking into ominous bass— puts him in the pantheon with Foster Hewitt and Danny Gallivan. Though he has always had his critics, pointing to shortcuts and omissions in his calls, Cole would doubtless respond with an "Ohhhh, baby," and a famous song title from his other obsession, Frank Sinatra. His way got it done.

57

Third Period

Jim Hughson

On March 22, 2008, *Hockey Night in Canada* play-by-play man Jim Hughson and his colour analyst, the former NHLer Craig Simpson, made *Hockey Night in Canada* history. The duo called the 3:00 P.M. EDT game between Edmonton and Colorado, then rushed to the airport and onto a charter flight to be in Calgary to call the Flames game against Minnesota. It wasn't punishment for breaking *Hockey Night in Canada* curfew—it had all been Hughson's enthusiastic idea of the perfect Saturday.

"I spotted that on the schedule in September," Hughson said at the time, "and I thought, 'I want to do that baby'."

Hughson's love of hockey, the kind of thing that makes him race time to squeeze two games into a day, has propelled him to the top of the game as *Hockey Night in Canada*'s premier game caller. It is also the thing that has defined his peripatetic life as a broadcaster.

"My hockey bag has been the one thing I've packed with me everywhere I've moved," he says. "Everywhere I moved I had no furniture, I didn't need it—I had a stereo and I had a hockey bag. It became my social conduit. Everywhere I went I made new friends. There was always a rink, there was always a league, there was always a pick-up game somewhere."

Hughson grew up playing hockey and watching *Hockey Night in Canada* in Fort St. John, the oldest European-settled town in British Columbia, founded as a trading post in 1794, in the northeast of the province.

Broadcasters Craig Simpson (left) and Jim Hughson (right) call the game between the Winnipeg Jets and Toronto Maple Leafs at the MTS Centre in Winnipeg on December 31, 2011.

Indeed, hockey *was* life on Saturday for Hughson as a boy in the 1960s. "There was only one channel of television and it was the CBC," he says. "*Hockey Night* was a staple, but at the same time, too, the local hockey team, the Fort St. John Flyers, were a senior team of some repute and their home games were Saturday night, too. So it was a balancing act."

Hughson played junior hockey at home, and watched his friends go off to play in the Western Hockey League, with a shot at a pro career. He knew it wasn't for him because of one simple reason: "Fear. I was always the fastest player on the team and there was a reason for that because I could get out of everybody's way."

When his high school drama class recorded radio plays at the local station on Sunday afternoons, Hughson was intrigued by the medium. When a neighbour who ran the station offered him a part-time gig on weekends, he was hooked. After a stint at the University of Victoria, Hughson returned to radio in Fort St. John. When the sports announcer at the station got a better-paying job in Edmonton, Hughson wound up in his chair. "I think I was the only guy left in the place that knew a puck from a football."

From there Hughson wound his way to CKNW in Vancouver, and called the two home games on radio while Jim Robson called them on TV during the Vancouver Canucks' improbable—and brief—appearance in the 1982 Stanley Cup final against the New York Islanders.

He left to do his first tour at *Hockey Night in Canada* in the 1985–86 season, then moved on to TSN, Sportsnet, and back to *Hockey Night* to stay in 2005. "What Sportsnet could never offer was the Stanley Cup playoffs," he said when he rejoined the CBC. "We're no different than players in that you want to be working on the last day of the season."

Hughson, known for his clear, articulate play-by-play, peppered with signature phrases such as "That's hockey!" or "Great save, Luongo!" (or whichever goalie he's covering), sums up his approach to work by paraphrasing a quote from a football player: "If I practise hard all week long then the game on Saturday is recreation."

During that week of practice, Hughson, in his office in White Rock, B.C., watches the games of the teams that he'll be broadcasting on Saturday. "I watch hours and hours of hockey, and break down the games…. I'm doing a lot of the things that I think coaches do."

On Friday, he flies to Toronto, and on Saturday, he goes to work—taking in the morning skate, checking in with his crew about the night ahead, which they've been emailing, texting, and talking about all week. "Mostly it's putting together notes, putting on a clean suit, and being back at the arena."

Hughson's broadcasting philosophy is simple: Treat the audience with respect, make sure all the tools are in place—the cameras, the tapes, the people—to tell the story of the game, and then do it. "At the end of the night, after a game, the question I always ask of myself, and ask of the crew I've worked with, is: 'Did we accurately tell the story of the game?'" he says. "And if you can walk away from the rink that night comfortable that you've told the story of the game, then you've done your job."

And the best place to do that job, for the man who took over the marquee play-by-play mantle from Bob Cole in 2008, is not in the Foster Hewitt Broadcast Gondola in Toronto, but in the city that gave the Leafs their greatest rivals. "There's probably not a better place in the world to go to a hockey game than Montreal. It's a real event in the city when there's a hockey game on," he says, but then realizes it's just a matter of degree. "Hockey games on Saturday in Canada are different than anywhere else. You don't get the same buzz in Chicago on a Saturday night that you do in Winnipeg or Vancouver because it's a tradition, because it's an event, it builds all day. If it's Saturday, it's *Hockey Night in Canada*. It's a special day to go to a rink in Canada."

Sidney Crosby Knocked Out of the NHL

It was no surprise when the Pittsburgh Penguins selected Sidney Crosby first overall in the NHL's 2005 entry draft. The draft had been nicknamed the "Sidney Crosby Sweepstakes" as the scoring phenom from Cole Harbour, Nova Scotia, had long been dubbed "The Next One." Expectations were huge that "Sid the Kid" would be the golden child to take the torch from Wayne Gretzky. *Hockey Night in Canada* has a camera on the pretender to Gretzky's throne as he hears the news, exchanges a proud smile with his father, then takes the stage where his new boss, Mario Lemieux, hands him his NHL jersey, Number 87. The number comes from Crosby's birth year, for when he steps on the stage, the player anointed to own the NHL is just 17 years old.

And soon, the records start to come. In 2007 Crosby became the youngest player to win the NHL's Art Ross scoring title—and the only teenager to win the scoring title ever in any of North America's professional sports. In case there were any doubters, Crosby added the Hart Trophy as the league's most valuable player, and the Lester B. Pearson Award, chosen by his peers in the NHL Players' Association to designate him as peerless.

In 2009, Crosby led the Pittsburgh Penguins to a Stanley Cup championship, and at age 21, became the youngest captain in the history of the NHL to do so. In 2010, Team Canada goalie Roberto Luongo confirmed Canucks fans' fears that he'd somehow blow the gold medal game in the Winter Olympics, by letting in the tying goal with twenty-four seconds left in regulation time. So Crosby, now wearing the hero's cape as "Captain Canada," had to skate in to save the day—and fragile Canadian hearts—by scoring the gold medal winner seven minutes and forty seconds into overtime.

It was 2011, though, that changed Crosby's world, and the NHL. Crosby had

58

Sidney Crosby can't see Washington's David Steckel approaching at speed from behind. Steckel hits Crosby's head with his shoulder with such force that Crosby is knocked to the ice. Steckel was not penalized for the hit.

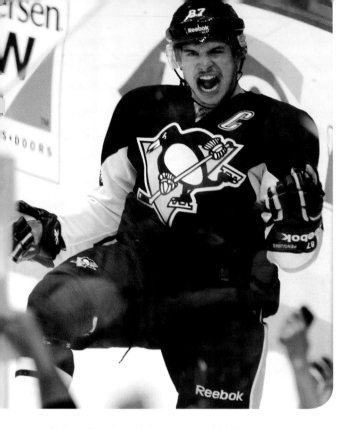

Sidney Crosby celebrates a goal in his return to action against the New York Islanders on November 21, 2011. The game was added to the *Hockey Night in Canada* schedule at the last minute when Crosby announced his return. The show had followed Crosby since he was a kid, shooting pucks in the basement at his family's clothes dryer.

been the centre of negative attention from other players—and their jealous parents—ever since his prodigious talent became apparent in childhood. In an interview with CBC's *The Hour* in 2001, the 14-year-old Crosby, his voice just breaking into manhood, explains how he deals with the on-ice mugging and abuse that his talent provokes. "The game they're playing isn't my game. My game is making plays, and making things happen, scoring goals. If they're doing things to prevent me from doing that then they're doing their job and I'm not doing mine."

On New Year's Day 2011, Crosby and the Penguins are playing Washington in the Winter Classic. Crosby is looking up-ice when Washington's David Steckel does hockey's version of a drive-by, felling Crosby with a shoulder to the side of the head. Four days later, Tampa Bay Lightning's Victor Hedman checks Crosby from behind into the glass. The Next One is out of the game for the rest of the season and the first twenty games of the next with what doctors call a "mild concussion." Crosby calls it brutal.

Crosby's injury, and his absence, hit the NHL hard. The February 6, 2011, game between Washington and Pittsburgh on Super Bowl Sunday saw an audience decline of half a million viewers in the United States because Crosby wasn't there. As the NFL was dealing with players developing dementia or committing suicide years after they retired due to the cumulative effects of head injury, the NHL was having to do the same. A Satellite Hot Stove segment three days after Crosby's January 5 concussion showed that the path hockey's managers should take in dealing with head shots—to make all contact to a player's head susceptible to suspension—wouldn't be as easy as Crosby and his agent hoped.

Hot Stove panellists Eric Francis and Pierre LeBrun, both journalists, argued with former player and GM Mike Milbury, who was under no illusions about what the "soft guys" wanted when it came to contact. "Why don't we all go listen to a Peter, Paul and Mary record," he fumes, as Francis and LeBrun look on in bewilderment to Milbury's invocation of how "mean and nasty" was fine back in his day. "I mean, what the hell are we doing here?"

"It's a hit to the head," LeBrun says in exasperation. "Have you been following the league in the last year?"

Team owners had been paying attention, and in June 2011, the NHL's Board of Governors changed the wording to Rule 48, which deals with hits to the head. "Now, the confusion some of the players have expressed in the past as to what direction they're approaching a player, what direction a player is facing, east, west, north, south, that has all been taken out," said Brendan Shanahan, the former Detroit Red Wings star who was appointed NHL Senior V.P. of Player Safety and Hockey Operations that month. "Anywhere on the ice, coming from any direction, you target the head and make it a principal point of contact, you'll be subject to a two-minute penalty on the ice for Rule 48. You'll also be—as with all two-minute penalties or non-calls—subject to supplementary discipline."

After undergoing an alternative medicine protocol conducted by chiropractic neurologist Ted Carrick, who had helped NHL players with head injuries by using non-invasive exercises to help heal the damaged brain, Crosby felt good to go. On November 21, 2011, *Hockey Night in Canada* was there to witness the triumphant return of one the brightest stars in its substantial firmament.

The Pittsburgh fans treated Crosby to the kind of ovation a saviour might expect, but the question on everyone's mind, including Crosby's, was whether he would be as good as before. Less than six minutes into the first period, Crosby begins his answer. "Here's Crosby with a burst of speed, up the middle, gets open, and scores!" calls play-by-play man Jim Hughson as Crosby takes the puck across the New York Islanders' blue line, splits the defence, and backhands the puck into the net. "Welcome! Back! Sid!"

Crosby would add another goal and two assists to punctuate his glorious return to form, but his story was far from over. He played just seven games before an elbow to the head from Boston's David Krejci sidelined him until March 2012. When Crosby finally came back, he added an assist on a March 15 Penguins victory over the New York Rangers. Despite playing only twenty-two games in the 2011–12 season, Crosby's 37 points were good enough to put him over the 600-point mark. All who love the game hope he stays healthy enough to reach 1,000, with the help of zero tolerance to head shots from peewee to pro.

59

Coach's Corner, Part 2

In the volatile world of ratings-driven network television, Don Cherry has become as dependable as winter ice in Kingston, Ontario, his hometown, which he has enshrined over three decades of TV life as hockey's answer to, well, himself. In that time, Cherry has metamorphosed from an unemployed hockey coach picking up extra TV work for $1,500 plus expenses, to a multimillionaire performance artist whose seven-minute segment is "must-see TV" for hockey fans and passers-by each Saturday night and during the NHL playoffs. His fans even voted him the seventh greatest Canadian in history—just after Prime Minister Lester B. Pearson, who won the Nobel Peace Prize. For millions of people, the pugilistic Don Cherry, and his adroit television partner Ron MacLean, have become the public face of *Hockey Night in Canada*.

Cherry's early *Hockey Night in Canada* years in the 1980s gave little hint as to what he would become. Segments featured him speaking with well modulated knowledge—and the occasional dropped "nothink" or "somethink"—to hosts Dave Hodge or Dick Irvin, who engaged him with amiable wariness. On occasion, he was featured orating alone in a swivel chair in front of an ominous black background, like a character out of hockey's version of *Dr. Who*.

In 1986, Cherry found his perfect foil when Ron MacLean was summoned from *Hockey Night in Canada*'s Calgary base to take over hosting duties from Dave Hodge, who had left the show after his on-air pen-flipping incident created an impassable crevasse between him and the CBC.

MacLean was in many ways as accidental as Cherry. Ralph Mellanby, *Hockey Night in Canada*'s innovative executive producer, who created Coach's Corner, calls him "the great surprise."

Don Cherry and Ron MacLean form one of television's most unusual and successful partnerships, attracting millions of viewers to their weekly Coach's Corner segment.

In the mid-1980s Mellanby "would look at his tapes and say, 'Geez, I don't think MacLean will ever make it. He's too corny.'" Mellanby was no longer with *Hockey Night*, but Ron Harrison, the show's new executive producer, wanted to give him a shot, and John Shannon, who became *Hockey Night in Canada*'s executive producer in 1994, worked with MacLean to help him improve. Shannon told Mellanby that someday, MacLean would be "the best host we ever had."

Today, Shannon thinks he is. "The show doesn't work if Ron isn't there," Shannon says, and neither do the Olympic Games and other big-ticket CBC events which MacLean also hosts. He's also won eight Gemini Awards as Canada's best sports broadcaster—a long way from his days as a teenage DJ in Red Deer, Alberta.

And then again, maybe not. MacLean's success as Cherry's sparring partner lies in his Everyman qualities, albeit an Everyman who is a quick thinker with a penchant for puns. A former hockey referee, MacLean also brings a usually clear-eyed view of the rule book of life to bear on some of Cherry's offsides.

Indeed, the template is set in one of their earliest duets, at the beginning of the 1987–88 season, illustrating the tensions of their dynamic.

Coach's Corner opens with the familiar vaudeville fanfare, along with a humble triptych of Cherry with his beloved bull terrier Blue, then alone, and then with Blue again. Cut to MacLean in a blue *Hockey Night in Canada* jacket, and Cherry in an uncharacteristically quiet checked number, sitting behind a desk. MacLean says, "This NHL season's now ten games old, already we've had five players handed multi-game suspensions for attempt to injure or deliberate injury; we've had a coach and an official suspended for three games; we've had the number two draft pick into the stands fighting with fans. Don, this is no longer a debate over whether we should have fighting or not in the NHL, it seems to be a blatant disregard for the rules."

Cherry, a pained smile playing on his face throughout this, comes out swinging. "You know what gets me, we pick on hockey so much!" He then answers the question by yelling at MacLean for the public indifference to recent baseball bad behaviour. "We're paranoid here! We're paranoid here!"

MacLean calmly stands up to this: "Sometimes when I don't have an answer to a question I cite other examples. This issue concerns hockey."

The segment ends with MacLean summing up their next twenty-five years: "Don Cherry will be back next week, and the week after that. What's unfortunate is we'll probably still have this conversation about what's wrong with hockey."

Cherry and MacLean sometimes stray from talking hockey, and since their audience is so large, their comments can't escape notice. Their vigorous dialogue about Canada's decision not to fight in Iraq was so polarized and polarizing that it was removed from the CBC website.

When Ron MacLean appeared to be leaving *Hockey Night in Canada* due to contract issues, public outcry was so loud that he was rewarded with a handsome contract to keep the show rolling.

Cherry's seemingly overnight transition from colourful coach to bombastic defender of the faith has its origins, fittingly, in a hockey brawl, in January 1987. "The punch-up in Piestany," says Cherry's son Tim, who produces Cherry's successful "Rock'em Sock'em" video franchise, and who wrote the first bio-pic of his father, *Keep Your Head Up, Kid* (and co-produced the second, *The Wrath of Grapes*). "I think that's when Dad's popularity really took off."

The punch-up was a bench-clearing brawl between Canada and the USSR at the 1987 World Junior Championships in Piestany, Czechoslovakia. Cherry was working as an analyst, and when the game was disrupted by the fight, he defended Canada for standing up to the Soviets, whom he squarely blamed for the brawl. Host Brian Williams was clearly offended by Cherry's flag-waving stance in the name of violence, and Tim Cherry says he thought his father's TV jig was up. "My mom and I were sitting there and we both knew this could easily be the end of Dad's career. And it turned out to be the opposite. It cemented the idea that he's going to stick up for Canadians. Because *nobody* was saying what Dad was saying."

And so it has continued. If the Cherry–MacLean team wound up on Sigmund Freud's couch for analysis, their dynamic would nicely fit within his theory of human psychology—Cherry is the unrestrained id crossed with the moralizing, critical super-ego, and MacLean is the "real world" ego who skates between the two, trying to referee. When things go wrong it's because the roles get reversed, and MacLean starts saying things that one might expect from the mouth of Cherry.

MacLean is at his best when he lets Cherry off his leash to romp through the topic of the day, then reins him in and cools things down to ice level. Which, of course, is where Cherry—the blue-collar idol in a custom-made starched white collar—lives. He has worked up his act to the point where a taxpayer-subsidized pointy-head would see him in his current opening montage robes and crown as an example of postmodern irony, and a taxpayer would see him as a fearless defender of their values.

Of course, Cherry's genius is that he has his finger firmly on the pulse of his people, wherever they may turn up. Tim Cherry recounts a visit he made to London with his history-buff father, who wanted to dress up in his Coach's Corner duds to visit the Imperial War Museum. "I said, 'You're in England! You're an ocean away from your fans.' But he says, 'Nope, I've gotta get dressed up.' So we're at a nice hotel in downtown London, we go out, and the black cab comes up, and the door opens and then out comes a guy who says, 'Hey, Don Cherry! I'm from Wolf Island!' Not only was the guy from Canada, he was from where Dad has his cottage!"

Coach's Corner is a guy's world, and women are largely absent. To be sure, his beloved wife Rose won frequent mentions on Coach's Corner. When she died of cancer, a rose appeared each week in his lapel to commemorate her. Cherry will wear pink to help promote breast cancer research, and mention a hockey mom, or a fallen Canadian female soldier. But the overarching theme, be it in discussing hockey, or in praising the Canadian troops, is that Canadian manliness trumps all things.

Cherry's performance is based on the creation of an ideal Canadian hockey player, and by extension, the ideal Canadian—male, Anglo, tough, honest, never-say-die. It's one that Cherry knows intimately, because he invented it. Don Cherry is not the God of the Old Testament, but he operates in the same way. Making man in his own image, throwing a few thunderbolts, and letting us think we live in a universe in which the good guys have a chance to win.

The Jets Return to Winnipeg

On October 9, 2011, *Hockey Night in Canada* gave the country something that it hadn't heard for nearly fifteen years—the roar of a Winnipeg crowd celebrating a Winnipeg Jets goal.

"Brett MacLean hovering around the net," calls play-by-play man Jim Hughson, his voice rising as the Jets buzz the Montreal Canadiens. "So is Antropov, who just got pitchforked down! The shot gets through, where's ...? and Antropov scores!"

No matter that the score is now 5–1 for Montreal, the sold-out crowd in the 15,004-seat MTS Centre—many of whom had paid nearly $2,000 for this ticket—stood in raucous ovation for a single goal that was a triumphant sign of life after years of pain. "Listen to this crowd!" exclaimed *Hockey Night in Canada* colour analyst Craig Simpson. "Welcome back hockey!"

Two minutes and twenty-seven seconds into the third period, Nick Antropov finally did what Winnipeggers had been waiting for ever since the Jets, like snowbirds, headed south to Phoenix in 1996. Professional hockey had thrived in Winnipeg with the arrival of the WHA's Jets in 1972, with Bobby Hull offering instant legitimacy (in exchange for $1 million) by signing on to play hockey beneath the imperious gaze of Queen Elizabeth, or a 23-foot-high painting of her hanging in the rafters of the Winnipeg Arena.

After fifteen years away from home, the Winnipeg Jets celebrate their first goal back where they belong on October 9, 2011.

The public passion for the return of the Jets saw ticket prices at Winnipeg's sold-out MTS Centre reach nearly $2,000 for the team's home opener.

The team changed professional addresses in 1979 when the WHA folded, and moved into the NHL. The new neighbourhood had become a hostile one by the 1990s, though, with the NHL looking to make hockey sizzle in the U.S. Sun Belt. Teams popped up in San Jose, Tampa Bay, Anaheim, Miami, Nashville, and Atlanta, while Minnesota moved to Dallas, and Hartford to Carolina. In the middle of the decade, the Quebec Nordiques went to Denver to become the Avalanche.

The Nordiques' emigration made Winnipeg Canada's smallest-market team, and despite a passionate and knowledgeable fan base, the Jets revenue stream—and the sinking Canadian dollar—couldn't keep them aloft against the power of the large-market and the U.S.-based franchises. Fans held rallies to build a new arena and sell season tickets. Counter-rallies came from a group called Thin Ice, who were opposed to spending public funds on a hockey rink when society had more demanding causes.

In the end, the Jets moved to Phoenix, and became the Coyotes. Life in the desert was not much better, with the franchise roiled by ownership troubles and lacklustre performance, failing to make the playoffs from 2002 through 2009 despite having hockey genius Wayne Gretzky behind the bench from 2005 to 2009. Then they went bankrupt.

Meanwhile, the Atlanta Thrashers were suffering from dismal attendance and a mediocre record in a city where football in all its forms—NFL, college, high school, pick up in the park—rates higher than hockey. On May 31, 2011, Winnipeg businessman Mark Chipman announced—at Winnipeg's fabled intersection of Portage and Main—that the True North Sports & Entertainment partnership had bought the Thrashers, who would be heading north to North American sports' second smallest pro market (after Green Bay). Four days later season tickets went on sale, and seventeen minutes later they were gone.

Canada's Prime Minister Stephen Harper showed up for the Jets' return to the country that gave the world the game, along with Gary Bettman. The NHL Commissioner had been skating the thin ice of credibility to Canadians who didn't like his mantra that "we don't like to move franchises" when they'd been on the wrong end of two of those moves. Now there was some comeuppance.

Fittingly for Winnipeggers, *Hockey Night in Canada*'s broadcast of the Jets' return home came on Thanksgiving Sunday night, and despite the distraction of turkey and tryptophan, more than 1.8 million Canadians tuned in. There was

The Winnipeg Jets played their last game before their move to Phoenix on April 28, 1996. Despite a 4–1 playoff loss to Detroit, they received a standing ovation of farewell.

an overwhelming sense not of revenge, but of redemption. An essential kind of winter life had returned to Winnipeg, and the country was glad.

"Welcome, everyone, to a once in a lifetime event in Winnipeg," said Jim Hughson, after a twelve-minute opening ceremony. "We're in the heart of the nation, and you can feel the heartbeat of hockey."

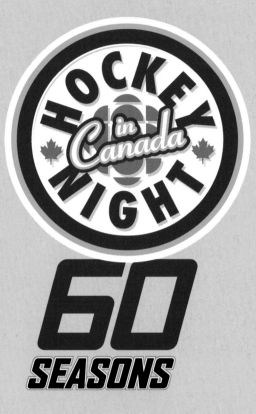

OVERTIME

Hockey Night in Canada begins on a Wednesday. That's when the production team meets on the fifth floor of the CBC Broadcast Centre in Toronto to talk about Saturday's game.

Rather, Saturday's *games*. Since the advent of the doubleheader in 1995, there are at least two games going out into the world on a regular *Hockey Night* broadcast, travelling far beyond the borders of Canada and the United States, and that planet whence Vancouver's Green Men come. The images rocket into the exosphere, then bounce off geostationary communication satellites 22,000 miles above the earth's equator, and back down to TV sets in Canada and the U.S., and to satellite dishes and Canadian Armed Forces units around the world.

On this upcoming Saturday in late March 2012, there will be five TV telecasts to produce, each one presented as if it's the only game in town. The mood among the dozen people in the *Hockey Night* production meeting is calm and focused, like a dressing room before the Stanley Cup finals. There are hockeyesque nicknames—"Spearsie" is Brian Spear, senior producer, who runs the meeting. "Houghie" is Jim Hough, who will direct the Montreal Canadiens game from Philadelphia, and who bears a historic lineage. He's the son of Ted Hough, the man who ran *Hockey Night* for MacLaren Advertising and its subsidiary, the Canadian Sports Network, from the 1960s until 1986. And there are things to think about beyond this weekend.

Despite having five games airing in three days, four of them in the same time zone, the Stanley Cup playoffs are also less than two weeks away. The Toronto Maple Leafs will not be gracing them. This means there will be no home games for anyone in this room come April 11.

The playoffs also pose another problem, as teams zip up access to journalists at a time of year when the maw of *Hockey Night*'s audience is even more voracious than usual. "We'll have to shoot a couple of Inside Hockey stories in Vancouver," Spear says, when they cover the Canucks at home next week, before the season ends.

They also plan a playoff preview show for Tuesday, April 10. It will go out live to Atlantic Canada at 8:00, taped to everybody else, featuring the show's core crew. "It's Ron [MacLean] hosting, P.J. [Stock] and Kelly [Hrudey], Elliotte

[Friedman] on the iDesk," says Mike Dodson, one of the team. There will be a live studio audience, a live band—Cuff the Duke—and hits from the Canadian cities that make it into the playoffs (two in the end, Vancouver and Ottawa).

In today's meeting, everyone knows what they have to do come Saturday, so this is about tweaking specifics. They discuss the tease, which opens the show with Nickelback's cover version of "Saturday Night's Alright for Fighting." They'll steal some time from it to cover the pre-game show. Spear reports that Cassie Campbell is likely to be sent to the Ottawa–Pittsburgh game, so Andi Petrillo, who joined the *Hockey Night* team as a reporter and host of the new segment, Game Day, will work the New York Rangers–Toronto tilt at home.

"Mike Milbury will be on satellite, I just don't know where yet," says Spear, as he sorts the Satellite Hot Stove. "Eric [Francis] and Elliotte are here in studio." Then he moves the discussion a week down the road, to the show that will feature the short list of towns competing to host Kraft Hockeyville. The first prize is serious: $100,000 in arena upgrades from Kraft, as well as getting to host an NHL pre-season game and a *Hockey Night in Canada* broadcast.

Kelly Hrudey at his familiar spot behind the desk. Hrudey's warmth and exhaustive knowledge of the game made him a star twice over once his playing days had come to an end.

The issue is how to have all five communities fed live at the same time, and there's another problem: figure skating. The team speaks in a kind of colour code as they try to sort it: they're losing green and pink, which will be helping out on the figure skating telecast.

The colours become apparent in the CBC studio where *Hockey Night in Canada* is controlled. A bank of video monitors glow along a wall opposite the crew who mastermind all the games on this Saturday night. Red, blue, green, and silver monitors are for video playback; the camera monitors are all numbered. The light in the control studio is dim, more like a swank cocktail bar at midnight than the room responsible for what millions of hockey fans are going to see tonight. They're connected to the various "trucks" and to their *Hockey Night* production crews who are on-site at the five arenas that will supply the feed for tonight's menu.

Despite the clock ticking down on a very busy broadcast night, the ambience is of professional calm. They've done this before—tonight, they're just doing more of it. Trevor Pilling, the show's affable executive producer, oversees the control room from the back deck of a double row of desks, facing the monitors. He views the technology before him as one big vehicle driving through the ether.

"TV sports is very producer driven," Pilling says. "The producer is the navigator. The director is the driver, while the switcher [the person who switches camera shots when the director calls a camera or video playback number] is the engine. And the audio guys are the drive train in the engine."

Pilling joined CBC in 1994 and the sports division in 1997, working on several Olympic Games and Grey Cups. But he always had his eye on hockey, even as a nineteen-year-old, when his NHL dream was dust. At the time, Pilling found himself working on his first live sports TV show. "It was a CIAU basketball game and it was a horrible show, it had only two functioning cameras. But on that day I was so energized, I knew what I wanted to do, and clearly remember saying it to myself: 'I want to work for *Hockey Night in Canada.*'"

Pilling caught up with his dream in 2010, when he became *Hockey Night*'s executive producer. He has all the TV gear a producer could want, and the personnel to deliver—and not always just what we'll see on camera. On his left are two crew who watch all the other NHL games on TV, log what happens, and post comments about them on Twitter. On his right is Kathy Broderick, expert at getting footage quick, and also the lead producer on Coach's Corner. There's a monitor that's live showing where Cherry and MacLean will perform their duet in the studio, and a technician enters before Don Cherry arrives to crank the seat of the stool higher, then sits on it to give a visual (it wouldn't do for Cherry to be lower in a shot than Ron MacLean). When Cherry arrives, he joins MacLean to look at video clips of items they might use on Coach's Corner.

One of the clips concerns Cherry directly. The NDP are holding a leadership convention, and a panel of NDP pundits wind up talking about Cherry. MP Pat Martin says if the NDP wins the next election, they'll make Cherry an "honorary left-wing pinko"—quoting Cherry for disparaging remarks he made about same. Stephen Lewis, Ontario's former NDP leader, half-jokingly says when the NDP forms a national government, "the first Order-in-Council would be to take Don Cherry off the air forever." Cherry laughs when he views the clip, but he doesn't use it in Coach's Corner that night.

There are other rooms nearby that contribute to the production. The audio guys preside over their console next door, while down the hall, a team of college-age people log all 1,230 regular season NHL games. The digital log is invaluable for calling up clips of plays that producers or on-air talent want to use. In real time. "Unlike football, where you have the story on Monday morning," says Pilling, "we have games to cover every night."

The show's stars, Kelly Hrudey, P.J. Stock, and Elliotte Friedman, all pop in and out to say hello to the control room. They're relaxed and knowledgeable—both Stock and Hrudey are NHLers—but humble about it, having grown up watching *Hockey Night in Canada*, too, and respectful of where they are and the history they carry. They are heirs to a legacy, whose names will one day be stamped on a whole generation's memories of the game. But they are not so unlike the viewers at home, and it is that love of the game, and love of knowledge of the game, that make the *Hockey Night in Canada* stars seem more like friends than distant celebrities. It seems to the viewer that you could easily continue their TV conversation in person over a beer—and that they'd even buy the first round.

There's also the Lotus Lounge for MacLean and Cherry to relax in and watch games. There's a camera in the lounge, with sound, so Pilling can keep an eye and ear on the talent. "If we notice a need to pump them up, we'll show them something cool" from one of the games in play.

Then suddenly, it's game time. "Have a good night, everybody," Pilling says to his colleagues, then the director calls out, "We're on!" For the next six hours or so, *Hockey Night in Canada* will broadcast its games, Coach's Corner, the Satellite Hot Stove, the Chevy iDesk "inside hockey" items from Elliotte

Kevin Weekes and Scott Oake with defenceman Jack Johnson (centre). *Hockey Night in Canada* personalities bridge the gap between fans and players, and have earned the trust of both.

Friedman, and rinkside reports from Scott Oake, Cassie Campbell, and Andi Petrillo. Play-by-play will come from Jim Hughson, Bob Cole, Mark Lee, and Dean Brown. Game analysis will come from Craig Simpson, Glenn Healy, Greg Millen, Garry Galley, Kevin Weekes, Kelly Hrudey, and Mike Milbury, while Oake and Weekes will close it all down with After Hours, when the Vancouver game ends around 12:30 A.M. Eastern time on Sunday.

As it happens, Pilling will be watching the action in the control room, and emailing or texting with his various crews, as well as with CBC execs watching at home and with CBC News Network, who want to put updates on the NDP leadership convention into the game. He'll also tweet on *Hockey Night in Canada*'s website, pointing out the various developing storylines, or responding to viewers' questions. "We have to stay nimble and flexible," Pilling says. "So many Canadians feel they have a part of this show."

Generations of them, in fact. For what George Retzlaff and Gerald Renaud figured out in 1952 still informs the template, and what Ralph Mellanby invented as *Hockey Night in Canada*'s revolutionary executive producer, drives the show's sensibilities.

"I didn't really want the job because I wanted to be the next Norman Jewison," Mellanby says today, still producing television well into his late seventies. "I wanted to do movies and big entertainment. For me it was a new adventure. I thought I'd last two years."

Mellanby lasted nearly a quarter of a century. When he first came on board in the mid 1960s, the show's sponsor, Imperial Oil, was "very happy with the coverage, but very unhappy with the lack of innovation and very unhappy with the intermissions and pre- and post-game, of which there was none. There was none!" Mellanby is still incredulous. "They just come on from Maple Leaf Gardens—'This is Bill Hewitt!'—or whoever it was, and they'd drop the puck. At 8:01. I said, 'This show needs an opening, like a Broadway show. You gotta have an overture. Who's playing, who are the stars?' They bought it into right away."

So along came Dolores Claman's iconic musical theme and a roster of Hall of Fame talent in Dick Irvin, Brian McFarlane, and Don Cherry (though not yet a Hall of Famer) and features like Showdown in the NHL and Howie Meeker's Hockey School and Bobby Orr and the Hockey Legends. Mellanby also stresses how much he valued working on the French version of the show, *La Soirée du Hockey*, and regards its fluid, nuanced play-play-play man René Lecavalier as "the greatest announcer in hockey history—and I include Foster in that."

Mellanby understood that as *Hockey Night in Canada*'s guiding hand, he was not just spicing up television, he was creating a brand. "Branding was a new thing," he says. "You gotta have the brand. That's why you have the music, and the logo, and the jackets. That's what American networks did."

Mellanby had worked extensively in the United States (and would win five Emmy Awards) and freely admits that he borrowed from ABC TV's genius producer Roone Arledge. ABC's *Wide World of Sports* had yellow blazers, so *Hockey Night in Canada* would have blue.

"The first ones were dark blue," Mellanby says. "We changed to the light blue ones because of colour television. They looked better."

Those cool blue *Hockey Night in Canada* blazers became so representative of the show's success as a brand that they became the most potent target of corporate revenge during the 1987 Rendez-vous series, a two game contest between the NHL's best players and the Soviet national team.

Since Rendez-vous '87 would be played at Quebec City's Le Colisée, and since brewery Carling O'Keefe sponsored advertising rights to the series, *Hockey Night in Canada* was barred from the premises since they were owned by Molson, Carling's fiercest rival. So, CBC Sports had to replace Dave Hodge and rookie Ron MacLean with Brian Williams, John Davidson and Don Wittman, and the iconic blue blazers were banned, too. Instead, the broadcasters wore the orange blazers of CBC Sports. But no matter what colour the jackets, or the personalities on screen, when the best hockey was played, it was played on the broadcast that set the standard for bringing the nation's game into the nation's living rooms.

The blue blazers are gone from *Hockey Night in Canada* now, too, but the spirit of the show that Renaud, and Retzlaff, and Mellanby did so much to create flows out to wherever new technologies will take it, looking forward to keeping the brand alive for the next sixty years. And it has a good chance of making it, for *Hockey Night in Canada* remains, at its essence, Canadians telling the story of themselves.

"It's not the Americans' game, it's not the Russians' game, it's our game," Mellanby says. "It's a very important part of our culture. John Diefenbaker told me one time that "our greatest heroes in Canada are hockey players." And that's true. It's part of being Canadian."

Photo Credits

All photos not listed below are courtesy
of Canadian Broadcasting Corporation.

2 Steven Taylor/Getty Images

8 Lou Skuce/Hockey Hall of Fame

11, 15 Courtesy of Mike Wilson

16 Imperial Oil-Turofsky/Hockey Hall of Fame

19 Glenbow Archives/Spring–1940 Review–page 15

20 Glenbow Archives/Salesmotor–1944–page 12-top

21 Glenbow Archives/Spring–1940 Review–pages 17-4, 17-5, 17-6

22 Courtesy of The Hockey News

48 Graphic Artists/Hockey Hall of Fame

66 Imperial Oil-Turofsky/Hockey Hall of Fame

72 Imperial Oil-Turofsky/Hockey Hall of Fame

74 Imperial Oil-Turofsky/Hockey Hall of Fame

81 Michael Burns Sr./Hockey Hall of Fame

91 Imperial Oil-Turofsky/Hockey Hall of Fame

94 Imperial Oil-Turofsky/Hockey Hall of Fame

108, 110 Steven Errico/Getty Images

112 Canadian Press

120 Imperial Oil-Turofsky/Hockey Hall of Fame

123 Graphic Artists/Hockey Hall of Fame

134 Frank Prazak/Hockey Hall of Fame

137 Graphic Artists/Hockey Hall of Fame

140, 144 Melchior DiGiacomo/Getty Images

Acknowledgments

This book had many helpers, and my deep gratitude goes out to all who gave me their time and expertise as the game clock ticked down. I'd especially like to thank Karen Bower, Joel Darling, Jim Hough, Kathy Broderick, Trevor Pilling, Bridget O'Toole, Anton Szabo, Michele Melady, Brenda Carroll, and March Thompson at the CBC; Nick Garrison, Mary Ann Blair, and Justin Stoller at Penguin; Lucie Grande at Molson; Imogen Brian; Greg Cameron; Paul Bruno; Ray Waines; and Natalie Tedesco for research. Special thanks to Paul Patskou, whose collection and knowledge of hockey history make him a national treasure. And to my wife, Nancy, and daughter Rose for their generosity in letting me skate long shifts with the book. Its victories are the results of many; any penalties are mine alone.

Index

Darling, Joel, 114, *195*, 257
Darling, Ted, 113, *114*, 149
Davidson, Jim, 239
Davidson, John, 244
Day, Clarence "Hap," *16*, 45, *150*
DeCourcy, Joe, 37, 40
DeJordy, Denis, 208
Denneny, Cy, 105
Dennett, Jack, *36*
Detroit Red Wings, 49, *55*, 87, *94*, 98, 113, 257, 268, 271, 281, 283
Detroit Vipers, 186
Dey's Arena, 105
Dornhoefer, Gary, *209*
Doucet, Roger, 172
Dryden, Ken, 173, 174, 175, 183
Dupont, André "Moose," 158
Dupont, Kevin Paul, 238

E

Eagleson, Alan, 90, 91, 143, 161, 198–201, *201*
Eastern Hockey League, 183
Edmonton Mercurys, 24, 265
Edmonton Oilers, 205, 225, 226, 232, 250, 264, 276, 279
Egoyan, Atom, 139
Elizabeth, Queen of England, 24, 240, 264, 304
Esposito, Phil, 176
Esso, 38, 41, 57, 59–60, 61, 75, 166, 168
Evans, Trent, 264
Expo 67, 99, 116

F

Faulkner, William, 28
Ferguson, Elmer, 87
Ferguson, John, 126–27, 172, *246*
Feyer, George, 38, 41
Finley, Charles O., 95
Fisher, Red, 149, 244
Fitkin, Ed, 44, 128
Fletcher, Cliff, 244

Foley, Tom, 39, *45*, 91
Follows, Ted, 57
Ford Motor Company, 118, 169
Foster Hewitt Productions, 13
Fotheringham, Allan, 154
Francis, Eric, 296, 297, 313
Friedman, Elliotte, *239*, 313, 315

G

Gaillard, Martine, 274
Gallivan, Danny, 70, *84*, 85–87, *86*, *92*, 134, 149, 175, 206, 208, 248, 286, 287
Game, The (Dryden), 183
"Game of the Week," 163
General Electric, 27
General Motors, 14, 118, 166
General Motors Hockey Broadcast, 14
General Motors Orchestra, 116
Geoffrion, Bernie "Boom Boom," 76
Giacomin, Eddie, 274
Gibson, Jack "Doc," 164
Gilbert, Gilles, 178
Goddard, Peter, 255
Good, Bill Jr., *132*, *133*, 134–35
Good Friday Massacre, 215–17
Gordie Howe Day, 103
Gordon, Bob, 153, 216
Gorman, Tommy, 105
Gould, Glenn, *25*
Green, "Terrible Ted," 126, 127
Greene, Lorne, 23, 41
Gregory, Jim, 181
Gretzky, Phyllis, 252
Gretzky, Walter, 252
Gretzky, Wayne, *188*, 189, 190, 205, 213, *224*, 225–29, *228*, 250–53, *251–53*, 266, 267, 270, *278*, 279, 292, 309
Gross, George, 31

H

Hamel, Jean, 217
Hammond, John, 230